MW00483958

Additional Praise for *Leading with Empathy*

"As technology becomes core, most leadership roles and value streams become more and more cross-functional, and organizations must move away from silos to survive. Breaking through these functional boundaries requires a deep understanding of others' roles, perspectives, and challenges. Gautham makes a very strong and unique case for empathy being a requirement among leaders in order for them to cultivate thriving workplaces that drive innovation."

—Dr. Mik Kersten,
Founder and CEO of Tasktop and best-selling
author of *Project to Product*

"Gautham's practical guidance in *Leading with Empathy* could not be more timely, as leaders grapple with supporting our teams through the ongoing challenges of the pandemic. Empathy is also the foundation to acting as an effective ally and using our voices to combat systemic racism."

—Jacqui Allard,
EVP Personal Financing Products, RBC

"In his book, *Leading with Empathy*, Gautham succinctly captures today's need to build a cohesive team and a positive professional atmosphere. With anecdotes from real-life experiences, the book talks about 'people management' and how leaders and managers should develop new traits such as patience, empathy, and the ability to relate to diverse situations. This book serves as a guide on how leaders should become responsible in creating an environment of trust and motivation, while leading form the front exhibiting the same traits, expected from team members. A must-read for all young managers and budding entrepreneurs!"

—Kaushik Madhavan,
Vice President–Mobility, Frost & Sullivan

"A strong leader is successful by having a vision and a drive for success, but they also have an empathy for their team that helps them inspire, motivate, and build loyalty. In this book, Gautham explores empathy in its many forms, like how recent world events such as the pandemic and racial inequity have changed us forever, and through this draws out lessons for us all to employ in everyday and in the workplace to drive a better future. His use of anecdotes, stories, and recollections helps bring these approaches to life and leaves the reader with approaches and strategies to help them empower their people and be better leaders."

—Martin Davis,
CIO and Managing Partner, DUNELM Associates Ltd

LEADING WITH EMPATHY

LEADING WITH EMPATHY

Understanding the Needs
of Today's Workforce

GAUTHAM PALLAPA

WILEY

Copyright © 2022 by John Wiley & Sons, Inc. All rights reserved.

Published by John Wiley & Sons, Inc., Hoboken, New Jersey.
Published simultaneously in Canada.

No part of this publication may be reproduced, stored in a retrieval system, or transmitted in any form or by any means, electronic, mechanical, photocopying, recording, scanning, or otherwise, except as permitted under Section 107 or 108 of the 1976 United States Copyright Act, without either the prior written permission of the Publisher, or authorization through payment of the appropriate per-copy fee to the Copyright Clearance Center, Inc., 222 Rosewood Drive, Danvers, MA 01923, (978) 750-8400, fax (978) 750-4470, or on the web at www.copyright.com. Requests to the Publisher for permission should be addressed to the Permissions Department, John Wiley & Sons, Inc., 111 River Street, Hoboken, NJ 07030, (201) 748-6011, fax (201) 748-6008, or online at http://www.wiley.com/go/permission.

Limit of Liability/Disclaimer of Warranty: While the publisher and authors have used their best efforts in preparing this work, they make no representations or warranties with respect to the accuracy or completeness of the contents of this work and specifically disclaim all warranties, including without limitation any implied warranties of merchantability or fitness for a particular purpose. No warranty may be created or extended by sales representatives, written sales materials or promotional statements for this work. The fact that an organization, website, or product is referred to in this work as a citation and/or potential source of further information does not mean that the publisher and authors endorse the information or services the organization, website, or product may provide or recommendations it may make. This work is sold with the understanding that the publisher is not engaged in rendering professional services. The advice and strategies contained herein may not be suitable for your situation. You should consult with a specialist where appropriate. Further, readers should be aware that websites listed in this work may have changed or disappeared between when this work was written and when it is read. Neither the publisher nor authors shall be liable for any loss of profit or any other commercial damages, including but not limited to special, incidental, consequential, or other damages.

For general information on our other products and services or for technical support, please contact our Customer Care Department within the United States at (800) 762-2974, outside the United States at (317) 572-3993 or fax (317) 572-4002.

Wiley also publishes its books in a variety of electronic formats. Some content that appears in print may not be available in electronic formats. For more information about Wiley products, visit our web site at www.wiley.com.

Library of Congress Cataloging-in-Publication Data:

Names: Pallapa, Gautham, author.
Title: Leading with empathy : understanding the needs of today's workforce
    / Dr. Gautham Pallapa.
Description: Hoboken, New Jersey : John Wiley & Sons, Inc., [2022] |
    Includes bibliographical references and index.
Identifiers: LCCN 2021028974 (print) | LCCN 2021028975 (ebook) | ISBN
    9781119837251 (hardback) | ISBN 9781119837275 (adobe pdf) | ISBN
    9781119837268 (epub)
Subjects: LCSH: Empathy. | Leadership.
Classification: LCC BF575.E55 P35 2022 (print) | LCC BF575.E55 (ebook) |
    DDC 152.4/1—dc23
LC record available at https://lccn.loc.gov/2021028974
LC ebook record available at https://lccn.loc.gov/2021028975

Cover image: © runeer/Getty Images
Cover design: Wiley

SKY10030916_102621

Dedicated to my mother.

She taught me the value of compassion and empathy in a highly technology-dependent world. Her actions transcended her self-needs, and she was always willing to help others.

Her approach to life and work instilled in me a desire to lead with empathy and improve human quality of life.

Contents

Preface

My mother was a strong and empathic human. She was also incredibly driven and motivated to help people, sometimes at her inconvenience. When I confronted her about this growing up, she told me that a person's existence is meaningless until they improve another's life, even if it is in some small way. She confided in me that was a primary driver for her becoming a doctor. Seeing that look of happiness and gratitude in her patients made her feel joy and empathy.

My mother was a busy person, being an ob-gyn at one of Bangalore's top medical facilities in India. She then gave it all up to support her husband's PhD in England, switching from being a busy doctor to a stay-at-home mom, taking care of me, and later my brother. I never once heard her talk about her old days or how she missed her life while at home. She had put her family first and spent her energy with her children's upbringing and emotional support for my father during his doctoral studies. I remember several occasions where she went out of her way to help the friends she had made during our stay there. One particular incident stands out in my memory. A friend of hers was going through a rough patch, and my mother wanted to cheer her up. Despite being in her third trimester with her second child, she cooked her friend's favorite food and took me with her to her friend's house, braving a snowstorm. We had to change buses in between, and I remember not being very happy or cooperative during the journey, but she bore it all with a smile and patience because she wanted to be there for her friend. I did not know it at that time, but she had a wealth of compassionate empathy in her.

When we returned to India, my mother decided to return to work. Our stay in England had exposed her to other aspects of humanity, adversity, and suffering, and she decided to focus her energy there. It was the late 1980s, and the AIDS epidemic had started to become a topic of public health and concern. My mother decided that this was the area she wanted to work in. She joined her Doctor of Medicine program in Microbiology, specializing in HIV/AIDS. She then went on to become a leading expert in her field. We used to have passionate and heartfelt conversations on her research, patients, and their unique stories.

I learned about Devi, a victim of human trafficking, at the age of 13. She was sold to a brothel and forced to have sex at such a young age, an act that could only be described as rape, sometimes 10 to 12 times a day. She had her first miscarriage at 14 and mistook it for heavy periods. Not being exposed to sex education or the concept of safe sex, she became pregnant again and had her first child at 15. The child died within the first six months, probably due to an auto-immune disorder. Devi did not know it yet, but she was infected with HIV at a young age and probably passed it on to her child. She was rescued from the brothel at 26 and was brought to my mother's hospital for a checkup. It was at that time that she found out that she had full-blown AIDS.

Feroz traveled from Bangladesh (the actual township escapes my memory) to Kolkatta, India, searching for a job and a better life. He had promised his family that he would establish himself and bring them over within six months. Not being able to hold a stable job in Kolkatta due to his drug use, he moved to Bangalore in hopes that he could have a fresh start. However, unemployment stress exacerbated his drug usage, and Feroz quickly became an addict. It had been over eight months since he left Bangladesh, and through a relative learned that his wife and three children—unable to repay the debts that they had incurred—had committed suicide by eating rat poison. Consumed by guilt, Feroz took to drug abuse to numb his pain. Not having any stable income and using all his earnings to purchase drugs, he became homeless.

Mary's uncle abused her at the age of 5. She grew up in a dysfunctional joint family and ran away at the age of 10. She worked as a maid until the age of 15 but told that her employers repeatedly abused her. She resigned to her fate and went into prostitution. She told my mother that she received more valuable gifts from her abusers than her work and figured that she could have a better life as a prostitute than a maid. She made that decision at the age of 14. She was diagnosed with HIV at the age of 17.

I still remember the pain and compassion in my mother's voice as she recounted these stories. I wanted to follow in my mother's footsteps and be a doctor to make the world a better place, and my mother, fully supporting me, shared her work and stories to motivate me. Unfortunately, being two years younger than my classmates, I was deemed ineligible to pursue medicine for another year. Rather than waste a year waiting for eligibility, my mother persuaded me to take up engineering, my father's profession. She said that there were many ways to impact humans and that opportunity would always present itself to people who had the desire to help others. I took that to heart, and though I pursued engineering and later computer science, I sought to apply my knowledge toward healthcare applications. As an extension of my master's thesis, I worked on a device that performed vagus nerve stimulation for patients who have epilepsy and seizure disorders. As part of my PhD, I worked on smart technology to improve patient quality of life in assisted healthcare. It gave me a sense of fulfillment, knowing that I was using technology to improve patient quality of life in a small way.

What I cherish most about those late-night discussions with my mother was her retelling of work stories and experiencing empathy for her patients. We bonded at a deep, emotional, and empathic level. I could sense my mother's passion for her research, her constant effort to improve people's lives, and her pain when talking about her interviews with drug addicts, women in prostitution, and sex trafficking survivors. I am grateful to have been exposed to such an influential parental role model who imparted a sense of empathy in me.

My mother passed away from cancer in 2009, and it impacted our family deeply. However, thanks to my mother and her guidance, I have made it my life's purpose to improve human quality of life through technology early in my career. I have had the good fortune to work with hospitals, assisted healthcare facilities, nonprofit organizations, and charitable institutions to help humans (and animals) through technology. I strive to channel my mother's passion into my work and interactions. I take every opportunity to drive awareness of empathy and its value in enterprises that believe predominantly in technology to transform their businesses. I have embraced the role of a digital humanist and storyteller, promoting workforce empowerment, empathy, and an enabling culture in organizations. My mother's empathic approach to humanity has helped me view challenges as opportunities to help others, especially in the workplace.

The first time I was given the opportunity of moving out of an individual contributor role and into management, I was nervous and scared. With a lot of trepidation (and a strong imposter syndrome), I took on the management role, as I viewed it as an opportunity to earn a seat at the table to champion my teams' wants and needs. It was a high-pressure job, and, being inexperienced, I made many mistakes along the way, which increased my stress and anxiety.

I was not a stranger to stress, having dealt with it throughout my life. I was two years younger than everyone in school, and while it did not seem like much, it was considerable pressure, especially in my formative years. My school and college were one of the top schools in my state, and there was an expectation that I, along with a few of my classmates, would excel in the final examinations with flying colors. I started suffering from tension headaches at the age of 12. Within a year, it became so severe that I was placed on medication until I was 15. I can still remember that sensation of dull, aching pain in my forehead, sides, and back of my head as if someone was hammering at my skull from inside. Those episodes lasted for hours at a time, and to compensate for lost exam prep time, I would get up early or sleep late to make it up. Stress and tension headaches were my study partners growing up.

These headaches went away when I entered college, probably because I didn't exert myself so much. But, like an old-time friend that you run into on social media, these headaches came back when I entered management.

Looking back, I believe that my move into management enabled me to spearhead numerous initiatives and institute processes and tools that improved my teams and organizations' quality of life. However, it came at a huge personal cost in terms of stress, anxiety, personal health, political capital, and emotional drain. Despite this toll on me personally, I still believe that deciding to be a strong champion for humans and their quality of life was one of the best decisions that I have made. The adversity that I faced allows me to truly empathize with humans at a genuine level, embodied by my mantra, **"Transform with Empathy."** This passion compelled me to write a book on empathy.

The world has undergone an unprecedented amount of adversity in the last few years. We have had hurricanes, tornadoes, racial inequality, riots, a global pandemic, wildfires, and unemployment, to list a few. There has been so much death, pain, stress, anxiety, and suffering in this world. It has been exceedingly challenging for optimists to find silver linings in this mountain of adversity that was 2020, and 2021 doesn't seem to be any better with the delta and lambda variants of Covid. However, it is essential to accept reality and the impact this hardship has had on humanity before we can look to emerge more resilient as a community. And that is what I have attempted to do in this book. *Leading with Empathy* is my attempt to elevate the importance of empathy in our technologically advanced world and champion human quality of life.

I start this book by exploring some of the events of 2020—the global pandemic and its impact on various industry verticals, racial injustice, and virtual schooling. I then explore empathy and how people can become leaders by acting with empathy. Employee empathy is a passion of mine, and I illustrate how empathy combined with technology can improve human quality of life in organizations, especially with a remote workforce. I have consciously not explored any political themes in this book. It is not because of my lack of belief in their crippling impact on humanity, but because I did not feel confident to have an optimistic or unbiased approach to the topic, especially as an immigrant still being put through the wringer of an unfair and draconian system.

As part of my work, I partner with enterprises on their transformation journey—a critical necessity for a world that has needed to go digital, remote, and contactless overnight. I have been lucky to amplify my call for empathy in the workplace through talks, keynotes, workshops, and executive mentoring. This book is an endeavor to elevate the conversation to all humans and another medium for recognizing what the world is going through and improving the quality of life of people around us, even if it is by a small amount. We currently face tremendous adversity, and there is suffering all around. My goal is to impress upon you the same message that my mother imparted to me. An opportunity will always present itself to people who have the desire to help others. All of us can choose to embrace our humanity and alleviate the less fortunate suffering around us. It does not require a massive amount of effort. Every small action counts.

Writing this book has been a wonderful, therapeutic, and fulfilling experience, but it has also been pretty frustrating at times. With the rate at which world events have been changing and rapidly evolving, I have found myself constantly catching up to them and revising my thoughts based on my learnings. Some of these events have been positive, such as vaccine administration to society, and restaurants and travel opening up again. Other events have been sad, depressing, or horrifying, such as the resurgence of COVID-19 through the delta variant, people making vaccination a political topic in the United States, or an uptick in racial violence. These are interesting and challenging times we live in.

In a way, the experience of writing this book has also been profoundly exhilarating, in the sense that I have been able to employ several Lean, Agile, and DevOps methodologies as this book moved from concept to consumption. Like other companies adapting to a dynamic environment, I went through a transformation of my own, albeit in a very personal way.

Finally, this book is also a eulogy to my mother. I am confident that she would have been a co-author of this book if she were still here, bringing her unique perspective, stories, experiences, and opinions. I have tried my best to channel her spirit and compassion in my writing. I hope you enjoy this book and join me in transforming humanity with empathy!

Dr. Gautham Pallapa

TRANSFORM WITH EMPATHY

Acknowledgments

Writing this book was more challenging than I envisioned but more fulfilling than I could have ever imagined. I was very close to my mother, and when I lost her to cancer in 2009, her death deeply impacted me. Since then, I have tried to emulate/extoll her virtues, spread awareness of her achievements, and cherish her memories. However, they always seem to have fallen short of capturing how amazing she was as a human being until I decided to dedicate this book to her. I have included several stories of how my mother shaped my life and made me a better person through her love, kindness, persistence, teachings, and discussion. I was not exactly an easy child, and I am forever indebted to her patience and for not having given up hope.

My wife, Rama, has been my rock throughout this journey. She has always been supportive of my endeavors, supporting me and staying by my side through thick and thin. Her ability to challenge my theses and provide a different perspective has kept me focused. I am eternally grateful that she does this with love and patience and still has not gotten exhausted from putting up with me and my craziness over the last 15 years. She is an immensely strong person, and I am fortunate to be a part of her life.

My son, Buddh, has been a treasure trove of learning, feedback, and a great partner in many of my experiments. Helping him adapt to virtual schooling, supplementing his emotional and physical development through a pandemic—reliving the joy of playing with Lego or soccer, coming up with inventive ways to entertain ourselves, grilling, Friday pizza and movie nights—these memories are priceless. Social distancing and lockdown enabled me to spend more time with my family than I have ever done before, and I feel blessed for that. Working with my son on experiments together, introducing Lean, Agile, and DevOps practices into his daily routine have been extremely rewarding. These experiences taught him to be emotionally aware, secure, and control his emotions, and he has given me valuable feedback if an experiment succeeded or failed. He was a champ and a trooper, though he might also be resigned to the fact that his dad was running social experiments on him and messing with his mind!

I also want to thank my son's friends and their parents, friends, teachers, caregivers, and other children who shared their perspectives, stories of adversity, stress, anxieties, and their approaches to handle and cope with the stress caused by the pandemic.

I am immensely thankful and indebted to my brother, Dr. Manu Pallapa, for reviewing the manuscript with a critical eye and a detail-oriented approach. His suggestions and perspective have helped me think many complex thoughts through, and break them down for better clarity and reflection. Our bond strengthened over passionate conversations around how our mother was empathetic and helped the community, and has made us closer than before. He has also helped keep me faithful to the book's premise and focused on core messaging instead of introducing tangential topics.

A few people have profoundly influenced my thinking and leadership style over the course of my career. Gene Kim with The Phoenix Project and his approach to DevOps methodologies started me down the transformation journey. Like many other leaders, I felt a strong resonance between the characters in the book and what was happening in my organization, and I made the book a mandatory read for my change agents before we embarked on our business transformation journey. With his book *Start with Why,* Simon Sinek helped me identify the purpose, the why, of our teams, and what business outcomes we wanted to achieve. Eric Ries with Lean Startup, and Nicole Forsgren, Jez Humble, and Gene Kim with *Accelerate* have greatly influenced my thought process. My friend Mik Kirsten with his book *Project to Product* has always been so insightful, and his take on flow and value management is phenomenal.

Various works by Dr. Brené Brown and Adam Grant have heavily influenced my thinking on empathy, compassion, and reciprocity have helped me cope with being an outlier in many respects. Daniel Pink has been an enormous influence in my initiative for helping the workforce, empowering and enabling a generative culture, and increasing psychological safety in the workplace. A few other authors I admire and have learned immensely from are Liz Wiseman, Malcolm Gladwell, John Maxwell, and Patrick Lencioni.

I have also been fortunate to have worked with many empathic leaders at Pivotal and VMware. Pivotal embodied empathy in everything that they did, and it showed in their work. I would like to specifically call out three outstanding individuals who are kind, empathic, and have always been there for me—Raghavender Arni, Chad Sakac, and Matt Nelson. Every idea needs strong champions to keep it alive, and these three leaders have championed my pursuit of enterprise and employee empathy, for which I am indebted. Additionally, the following leaders inspired me, encouraged my work, and channeled empathy in their actions—James Watters, Jeaninne Moya, Derek Beauregard, Jeff Arcuri, Mark Kropf, Steve Becker, and Duncan Winn. Pat Gelsinger, former CEO of VMware and current CEO of Intel, is a highly empathic person, and he embodied compassionate empathy in his actions, town halls, and communications. It was a great experience working with an empathic CEO, and his book, *The Juggling Act,* helped guide me with work-life balance. I am blessed to work with many of these leaders at VMware.

I am incredibly proud to be a part of an empathic team that transforms organizations with a holistic view and not just from a technological perspective. Jesse, Henri, Rick, Mark, Carl, Bernard, and JT—I enjoy working with you and look forward to many more pairings, interactions, and intellectual conversations.

Special thanks to Siobhan McFeeney and Mahil Maurice for their stimulating conversations, discussions, and insights as we collaborated on improving enterprise and employee empathy during business transformations. A shout-out to Tanzu (Pivotal) Labs and their passionate approach to be kind, do what works, and do the right things. Some of my best times at work were spent at their SF labs, and I missed being able to physically visit that location over the last year. I would be remiss if I did not specifically call out Pivotal Act, especially Ellie Ereira and Aly Blenkin. Our engagement with Mercy Ships was an excellent opportunity for us to exchange our thoughts on compassionate empathy and truly help people in need.

I have been lucky to have had some strong, empathic mentors—Lyssa Adkins, Thomas Squeo, and Maureen Mahoney—who have helped me grow not only through my career but also as a person. I want to give a special callout to Hunter Muller and HMG Strategy, Jayne Groll and Helen Beal from the DevOps Institute and its ambassadors, Mayank Mehta and Lisa Peng from Pulse, and the Project Management Institute. Our discussions and intellectual conversations have been fantastic and stimulating.

Thanks to everyone at Wiley who helped me convert my thoughts and ideas into a discrete, tangible artifact. Special thanks to Sheck Cho, executive editor, for championing my proposal and supporting me throughout this process, the editing teams for crisping up the content, along with Samantha Enders and the marketing team who helped synthesize my ideas into this book.

Personal development and growth are impossible without influence from interactions with friends, associates, colleagues, peers, and community members. Here are some notable people who have helped me grow in more ways than they know:

Swati and Abhishek Patil, Vidya and Sameer Rao, Sara and Kevin DeMers, Arvind Thapar, Jen and Dan Welch, Dinika Joshi and Prasad Sahasrabudhe, Asanka Abeysinghe, Swetha and Mahesh Kashyap, Madhu Venkateshaiah, Ajit Koshy, Shilpa Ramachandra, Kaushik Madhavan, Nidhi and Swarit Agarwal, Jason Foster, Sharath Sahadevan, Brian Peterson, Raj Rangaswamy, Santhosh Nagaraj, John Stong, Jeremy Hofstad, John Staup, Shane Heddy, Sina Sojoodi, Tony Hansmann, Tom Spero, Cornelia Davis, Tyler Jewell, DaShaun Carter, Jeff Hinds, Niki Theophilus, Joseph Barjis, Zach Gould, Dennis Rijkers, Artur Margonari, Jason Schreuder, Kathy and Dan Lanphier, Carrie Kenny and Shane Newman, Stacey and Rodney Parker, Gowri Chaganty, Steven Pratt, Pranav Patel, Pat Clark, Kelley Dean-Crowley, Greg Ahl, Matt Kirilov, Nancy Williams, Kookai Apilado, Rhonda Harvey, Songqing Liu, Kafeel Pasha, Stacy Skradski, Dan Werner, Christine Stanczak, Indradip Ghosh, Anita Kanavalli, Anand Rao, Niall Thomson, Dr. Guna Raj, Dr. Geetha Pugashetti, Aishwarya Suresh, Anup Vijaysarathi, my students and colleagues at PCCE Goa and MS Ramaiah Institute of Technology, my SPHS 93 friends, organizations that I have worked with, and people I have had discussions with and who trusted me with their stories.

Many people have been an influence and inspiration for this book, some of whom I never knew their name. Strangers who performed acts of kindness, people who demonstrated empathy when they did not have to. Some of the inspiration has not been positive, either. However, I want to acknowledge these people who suffer from apathy, insecurity, and hatred in their hearts. My earnest hope is that this book will help reduce such negative emotions and malintent in the world.

Acknowledgments

I want to acknowledge all of you readers, for purchasing this book and contributing to a good cause. A large portion of royalties received from this book will be donated to nonprofit organizations supporting the underprivileged, underrepresented minorities, and the homeless. By purchasing this book, you have made a difference in someone's life, performed a random act of kindness, and have positively impacted humanity. Thank you for helping.

And finally, humanity is not wholly defined without a spiritual perspective. I want to thank the Lord for protecting me through this complex journey of life and giving me the ability to express my thoughts and share my learning with my fellow humans.

Chapter 1

Introduction

The global pandemic of COVID-19 demonstrated how fragile humanity truly is, despite our technological, medical, and evolutionary advancements.

To say we are living in uncertain times is an understatement. In recent times, many of us have been scared, confused, and unsure of what could hurt us first: an unknown virus, a deepening economic downturn, or growing geopolitical tensions. Uncertainty about our future physical and financial health, combined with the pressures of required social distancing, has increased our worry and stress. All around us, we kept hearing stories of peoples' lives falling apart, incidents of injustice and cruelty, alarming mortality rates, and an unprecedented death toll. As a result of all these events, the number of people worldwide[1] experiencing high levels of psychological distress has noticeably increased since January 2020.[2]

Fear, frustration, panic, anger, confusion . . . we have all been dealing with these emotions (and many others) during these adverse times. News coverage and social media posts have managed to keep us in a constantly triggered state for long durations, making us paranoid, agitated, and insecure. What used to be normal is no more, and our lives have been affected in numerous disparate ways that we would have never anticipated or imagined. Mirthful conversations with friends over dinner and drinks on surviving a dangerous disease outbreak have slowly become a reality. Some people are unable to cope with these difficult conditions and are struggling with stress, anxiety, depression, and even suicidal thoughts.[3] It is crucial for us to demonstrate love, compassion, and empathy in each and every encounter.

Many people are scared to interact with humans even when necessary. More patients are missing critical in-person screenings or are coming to the hospital too late for potentially life-saving treatment. For people living with serious chronic conditions, these feelings of fear, anxiety, and worry were amplified, manifesting into various degrees of harm. Those with serious, acute conditions often avoided the hospital due to a fear of catching COVID-19 and consequently ended up sicker, or dying.

Alarmingly, from March to May 2020, visits to hospital emergency departments decreased by nearly 40 percent.[4] This was despite measures of how sick emergency department patients rose 20 percent between March and May. In Spring of 2020, non-COVID-19 out-of-hospital deaths increased, while in-hospital mortality has declined.[5] Almost half of these decreases (45 percent) were seen in patients with cancer diagnoses, heart attacks (40 percent), and strokes (30 percent). Some leading health systems believed the death toll for these individuals would reach levels comparable to COVID-attributed deaths if patients continued delaying their care.[6]

Social distancing guidelines, lockdown protocols, rapidly changing information about the virus, portrayal of the virus's danger on media, combined with changes in our external surroundings have all played into individual cognitive biases influencing how people perceived the threat of COVID-19 and influenced their decisions overall. To further complicate matters, rising unemployment also led to real trade-offs in care and affordability. Nearly half of Americans said they or someone they live with had to delay essential care since COVID-19 began.[7] Some countries have been suffering a debilitating second wave of the pandemic with a shortage of hospital beds, healthcare workers, medication, vaccines, and even oxygen supplies.

The COVID-19 pandemic put everything to the test—from healthcare systems to supply chains to social safety nets. It also tested our moral character. We didn't fail this last test, but *we didn't exactly make the honor roll*, either. Throughout lockdown, most of us behaved responsibly by practicing physical distancing and staying away from crowded places to flatten the curve. But as restrictions partially lifted, hundreds gathered unnecessarily in places like boardwalks, beaches, and parks, with no regard to safe distancing, just for a picnic. Many people resisted wearing masks in public, claiming an affront on their civil liberties, putting themselves and others near them at considerable risk.

Yes, isolation has been hard on many, especially in urban areas and small living spaces. But it was challenging to see people on the news and social media saying things like "I don't think this affects me," or "The pandemic is a hoax," or even, "I do not trust the vaccine and won't get vaccinated." It might have been challenging as well to see people with hearing loss, for example, suggesting the use of clear masks. If we have trouble considering the well-being of others in the midst of COVID-19, how can we begin to empathize with anyone outside of our own experience?

How we behave in these situations is important, even beyond COVID-19. Our actions demonstrate our ability to put the greater good ahead of personal desires. Without that capacity, we'll never tackle other global problems, from endemic poverty and climate change to the biggest test of our empathy: systemic racism.

Once vaccine rollout was widespread, people certainly felt pandemic fatigue and many were impatient with the slow progress. They wanted to make up for lost time and regarded the slow vaccine rollouts as bureaucratic incompetence. Administering a vaccine to the entire population is challenging and requires complex planning, logistical management, and tactical execution. There are established protocols to follow, procedures to adhere to, and demographics to cater to. There are horrendous reports of people trying to cheat the system by providing wrong information, buying a prioritized place in line, or impersonating elderly or essential workers.[8] A majority of these actions are by a section of society that has become entitled through their wealth and privilege and cannot comprehend a system of democracy where all people are treated equally. It is, therefore, appalling to see people complain about how an unfair system has singled them out and how they face injustice.

People of color and Indigenous groups face racial injustice every day. Those of us who live with racial privilege don't have that experience. Many people in developed worlds have never suffered severe hunger. They don't know what it's like to flee their home country to escape war. They have never had to worry about an unfair immigration system. A lack of lived experience doesn't relieve us of responsibility; it means we need to work harder at empathy. We need to work harder to understand how we might be connected to someone else's pain and to act accordingly.

Many of us understood that a relaxing day in a crowded park during a pandemic could help spread disease. We realized that our actions affected others around us—like healthcare workers, first responders, or grocery store workers who did not have the luxury of isolating themselves—a *butterfly effect*[9] at a global scale. Our daily habits are connected to climate change and to the Inuit communities most affected by melting polar ice. Our consumption habits are connected to workers in developing countries. From empathy, we can better understand this interconnectedness. And then we can move to action.

Above all, COVID-19 tested our willingness to make small sacrifices, to prioritize the safety of others before our own comfort, to think about others and how our actions affect our community. We

can give up coffee or take-out dinners for a month and make a donation to a group most affected by the pandemic. We can stand up for
an immigrant being harassed on the bus or speak out when a friend
or family member makes racist comments, even if it makes us
uncomfortable.

COVID-19 was a moral test of our time, assessing our ability to
think about others before ourselves and to take action for the greater
good. It was a test, but not the final exam. We still have the opportunity to learn. We can still build on the character strengths and fix the
moral weaknesses that COVID-19 laid bare.

Adverse Impact of a Global Pandemic

*There have been at least 209.2 million cases of COVID-19 world-
wide with 4.4 million dead.[10]*

The COVID-19 pandemic has led to a dramatic loss of human life
worldwide and presents an unprecedented challenge to public
health, global economy, hospitality, food systems, and the world of
work. The economic and social disruption caused by the pandemic
has been devastating: tens of millions of people are at risk of falling into extreme poverty, while the number of undernourished
people, currently estimated at nearly 690 million,[11] could increase
by up to 132 million by the end of the year. Numerous people are
having to make base decisions: feed the family, pay for a roof over
their heads, or pay for healthcare. Many cannot even afford to
choose two out of those three choices without falling into inextri-
cable debt.

Millions of enterprises also face an existential threat. Nearly half
of the world's 3.3 billion global workforce were at risk of losing their
livelihoods.[12] Informal and gig economy workers were particularly
vulnerable because the majority lacked social protection and access

to quality healthcare in addition to losing access to productive assets. Without the means to earn an income during lockdowns, many were unable to feed themselves and their families. For most, no income meant no food, or, at best, less food and less nutritious food.

The pandemic also affected the entire food system and has exposed its fragility. Border closures, trade restrictions, and confinement measures prevented farmers from accessing markets, including for buying inputs and selling their produce, and agricultural workers from harvesting crops, thus disrupting domestic and international food supply chains and reducing access to healthy, safe, and diverse diets. The pandemic decimated jobs and placed millions of livelihoods at risk. As breadwinners lost jobs, fell ill, and died, the food security and nutrition of millions of women and men came under threat, with those in low-income countries, particularly the most marginalized populations, which include small-scale farmers and Indigenous peoples, being hardest hit.

Millions of agricultural workers—waged and self-employed— while feeding the world, regularly faced high levels of working poverty, malnutrition, and poor health, and they suffered from a lack of safety and labor protection as well as other types of abuse. With low and irregular incomes and a lack of social support, many of them were compelled to continue working, often in unsafe conditions, thus exposing themselves and their families to additional risks. Further, when experiencing income losses, they were coerced into resorting to negative coping strategies, such as distress sale of assets, predatory loans, or child labor. Migrant agricultural workers were particularly vulnerable, because they faced risks in their transport, working, and living conditions and struggled to access support measures put in place by governments. In the future, guaranteeing the safety and health of all agri-food workers—from primary producers to those involved in food processing, transport, and retail, including street food vendors—as well as better incomes and protection, will be critical to saving lives and protecting public health, people's livelihoods, and food security.

During the COVID-19 crisis, food security, public health, and employment and labor issues—in particular, workers' health and safety—converged. Adhering to workplace safety and health practices and ensuring access to decent work and the protection of labor rights in all industries are crucial in addressing the human dimension of the crisis. Immediate and purposeful action to save lives and livelihoods should include extending social protection toward universal health coverage and income support for those most affected. These include workers in the informal economy and in poorly protected and low-paid jobs, including youth, older workers, and migrants. Particular attention must be paid to the situation of women, who are overrepresented in low-paid jobs and care roles. In fact, several studies found that, financially, women suffered disproportionally during the pandemic.[13] Different forms of support are key, including cash transfers, child allowances and healthy school meals, shelter and food relief initiatives, support for employment retention and recovery, and financial relief for businesses, including micro, small, and medium-sized enterprises. In designing and implementing such measures, it is essential that governments work closely with employers and workers.

Countries dealing with existing humanitarian crises or emergencies were particularly exposed to the effects of COVID-19. Responding swiftly to the pandemic, while ensuring that humanitarian and recovery assistance reaches those most in need, continues to be critical.

Now is the time for global solidarity and support, especially with the most vulnerable in our societies, particularly in the emerging and developing world. Only together can we overcome the intertwined health and social and economic impacts of the pandemic and prevent its escalation into a protracted humanitarian and food security catastrophe, with the potential loss of already achieved development gains.

We must recognize this opportunity to build back a better world for all, as noted in a press briefing issued by the United Nations Secretary-General. The UN is committed to pooling their expertise and experience to support countries in their crisis response measures and efforts to achieve the Sustainable Development Goals.[14] We need to develop long-term sustainable strategies to address the challenges facing the health and agri-food sectors. Priority should be given to addressing underlying food security and malnutrition challenges, tackling rural poverty, in particular through more and better jobs in the rural economy, extending social protection to all, facilitating safe migration pathways, and promoting the formalization of the informal economy.

We must rethink the future of our environment and tackle climate change and environmental degradation with ambition and urgency. Only then can we protect the health, livelihoods, food security, and nutrition of all people, and ensure that our *new normal* is a better one.

Apocalypse Bingo

First the pandemic, which divided us, economically devastated us; it has killed nearly 4.1 million[15] of us worldwide.[16] Then the racial unrest, erupting at the deaths of more Black Americans at the hands of police: George Floyd, Breonna Taylor, Rayshard Brooks, Daniel Prude—to name a few.

Combine that with extreme weather patterns. For only the second time in history, the National Hurricane Center moved into the Greek alphabet for storm names. The wildfires of 2020 were bigger, deadlier, and more frequent than in years past. For months in several West Coast cities of the United States, people could not breathe properly.[17] Many were evacuated, lost their homes, and there was widespread destruction. On a personal front, we almost got evacuated ourselves and experienced a level of anxiety and stress that we had never faced before. We also caught a glimpse of an inevitable bleak dystopian future with red skies, an ash-covered moon, and a blotted sun for days.

In record numbers, humans have been anxious, worried, sleep-deprived, distracted, and depressed. The COVID-19 pandemic's triple whammy of an invisible and omnipresent threat (coronavirus infection), profound disruptions in daily life, and uncertainty for the future thrust many people into a chronic, high-stress state that is, let's just say, less than optimal for rational thinking or any other sort of higher-order cognitive functioning.

Many social forums and social circles started referring to all this adversity as *2020 bingo* or *Apocalypse bingo*. They made it a game of checking off items from a master list of apocalyptic scenarios: Australian wildfires, a plague of locusts and cicadas, war in the Middle East, an asteroid larger than the Empire State Building passing by Earth, solar flares, and increased seismic activity in Yellowstone suggesting reactivation of the supervolcano are but a few examples on the apocalypse bingo card. Several memes emerged as part of this macabre humor.[18]

While the COVID-19 pandemic raged on worldwide, the immediate mental health impact of this collective trauma is coming into focus even as the outlook for long-term psychological effects remains considerably fuzzier.

Are we experiencing a pandemic of mental illness? Much has been reported about the ill-termed "mental health pandemic" that seems to be surging through the United States and other countries in lockstep with lockdowns and the death, societal disruption, and economic devastation of the viral pandemic. Many experts have sounded the alarm for an approaching tsunami of psychological maladies that could sink an already overburdened mental health-care system.

A growing cache of data seem to bear out those fears. A recent population survey conducted in April and May found a threefold increase in depression since the pandemic began.[19] The researchers examined mental health problems relative to 13 pandemic-specific stressors, including loss of a job, death of someone close to you due to COVID-19, and financial problems. The more stressors people reported, the more likely they were to also report symptoms of anxiety and depression. Other studies show similar rises. From April to October of 2020, the National Center for Health Statistics partnered with the Census Bureau and tracked anxiety and depression symptoms among Americans in household pulse surveys, finding a sharp rise in both.[20]

Impact on Families and Society

The economic and social disruption caused by the COVID-19 pandemic affected millions of people worldwide. It rattled pretty much every segment of life, including education, economy, religion, employment, tourism, entertainment, sports, food, security, and posed significant challenges to the global economy. Research has shown the pandemic's significant impact on the psychological well-being of families and overall society and how it has changed the way we work, eat, and interact. Social distancing has led us to a more virtual experience both personally and professionally. Let's take an in-depth look at how the pandemic has affected families and society over the last year.

Impact on Families

COVID-19 was a seismic shock for everyone, even for the financially stable families who did not suffer any income loss from lockdown closures and social distancing. Many people have lost their jobs; some are working on remote jobs from home, and others associated with healthcare cannot meet their families to protect them from virus exposure. Families living in poverty with dependent children and less-educated parents were more adversely affected by the pandemic's emotional, physical, and financial implications than others.

Many single-income families were hit hard when their livelihood was affected by the lockdown and shelter-in-place. Many of these families did not have savings to fall back on, having lived paycheck to paycheck on a minimum wage that hardly covered the inflation rate or price increase of commodities due to the pandemic. Families have also struggled with the additional costs of raising their children at home, most notably from closed schools and childcare. The financial hardships during the pandemic have forced people to make significant changes in everyday routines and with limited resources.

Increased Responsibilities

Traditionally, women were already carrying the primary load as caregivers before the onset of the pandemic. According to a Pew Research Center survey conducted in the United States,[21] 59 percent of women reported that they perform more household chores than their spouse or partner. The same study revealed that only 46 percent share equal domestic responsibilities with their partner. These numbers are worse in developing countries or nations with poor women's rights.[22]

With the abrupt crises and closure of schools and daycare centers worldwide, the workload dramatically increased for women. As with all times of stress and anxiety, families and the community at large found comfort in the caregiving nature of women. Women are expected to take care of their families and household duties without any additional support. Some men are now more involved with their families, but that percentage is still low overall.

Difficulty in Achieving Work-Life Balance

The pandemic has allowed men to put their share in childcare and housework, and that's the best way to achieve work and family life balance during these challenging times. Parents juggling a full-time job and homeschooling find it challenging to balance their work schedules and their kids' homeschooling schedules. Furthermore, there is a vast discrepancy in the quality and effectiveness of homeschooling, which depends on the parent's education level, language, physical and psychological health, and availability of computer skills along with Internet connectivity.

Homeschooling Children

Reliance on homeschooling had a massive negative impact on children, particularly for underprivileged communities. Virtual schooling was exceedingly challenging for children with special needs and their caregivers. Children experienced considerable stress and anxiety adapting to new communication methods with their teachers, video conferencing solutions, and loss of physical interaction in a familiar setting (school classrooms). They could not spend time with their peers for group learning or go to recess to play with their friends. Child development has been severely impaired due to virtual schooling. We may not know the true long-lasting effects of this forced isolation on the world's children for many years.

Impact on Birthrates

The COVID-19 crises created a baby boom with millions of people stuck at home cut off from reproductive healthcare. Around 140 million babies were born worldwide in 2020.[23] The United Nations has already predicted that about 47 million women were unable to access contraceptive measures during the lockdown,[24] leading to unwanted pregnancies. Just as expected, after roughly 10 months into the lock-down, there was a huge baby boom worldwide.[25] Although social distancing urged partners to meet less and financial instability caused many families to stop having children, the lockdown has led to increased planned and unplanned pregnancies.

Despite the fact that there was a considerable spike in birthrates throughout the world, it was a significant concern for poverty-stricken and underdeveloped nations.[26] In India, about 1.85 million women were unable to access contraception and safe abortions during the lockdown. Pandemic-linked deaths in children are projected to be at least 10,000 per month in Latin America, South Asia, and sub-Saharan Africa.[27] A study from the Standing Together for Nutrition Consortium predicted that over 12 million children would suffer from undernutri-tion, wasting, or severe malnutrition due to the pandemic.[28]

Societal Impact

COVID-19 has severely affected many communities. In particular, vulnerable communities with entrenched poverty, limited employ-ment flexibility, and overcrowded housing faced significant chal-lenges. The health and economic impacts of the virus are being borne disproportionately by poor people. They continue to affect the most vulnerable populations, including older citizens, disabled peo-ple, youth, and Indigenous people. Other people at a disadvantage include the homeless, who are more exposed to the danger of the virus in tent camps and other close quarters. Similarly, refugees and migrants also stand to suffer from the pandemic and its aftermath.

Social Relationships

COVID-19 disrupted people's social relationships and the ways they used to connect with their loved ones. Some people felt isolated physically and emotionally, and others felt more connected to their families, friends, and social networks than they typically do. The ban on personal gatherings promoted the unconventional activities of maintaining social distancing, such as birthday parades on birthday parties or balcony sing-along for concerts. Awkward socially distanced get-togethers in cul-de-sacs or front yards substituted socializing at bars or favorite hangouts. Driveway or drive-by conversations replaced meeting friends and chatting. Children were continuously cautioned to be six feet apart, don their masks, and not have physical contact during playdates.

Domestic Violence

Many countries reported an increase in cases of domestic violence during the lockdown.[29] Unemployment, financial insecurity, and stress were significant contributors that led to the increased aggression at home. Several news outlets reported a surge in domestic violence during the COVID-19 pandemic in the United States.[30] With people confined to their homes, there was a potential increase seen in intimate partner violence (IPV). The lockdown measures were intended to protect the public, but they left many IPV victims stuck with abusers unable to connect with services and ask for help safely.

Surveys conducted worldwide have shown a significant increase in domestic violence cases since January 2020. *The Guardian* reported a surge in domestic violence during the COVID-19 pandemic in the United States.[31] The UK's largest domestic abuse charity, Refuge, reported a 700 percent increase in calls to its hotline in a single day.[32] According to the *American Journal of Emergency Medicine*[33] and UN women[34]—a United Nations entity dedicated to gender equality and empowerment of women—the cases of domestic abuse increased by 300 percent in Hubei, China; 33 percent in Singapore; 25 percent in Argentina; 30 percent in France; 30 percent in Cyprus; and 50 percent in Brazil.

Religious Impact

Religious and devout people visit places of worship to receive hope, peace of mind, strength, and spiritual guidance. Due to the pandemic, churches, temples, mosques, and other places of worship had to close overnight, affecting people of all faiths. There were the cancellations of services, festivals, observances, pilgrimages, and Sunday schools. People felt isolated and alone. Many religious organizations offered worship services through video conferencing and live streaming. However, people have expressed that they do not feel the same spiritual connection and peace as before.

Diwali, the festival of lights in India, is usually celebrated by over 800 million people worldwide. This festival involves the lighting of lamps, exchanging gifts, celebrating with friends and family, and lots of fireworks. COVID-19 restrictions severely limited these activities, with an estimated 60 percent reduction in social interaction.[35] Other religious events have been significantly impacted as well. About 4.55 million tourists visited Israel in 2019, but this was reduced by 81 percent in 2020[36]—a mere 850,000 tourists. Hajj, Islam's most important annual pilgrimage, which usually has more than 2 million people attend every year, was limited to only 1,000 people due to social distancing and crowd control measures implemented by Saudi Arabia. International travelers were barred from the Hajj for the first time in decades.[37]

Advocates of many religions appealed to their followers to take safety precautions and embrace their spirituality to deal with challenges related to global crises. Muslim clerics emphasized the government regulations by issuing *fatwas*[38] and encouraging their communities to practice social distancing and self-isolation. Pope Francis urged Christians to follow the protocols and stay united in difficult times. The unprecedented global crises made millions of Americans embrace worship as an essential part of life.[39] According to a PEW Research Center report,[40] more than half of adults admitted to praying for an end to the virus, with women and the elderly constituting a large portion of the adults.

Pandemic Pets

Many pet owners were shocked to hear news reports that a small number of cats and dogs were infected with the COVID-19 virus, probably by being exposed to someone who was COVID-19 positive. There were also other reports of animals being potential carriers of the virus, and some people were reluctant to keep their pets due to the fear of transmission. The Centers for Disease Control and Prevention (CDC) issued a statement[41] stating that there was no evidence that animals play a significant role in spreading SARS-CoV-2, the virus that causes COVID-19, to people. They also said that based on the limited information available to date, the risk of animals spreading COVID-19 to people is low.

Despite that initial fear, the number of people adopting more pets during the lockdown also increased. People stuck at home are using pets to endure the challenging time and comfort them. People dealing with mental health problems self-reported that their pets helped improve their mental well-being, and they experienced stronger bonds with them. Also, pet owners reported feeling less lonely than those who didn't own pets. Pets constituted an important source of emotional support and helped people filling the gap created by the lockdown.[42]

Divorce Rates

With everyone locked in together for long periods and with high levels of stress and anxiety, relationships have been strained and stretched to their limit in many cases. During the COVID-19 pandemic, divorce rates skyrocketed, and lockdown created a make-or-break environment with people having relationship realizations. In the United States alone, the divorce rate increased by 34 percent.[43] Relationship counselors rank financial problems, boredom, mental health issues, disagreements about parenting, and division of labor in the house as the most common sources behind relationship trouble. The most affected couples had bumpy relationships long before the pandemic, and being couped up with the stressors further amplified during the lockdown, leading toward separation.

Humanity Needs Empathy Now More Than Ever

The ongoing coronavirus pandemic, political turmoil, and revelations about systemic racism and sexism have been heart-wrenching for people and their families all over the world. Millions of people have reported that they struggle to put enough food on the table. Just in the United States, over 26 million adults said they could not feed their families properly in 2020 due to hardship[44] and an additional 24 millions adults are undergoing some form of food insecurity.[45] Families suffering from unemployment also have had to grapple with an inability to pay rent or mortgage. Studies have shown that renters of color face food and housing hardships, in addition to difficulty covering expenses such as utilities, car payments, or medical expenses.[46]

Over 1.6 billion workers were impacted or unemployed due to the pandemic out of a global workforce of 3.3 billion![47] That is nearly half of the global workforce affected or at risk of losing their livelihood. Unemployment rates have jumped since April 2020 to levels not seen since the Great Depression of 1929, and it is depressing to realize that these rates will continue to grow until conditions improve globally.[48] Job losses have predominantly centered in low-paid industries, part-time jobs, and the gig economy. A recent US Congressional Research Service report stated that part-time workers experienced an unemployment rate almost double that of full-time workers in April 2020[49] and, as expected, racial and ethnic minorities had high rates of unemployment through all of 2020.

The last two years have been ones of losses, not just in lives but also in jobs, security, safety, belonging, familiarity, love, emotional health, and well-being. People have been afraid to venture outside their homes, and many have become depressed or have severe anxiety bouts. In senior living and care communities, people have been suffering from an atmosphere of fear, from contracting the virus and from the isolation and new realities the pandemic has triggered. Most of us want to step up and contribute to solutions but are hard-pressed to know what we can do as individuals and as long-term care teams.

Finding the Silver Lining in These Dark Clouds

It is difficult to see the silver lining from this devastating pandemic, in addition to all the adverse events since early 2020. However, being a naive optimist, I firmly believe that there are some positives to all our suffering:

- **There is a vaccine (in fact, there are several!).** Scientists across the world rallied together with a singular purpose of finding a vaccine for COVID-19. Humanity could not afford the long cycles of rigorous testing, but at the same time, they needed a level of confidence that the vaccine would work en masse. People worked around the clock, put themselves at risk, and pushed the boundaries of medicine, technology, human endeavor, and grit.
- **Stronger relationships.** The pandemic has given people a chance to spend more time with their families and build

genuine relationships. Parents are becoming more involved with their children. Family bonding has strengthened, and children are communicating better with their parents. People have found more ways to reconnect with their loved ones as sources of mutual support, advice, and care. On a personal note, I spent over 900 extra hours with my family and am grateful for the social distancing protocols to have given me a chance to create some beautiful memories with my wife and son. I could not have done this if we were not on a lockdown.

- **Better hygiene.** We finally learned how to wash our hands properly in 2020! Our smartwatches now have apps that train us to wash our hands appropriately and for the right amount of time. People are now more aware of how important it is to practice hygiene, and it's no longer just a good habit but a skill you need to survive. The pandemic made us cognizant of maintaining our hygiene by sanitizing our hands after touching anything, covering our mouth while coughing or sneezing, and washing hands regularly. We also learned to gauge how much six feet distance is and respect people's personal space.

- **Reduced air pollution.** With the shutdown of economic and commercial activities, people were confined in their homes. Traffic volume rapidly plummeted by over 80 percent, making a significant drop in the air pollution rate.[50] NASA satellites have documented a substantial reduction of 20 to 30 percent in air pollution.[51] As all the social, industrial, and urbanization activities stopped, nature bounced back and improved various environmental parameters, including air quality, noise pollution, and cleaner rivers.

- **Increased kindness.** Social distancing has affected people's relationships and their compassion toward others. As life slowed down and with nowhere really to go, people started acknowledging, conversing, and even, in some cases, caring for their neighbors and the community's health and well-being. People are cooking meals for the needy, offering emotional and even financial support to those in need, and performing supermarket runs for those unable to leave their homes.

- **Prioritizing life over work.** Many people have started to slow down and enjoy the time with their loved ones and friends. They have created new memories and experiences within the confines of their homes, in many cases strengthening their relationships. Work-life balance has become a more important aspect of many people's lives. Even though many people were sequestered in their homes for long periods, they created innovative ways to enjoy themselves.

As an optimist, I see these signs and feel hope that things will work out eventually. However, as a pragmatist, I know that we cannot rest on these meager triumphs alone. We must endeavor to bring more hope, cheer, and positivity into the world. But how do we heal a world that has endured an exponential amount of pain and suffering in such a short time?

Proposing: Empathy as a Prescription for a World Overwhelmed by Adversity

Empathy is the powerful driver of breakthrough change toward achieving a much more just, caring, and compassionate world. *Now,* as individuals and teams, we can bring new energy and determination to making empathy a way of life that infuses all of our activities and relationships and sparks inspired positive change.

Says Jamil Zaki, in his groundbreaking 2019 book *The War for Kindness: Building Empathy in a Fractured World:* "Empathy is in short supply. Isolation and tribalism are rampant. We struggle to understand people who aren't like us, but find it easy to hate them."[52]

Studies show that we are less caring than we were even 30 years ago. In 2006, then-Senator Barack Obama said that the United States is suffering from an empathy deficit. "As you go on in life, this quality of empathy will become harder, not easier . . . we live in a culture that discourages empathy."

According to Zaki, empathy is a skill that we can develop and sharpen over time. By working on this skill, we can improve our ability to be empathic and utilize it in our everyday life. This point of view resonates deeply with me. I believe that while some people might have a genetic disposition to higher levels of hormones that trigger empathy,[53] a more significant influence on developing empathy resides in our support networks, environments, experiences, cultural backgrounds, and interactions. My wife comes from a close-knit joint family with stronger bonds, while I come from a nuclear family.[54] I have been fortunate to have had an influential empathic role model in my mother growing up; however, my wife has much more empathy than me, perhaps because of her more robust support structure and family bonds.

Lead with Empathy

Overwhelmed, angry, weary, confused, concerned, impatient—these feelings can paralyze organizations and people alike. But it doesn't have to be that way. Why not seize the moment and become the empathic leader that the world needs right now? Why not use this unique opportunity to focus everyone on strengthening our empathy muscles for the good of ourselves, our families, our communities, and our world, while we also proceed to pursue sorely needed systemic changes?

Each of us has a unique personality. That makes us different, but equally we all have lots in common and are connected in so many ways. We live in our own realities that are defined by our senses and our own experiences. But we are social beings and it is of utmost importance to our personal development to experience other people's realities. Our ability to communicate and understand our and other peoples' emotional states are keys to maintaining our relationships. When we observe someone experiencing joy or sadness, we are experiencing a similar sensation to a certain extent. Being empathetic means thinking further beyond ourselves and our own concerns. It shows our ability to put ourselves in another person's position to feel what they are experiencing.

Empathy is a very vital aspect of our daily lives. This is because it enables us to show compassion to other people, relate to our friends, loved ones, colleagues, and even strangers, hence affecting the world positively. As we embrace our role as empathic leaders, we also need to be cognizant of the difference between sympathy and empathy. Sympathy is driven by feelings of pity or concern for another person without really comprehending what it feels like to be in that person's situation. One can feel sympathy for homeless people, someone crying on the street, or painfully hobbling along with crutches on an icy footpath. However, empathy refers to the ability to imagine oneself in another's situation; experience the emotions, ideas, or opinions of that person; and take action to help reduce pain and suffering for the other person.

Empathic leaders are in short supply in the workforce as well. The stereotype of a workforce leader has been military in nature with no leeway for human emotions. This behavior suppresses any dredge of feeling in the workplace, and people are hesitant to demonstrate emotion lest they be judged weak and ineffective. It is imperative that we destroy this leadership stereotype if we want to enable our fellow humans. Genuinely understanding the need of team members, being sensitive to team needs, and selflessly striving to increase psychological safety in the organization are some benefits of an empathetic leadership style.

From a global perspective, empathy is infinitely important particularly if it ends in compassion. Empathy motivates people to step in and help those who have been struck by major disasters even if they are total strangers. Empathy brings out the best in us and improves the global quality of life. ***When you lead with empathy, you are empowering humanity in the face of adversity.***

How This Book Is Structured

Simon Sinek transformed how leaders can inspire people to take action through his influential book, *Start with Why*. He has been a great inspiration to me. As a tribute to his influence on my personal thinking, I have espoused his powerful idea, The Golden Circle, to inspire and motivate humanity in these adverse times. *Leading with Empathy* is a call to action for becoming empathic leaders in a world that has suffered so much strife and misery.

In the first part of the book, I explore *why* humanity has undergone so much adversity in recent times. I start with the impact of the COVID-19 global pandemic and events since 2020. While it can be traumatic and painful to some, this first step of acknowledging why there is so much suffering in recent times is vital to our leadership transformation. I examine the impacts of COVID-19, unemployment, Black Lives Matter demonstrations, and the economic downturn. These topics could trigger bouts of pain, anxiety, suffering, loss, and sadness in many of us who have undergone adverse episodes, especially over the last year. My intent is not to generate pain; instead, it provides visibility to human suffering, and I profusely apologize in advance if these topics invoke pain for you. I dedicate a chapter to stress and anxiety, proffering insight into why the pain and suffering have impacted us profoundly in recent times. Part 1 is aptly called Adversity.

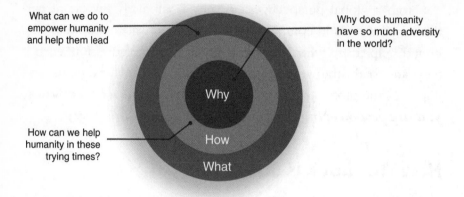

Figure 1.1   How this book is structured.

Part 2 of the book helps us understand *how* empathy has emerged as a panacea to combat the anguish and suffering that the world has undergone. I examine how elevated stress levels and anxiety affect us physically, mentally, and emotionally and how we can overcome the impact of stress and anxiety in our lives. I then discuss emotional intelligence and empathy. We take an in-depth look at the types of empathy, benefits, and impediments to empathy and how we can enable empathy in people.

I then present how empathic leadership can empower humanity in the face of adversity. I provide anecdotes, stories, and personal musings throughout the book to underscore the topics discussed and grant visibility to the suffering around us and how people have stepped up and led with empathy. I also share exercises and tips to reduce stress and anxiety and improve happiness and positivity.

The third part of the book is all about empowerment and what actions and steps we as empathic leaders can embrace and initiate to enable the workforce, people around us, and our loved ones in these challenging times. Empathy in organizations has been a passionate topic for me. One of my two primary beliefs is that happy people are productive people. I firmly subscribe to the idea that people will be happy when they are a psychologically safe and work in a positive organizational culture that nurtures trust, collaboration, and innovation that embraces failure. This necessitates enterprise and employee empathy. I examine what steps empathic leaders should take to promote empathy in the workplace, especially for a remote workforce—a relevant topic right now.

Throughout this book, I have tried to refrain from using many of the cliches that have become mainstream over the last few years. However, there are occasions where I might have inadvertently succumbed to parroting them. I highly encourage you to chuckle at those instances and either substitute the phrase with your choice of cliche or roll your eyes and let out a deep sigh. Shake your head sagely if you are reading the book in a public setting for extra effect. Feel free to even tweet about it with #empathicleadership or #leadwithempathy and express what went through your mind when you encountered the cliche. I look forward to reading those gems on my Twitter feed.

Leading with Empathy is intended to help people relate to their personal experiences as we explore various topics throughout the book. It is a call to action for people to lead with empathy. I have included exercises, tips, and activities to promote empathic leadership, reflection, and introspection and ways to start the dialogue about empathy and its dire need today. Each chapter also ends with a few points for reflection and introspection. I encourage you to use these not only for your personal growth but also as conversation starters with your fellow leaders. You don't have to wait until Part 3 to take action.

Together, we can lead with empathy and strive to elevate humanity in the face of adversity.

An Exercise to Reduce Stress

Here is a simple exercise that you can perform any time you feel overwhelmed by stress or anxiety.

Close your eyes. Take three deep, slow breaths. Now relax your shoulders and assume a comfortable position. It could be leaning back in your chair, your favorite place on your couch, or even on the floor. The objective is to be comfortable and relaxed.

Next, with your eyes closed, think of a memory or event that brings a smile to your face or warmth in your heart. Focus on that happiness or warmth that you feel when you relive that memory.

Keep breathing and continue to keep your eyes closed. Let that warmth spread all over you down to your fingertips and toes. Allow that feeling of happiness to envelope you and bask in it. Go back in time and think hard about how you felt then. Where were you at that time? What was the weather? Who was with you? Did you smell anything nice? What were your fingers feeling?

Spend some time in that memory. Then, slowly open your eyes, take three more deep breaths, and get up.

Hopefully, you feel relaxed and less stressed after this exercise. Repeat this whenever you feel overwhelmed and need some calm.

Reflections

- How has COVID-19 affected you and your loved ones?
- Do you have examples that can differentiate *sympathy* from *empathy?*
- Have you ever performed an act of kindness that influenced a stranger's life?
- Has some stranger performed an act of kindness that influenced your life?

Part I

Adversity

Chapter 2

The Toll on Humanity

2020 was a tough year to be an optimist. It was hard to find a silver lining in the tempestuous clouds of adversity.

Delilah was a single mother to three young children and worked at a clothing store, making about $10 per hour. When the lockdown occurred, similar to many other retail stores, her store shut down, and she was laid off. She was distraught and, like millions in her situation, hoped that the shelter-in-place and the lockdown orders would be temporary and she could get back to work. Her children were all at home and thankfully were able to join their classes through Zoom from Chromebooks provided by the school district. Her neighbors were considerate enough to share their WiFi password with her children, allowing them to continue learning without interruption. The money that she stashed away over the years disappeared within four months. She was late on rent but was rescued by the eviction moratorium act, which prevented landlords from evicting defaulting tenants until March 2021. She received a stimulus check of $2,400 and used it to pay utilities and rent. That left her with a mere $130 that she saved as emergency medical funds for her children.

With brick-and-mortar stores closed indefinitely, Delilah found a job at a nearby grocery store that paid $8.25 per hour. The work was taxing and stressful. She was always afraid of getting infected by the pandemic and carrying it into her home. Her children were under strict orders not to have any physical contact with her until she had sanitized herself and changed her clothes. She said that it was hard on her five-year-old to suppress his urge to run and hug his mother after her long shift. Her other two children were understanding, but it affected them as well. There was always a looming threat of contracting COVID-19 in their house. For Delilah, there was an added fear of losing her only source of income, that heat and water would be shut off (especially during winter), and of being evicted by her landlord once the moratorium date expired. She did not know where she would go or how she would afford to support her children's virtual schooling if that ever happened. She said that the best thing she could do was live one day at a time and pray that things did not get worse.

Adversity on a Global Scale

The COVID-19 pandemic caught most of the world unprepared. Not only were people with varying demographic and socioeconomic characteristics differentially susceptible to COVID-19, the ability to cope, response, recover, and adapt to the pandemic and its social and economic consequences varied across population subgroups as well as institutional and geographical contexts.

Over the months, we saw significant economic impact of the coronavirus on financial markets and vulnerable industries such as manufacturing, tourism, hospitality, and travel. Travel and tourism, which account for 10 percent of the global GDP and 50 million jobs worldwide,[1] along with hospitality companies, closed down, affecting small and medium companies globally. This, in turn, affected millions of people, typically the least well paid and those self-employed or working in informal environments in the gig economy or in part-time work with zero-hour contracts. Some governments announced economic measures to safeguard jobs, guarantee wages, and support the self-employed, but there was a lack of clarity in many countries about how these measures would be implemented and how people would manage a loss of income in the short term. Behind these statistics lay the human costs of the pandemic, as discussed in Chapter 1.

In this chapter, I explore two broad themes of global impact. The first theme is *societal*, where we examine how adversity has impacted humanity overall. The second theme is *financial*, and we investigate the economic ramifications of the pandemic and its aftermath.

The Impact on Society

COVID-19 had an incapacitating impact on humanity. It affected the way we work, socialize, interact, and operate as a society. Lockdown procedures ground all forms of travel to a halt, which caused a ripple effect to the hospitality industry, trade, supply chain logistics, and manufacturing. Overnight, people had to adapt to new modes of working, learning, and surviving, causing considerable stress and anxiety.

Loss of the Familiar

Social distancing and lockdowns induced social challenges in our communities. People lost the ability to perform their regular routines—activities that had become ingrained in their psyche as a part of their identity. People had to stay at home as offices were closed, eliminating the familiar morning scramble to get out of the house and beat office traffic for many. Relying on restaurants and eateries for lunch was not a viable option initially, requiring people to learn or utilize their culinary skills daily. It felt like the entire world was learning to bake bread or use an instapot!

Many people reported being bored or concerned about putting on weight; others reported that loneliness and isolation triggered considerable traumatic stress, confusion, and anger, all of which were exacerbated by fear of infection, having limited access to supplies of necessities, inadequate information, or the experience of economic loss or stigma. This stress and anxiety led to increased alcohol consumption, as well as an increase in domestic and family violence.[2] The closure of schools and childcare to combat the spread of coronavirus contributed to this stressful situation and created additional pressures on working parents. It also affected children in many ways: loss of bonding with peer groups, loss of proximity with a parental figure (teachers), loss of familiarity (schools/daycares), and stress of adapting to a virtual schooling methodology.

Social distancing and lockdowns also meant that many of our favorite pubs, bars, and restaurants shut their doors for extended periods of time. Even on reopening, venues had to adapt their seating arrangements and run at a lower capacity, which in some cases was not financially viable. Many restaurants, bars, and local hangouts shut down permanently. Swathes of local culture have been lost forever.

Social distancing and the rules enforced on large gatherings also meant that the on-location events industry has taken a huge hit. Festivals and sporting events, such as the National Collegiate Athletic Association basketball tournaments, College World Series, Formula 1 season, Glastonbury Music Festival, and Wimbledon have had to be either postponed or canceled, drastically affecting the many people employed directly by these large-scale events, as well as for hotels and restaurants in their vicinity and other indirect employment. Everyone from the performers to the organizers and from the caterers to other nearby businesses felt this impact. Even patrons of these shows were affected when ticket sellers refused to refund their tickets. The Tokyo Olympic Games, which was supposed to be held in 2020, was delayed by a year and had strict quarantine rules and COVID-19 measures. It was a commendable feat but not without consequences. Since the teams started arriving at Tokyo for the games,[3] over 380 positive cases of COVID-19 were reported.[4]

One positive thing we have seen in the last few years is the way communities have come together and supported each other through times of hardship using an empathetic approach. There is debate over whether our behaviors and habits have be changed permanently, but our reliance on certain social habits and comforts we had taken for granted has certainly been impacted.

Unemployment

1,600,000,000. One-point-six-billion! The figure is jaw-droppingly large.

The International Labor Organization (ILO) reported that over 144 million people were unemployed due to the pandemic, with an average unemployment rate of 6.5 percent.[5] At the peak of the pandemic, the United States, the largest global economy in terms of gross domestic product (GDP),[6] faced an unemployment rate of 14.8 percent.[7] Although these numbers dropped significantly after the COVID-19 vaccines started being administered to the population, we are still suffering in unprecdented ways. The ILO projects over 205 million unemployed by 2023.

That number does not represent the people on the margins of the world economy, from migrant workers to those employed in the gig economy, who are in immediate danger of losing their livelihoods. They make up half the world's workforce, and it is far from certain that their jobs will reappear. If we include these informal economy workers, then the number of unemployed people in the world skyrockets to almost 1.6 billion people! That is, 1.6 billion workers out of a global workforce of 3.3 billion had suffered some level of impact on their ability to earn a living due to the pandemic.[8]

There's a key question, even in a best-case scenario: How many of the jobs lost to COVID-19 will be lost for good, or at least for a

The Toll on Humanity

long time after the economic reopenings? That question is particularly acute in the service economy—restaurants, leisure businesses, small retail shops—and for the 1.6 billion strugglers in the informal economy worldwide.

Yet beyond the economic imponderables, long-term mass joblessness—possibly on the scale of the Great Depression in the 1930s—could pose major social and political challenges.

Work, especially for those living payday to payday, is essential to economic survival. But it's also central to people's identity, their sense of self-definition, even self-worth. Lack of work, on the other hand, can depress and embitter. A more recent example—the political fallout from the 2008 world financial crisis—is a reminder that one result can be a growth in the kind of anger and resentment on which populist strongmen often feed.

The good news that organizations like the ILO are emphasizing is that the employment crisis caused by COVID-19 is not limited to one country or region. Their hope is that, rather than focus only on the domestic imperative of getting each national economy back on its feet, governments will take shared, international action to address the needs of the "1.6 billion" in a post-pandemic world.

Hoarding and Profiteering Issues

The early stages of COVID-19 were a difficult time for supply chain logistics. When the pandemic first began and we did not know or understand the severity of this new virus, the United States went into a panic buying mode that has still not fully recovered. We had a severe paucity of information about the impact of COVID-19 on our health and well-being. At the same time, we kept hearing stories and accounts of how fast the virus was spreading, which made many people panic. And when people begin to panic, they resort to coveting and saving items that they feel are essential. Hoarding behaviors manifest during crises, and this is not unique to humans. Animals also have demonstrated the propensity to hoard during times of stress and adversity.

People started over-acquiring and hoarding essential items such as dry and non-perishable foods, toilet paper, kitchen towels, hand sanitizer, antibacterial wipes, bleach, disinfectant, nitrile gloves, masks, tissues, and pretty much anything that claimed to kill germs. As a result of mass overstocking, stores ran out of necessary supplies and could not restock as fast as items were flying off the shelves. Observing low inventory, people panicked even more, causing them to stockpile and create a shortage of these nonperishable goods.

The impact of this hoarding behavior on the community was terrible. Overwhelmed stores were unable to stock the hoarded items quickly. Hospitals, caregivers, and assisted homes had a shortage of medical supplies, hand sanitizer, and antibacterial wipes in many places. N95 masks were in deficit, putting healthcare personnel in considerable danger.[9] Some pharmacies ran out of certain medications due to overacquiring, putting patients who truly needed the prescriptions at significant risk.

Shortage of goods inevitably results in profiteering, price gouging, and black markets. It seems that some humans always exploit the fear, insecurity, and weaknesses of others because they are greedy. There are many stories of people profiteering and price gouging in the community. We have seen people sell supplies from their car trunks in parking lots. People have sold toilet paper for over $10 a roll and over $70 for a hand sanitizer bottle.[10] Even supermarkets got in on the action and increased their prices considerably, sometimes over 20 percent overnight. And it wasn't just these items. Some N95 masks and personal protection equipment (PPE) manufacturers inflated their prices by upward of 50 percent.[11] Many online sellers finally stepped in and introduced measures to prevent COVID-19 price gouging, an act that is a federal offense in the United States and several countries.

Perhaps the most appalling and famous hoarding story is about brothers Matt and Noah Colvin, who drove around Tennessee and Kentucky for over 1,250 miles and filled a uHaul truck with thousands of hand sanitizer bottles and an equal amount of antibacterial wipes.[12] They cleaned out the shelves from several stores and amassed almost 18,000 bottles of hand sanitizer. Matt listed these items on Amazon for anything between $8 and $70, way more than what he had paid for. This act was blatant profiteering and price gouging during a pandemic. Luckily, Amazon delisted his items, along with thousands of listings of face masks, hand sanitizer, and wipes from other similar price-gouging sellers. Walmart, eBay, and other e-commerce platforms followed suit. As a result of swift action from their online retailers, Colvin sat on a massive stockpile of sanitizer and wipes with no way to sell these items. At the same time, millions of people across the United States searched desperately for these items to protect themselves from the spread of COVID-19. Matt later donated two-thirds of his cache to a church, not because of the goodness of his heart, but because he wanted to avoid getting charged for profiteering and price gouging. Officials from the Tennessee attorney general's office seized the remaining third of his stockpile.

At the end of April 2020, the US Federal Trade Commission had to send warnings to multilevel-marketing (MLM) businesses telling them to stop advertising that their products can treat or cure COVID.[13] These businesses prey on stay-at-home mothers and military spouses at the best of times. But at the worst of times, when large numbers of people are already laid off and many families are having to make choices about work and child care, these businesses preyed on their fear without showing that 99 percent of distributors lose money, let alone the insane claims that the product has any medical uses.

Slowly, supply returned to normal; pasta sauce and taco shells found their way back on the shelves, followed by toilet paper, and finally, sanitizing wipes. After a few months, these products were in enough supply to be offered at sale prices again.

Lack of Trust in a Vaccine

Pain and suffering drive communities to resentment, cynicism, and paranoia. Trust in procedures goes down, and people question the efficacy of the systems that enforce those procedures. When a vaccine for COVID-19 was announced, hope was instilled in people, but that sentiment evaporated once vaccine administration began. How did we lose trust in the vaccination system? Did we ever trust the vaccination mechanisms, or did corruption and exploitation incidents drive people to distrust the vaccine rollouts?

The first group of people we need to look at are the so-called "anti-vaxxers." These are people who believe in conspiracy theories about vaccines. The "anti-vaxxer" movement has been around in one way or another since scientists invented vaccinations. People had fear and concern over the first vaccines for smallpox, mostly because they had never seen a vaccine before. In the 1980s, there were concerns over the DTP vaccine due to neurological side effects found in a small number of patients. But the beginnings of the modern-day mistrust of vaccines came from a now-debunked paper written by Andrew Wakefield in 1998. This article linked the MMR vaccine to autism and gastrointestinal disease.[14]

The media hyped this story. At that time, the rate of autism diagnosis was rising, and concerned parents were looking for a reason behind this. The Wakefield article was the center of a perfect storm. We know now that Wakefield exercised monetary and fraudulent practices to find a correlation between vaccines and the diseases, in addition to falsifying data. Since then, multiple studies have been conducted to refute the Wakefield article, but these newer studies have never received the media attention as the original Wakefield article.

Parents trapped in the echo chamber of anti-vaxxers on social media and friend circles increasingly choose not to vaccinate their children. Some cite religious beliefs, though most mainstream religions do not consider vaccination as taboo. Others questioned the efficacy of vaccines and said that better hygiene and living conditions were attributed to disease eradication. Some, not understanding how RNA vaccines work, claim that the vaccine is nothing but a willful introduction of the virus introducing fear into people. Another circular argument concocted by anti-vaxxers is that there is no need for vaccinations for infections that do not exist anymore. Of course, the reason for the infections not to exist is that vaccines are regularly administered to the population. Unfortunately, due to their conspiracy theories, fear-mongering, and disinformation tactics, anti-vaxxer propaganda has resulted in many outbreaks of vaccine-preventable diseases such as measles worldwide.

The fears about vaccinations in the black community are deeper rooted. Historically, black people in the United States were used as test subjects in medical experiments, many of them unknowing participants in these experiments. The most famous of these experiments was the Tuskegee Syphilis Experiment. This experiment was controlled by the US Public Health Service and later the Centers for Disease Control between 1932 and 1972.[15] The purpose of this study was to observe the course of untreated syphilis.

The study, conducted in conjunction with the Tuskegee Institute had 600 impoverished black men—399 men who had latent syphilis and 201 who did not. These men were incentivized to participate by being told that they would receive free government healthcare. These men were never told of their diagnosis and were given placebos or ineffective treatments for their disease. The men were told the "study" would last for six months, but it lasted for 40 years. None of the men were treated with penicillin, even though by 1947, that antibiotic was the standard treatment and wildly available.

The study only ended in 1972 because of a leak by epidemiologist Peter Buxtun. The July 26, 1972, headline of *The New York Times* was "Syphilis Victims in U.S. Study Went Untreated for 40 Years."[16] The study was officially terminated that November, and the federal government began to pay reparations to the participants and their descendants' families. It wasn't until 1997 that the sitting president, President Bill Clinton, issued an official apology.

This was not the only case of medical harm or experimentation conducted on the black community. Black women were experimented on without their consent[17] well into the 1960s.[18] These incidents are living memories. Many black people do not trust that the federal government will give them the same vaccine as others or that the vaccine would be safe for them. The speed at which pharmaceutical companies developed these vaccines and the swiftness of approving the vaccine's production and administration amplified the distrust. Many in the black community fear becoming the next unknowing subject of an experiment.

The third issue early on was line jumpers and corruption in the vaccine distribution system. In January 2021, a report was issued by the Guardian about a wealthy Canadian couple who chartered a plane to the Yukon territory and posed as hotel workers to receive vaccines meant for indigenous peoples.[19] In Los Angeles, the codes needed to make vaccine appointments were being stolen and used by those not yet eligible for vaccination.[20] In Florida, young women dressed up as older adults to procure the vaccine and were caught when they returned for their second dose.[21]

Countries vouch not to let anyone get preferential treatment during the vaccination process, but it has been challenging not to let unconscious bias seep in. The rollout protocols intended that healthcare and frontline workers, along with the elderly, would be targeted first. However, it was hard to adhere to those intentions with privilege and elitism so rampant in our society. Cases of discriminatory and preferential treatment during vaccine distribution were continu-ally on the news and once again exposed the deep-rooted problem of systemic racism and discrimination toward minorities. Many wealthy, privileged, and connected elites in an advantaged position economically and socially had no difficulty violating the protocols to procure access to the vaccine. In contrast, society's vulnerable mem-bers had to wait patiently, every day filled with fear and apprehen-sion, isolated from their loved ones, and praying each day that it might be their lucky day.

To reach the public as quickly as possible, many state govern-ments created community vaccine clinics and mobile access pro-grams, sometimes targeting people of color, where vaccines are being administered at churches, local pharmacies, and mobile units, rather than the mass vaccination sites that we have seen in other places. This was meant to get the vaccine out to more people in vul-nerable and low-income areas. First, many in those communities could not drive to those mass vaccination sites. Second, others in that community saw vaccinated people and realized that it is safe, with the operating thought that more people would get vaccinated because it was conveniently available.

We watched high-profile individuals: the president, vice presi-dent, Jesse Jackson, former President Obama and former first lady Michelle, and others be vaccinated on TV while many others recorded their vaccinations and posted them on social media with their vac-cination cards or "I got the vaccine" picture frames.

Some people felt that these vaccines were rushed through trials and approval expeditiously, quicker than any other vaccine in recent memory, at least. But this "feeling" isn't true. Scientists were not start-ing from scratch. COVID-19 is a part of the SARS family, and scien-tists had been studying and working on a vaccine for SARS for years. There was an unprecedented worldwide collaboration in addition to enormous funding to find a cure for the global pandemic. That is not the traditional approach. When there isn't a global pandemic, there are issues with finding enough people to test the vaccine, getting the cooperation of various governments. Many other challenges that scientists developing a cure would have faced were eliminated because almost every government incentivized vaccine development and administration.

Once the vaccine became readily available, it hit a new roadblock: Everyone who was eager to be vaccinated had received the vaccine, and COVID-19 cases fell precipitiously. But COVID-19 didn't disappear, and variants of the virus became prevalent. The public also started getting mixed messages. If you get vaccinated, you don't need a mask. Get vaccinated, but still wear masks. Get vaccinated, even if you have had COVID-19. Don't get vaccinated if you have had COVID. As treatments became more understood and more and more people were surviving COVID, the urgency to get vaccinated declined. Young people, especially, often decided they were willing to take a chance with COVID rather than receive a new vaccine.

There have been an increasing number of peer-reviewed studies on COVID-19 emphasizing the efficacy of the vaccines, and how they have contained the spread of the virus, but this isn't the information that the general public hears. People receive most of their news through social media headlines and snippets and do not perform their due diligence of reading through shared articles to understand the facts. Many of these articles are not from verified sources, are paid pieces, cherry-picked facts, conjecture, or hearsay, but social media lends them legitimacy. The more these spurious articles are liked and shared within the community, the more they become the truth. Perception has genuinely become a reality, and people have difficulty deciding between what is real and fiction. Social media companies have begun to label certain news and claims as false. However, false information is easy to create, and rumors are spread so quickly online it is nearly impossible for these sites to control the spread of all misinformation.

Racial Inequality and the Pandemic

COVID-19 has exposed deficiencies and administrative flaws at institutional levels while revealing how the system is racially discriminatory toward minorities. Racial inequality emerged through a rising number of cases among Black and Hispanic communities, spurred by the prevalence of the employment disparities. This, in turn, gives rise to social and economic discrimination and has been a hot topic of discussion and contention for decades.

Latino and African American communities have been three times more likely to be affected than their white counterparts, while the mortality rates were 5.5 and 6.7 times higher for black adults than white adults.[22] It emphasizes the disparity in living conditions, employment opportunities, and access to healthcare among these communities. This inequality has put some communities at a greater risk of contracting and dying from the virus than racially preferred white people.

Racial discrimination impedes protecting the fundamental right of equal access to essential healthcare and housing facilities to everyone regardless of their race and gender. COVID-19 has exposed ground realities and systemic racism being practiced by institutions meant to protect all races. While we can give the benefit of the doubt to some practices that caused unintentional consequences, the majority of cases reflect inherent systemic racism and have put the lives of racial and ethnic minorities in critical danger, increasing their morbidity and mortality rates.

Anti-Asian Sentiment

While the United States has a harrowing history of racism against the black community, it also has a long history of racism against Asians. Politics has fanned the flames of xenophobia and racial discrimination, inciting people who are already insecure, creating convenient scape-goats to blame for their suffering and adversity.

Asian Americans have been dealing with an uninformed public believing/blaming all Asians for the COVID-19 virus. It does not help when the former president of the United States callously called COVID-19 the "China Virus," stigmatizing people of Asian heritage. At the beginning of the pandemic, President Trump or members of his administration used the phrase "China Virus," "China Flu,"[23] or "Wuhan Virus" more than 20 times in March 2020.[24] This behavior provided a false sense of personification to a pandemic and legiti-mized victimization of an entire ethnicity. Over the following year, xenophobic violence, racist attacks, and hate crimes rose, in many cases due to direct and blatant encouragement from government leaders and people in power. Asian racism is on the rise as well. The Trump administration clearly fanned the flames of this ethnic hatred, and though it is not in office anymore, we are experiencing the repercussions of these acts of incitement.

Between March and December of 2020, the organization Stop Asian American and Pacific Islander hate[25] has reported more than 3,000 incidents of Anti-Asian hate crimes.[26] The city of New York reported a 1,900 percent increase in Anti-Asian hate crimes.[27] Let that sink in for a minute—1,900 percent increase of anti-Asian hate crimes. To put that in perspective, the Dolby Theater in Los Angeles can seat around 3,400 guests during the Annual Academy Awards (Oscars). The people at this event celebrate achievements over the year and are all part of the actors' community. Now, imagine a same-sized group of people who were not celebrating acting and the magic of movies, but instead xenophobia, violence, and hate crimes against Asians. This group would have to rent a large football (or soccer) stadium to host their annual racial hatred conference in 2020, and even then, they would need to use a portion of the field for standing room entrants.

In March 2020, a New York representative introduced a resolution to condemn anti-Asian rhetoric.[28] While this resolution passed the New York House, 164 Republicans voted against it. She received racist voicemails mentioning the "karate kid virus" and "Chinese virus." The representative said in an interview with a news outlet, "Our people are getting attacked. Our people are getting harassed, spat on, beat up, slashed. Please, somebody, pay attention. Please, notice us. Give me confirmation that I am American, too. I just haven't been able to feel that in a long time."

By 2021, the news finally began prominently speaking about anti-Asian racism and crimes. In February 2021, an Asian man was stabbed with an eight-inch knife in the back in New York City's Chinatown.[29] The criminal was with attempted murder and assault but not hate crime since the police had no proof that the criminal saw the victim's face before stabbing him.[30] Many Asians were notably concerned with how the rest of the world would treat them during their Lunar New Year celebrations. They feared that they would not have the freedom to celebrate with their family or even express their emotions during this joyous event.

Former New York Knick and current member of the Santa Cruz Warriors Jeremy Shu-How Lin reported being called "Coronavirus" on the court during a game.[31] Lin has stated that he would not publicly reveal the player who called him that racial epithet on the court because that was not his point.

A Spanish teacher in Sacramento was caught on video explaining to her students that if people's eyes slant upwards, they are Chinese; if they slant down, they are Japanese, and straight one can never really know.[32] Such comments are not only abusive to Asian children, it can permeate other aspects of life and allow bullying, taunting, and scar children.

In March 2021, a shooting spree at three spas in Atlanta, Georgia, United States, resulted in eight people killed, six of whom were Asian women. This act was identified as a targeted killing of Asians, and this event triggered mass protests against anti-Asian violence across the world.[33] Attacks on Asians in 16 of the largest cities in the United States increased by a shocking 164 percent in the first quarter of 2021 alone,[34] with reports of hate crime almost every day.[35]

These problems are not just happening in the United States. This phenomenon is a global crisis[36] and is rooted in hate and xenophobia. Racism was always prevalent in the human race. The strain on society generated by the pandemic has resulted in scapegoating, scare-mongering, and targeted racial hatred. Many governments have not focused on this issue as their resources were tied up battling a devastating pandemic, allowing this hatred to fester and spread. Some governments actively fan the flames of racism, allowing society to burn and turn upon themselves, permitting racists to express their deep-rooted xenophobia in violent ways, sometimes engaging in this rhetoric themselves, and exploiting their base fears.

Are there any takeaways from these events? This generation of Asians, especially Asian-Americans, is going to publicize what is happening to them. These men and women are using their phones to record the racism occurring to them or others around them. The perpetuation of the "model minority" myth allows the general public to believe that Asians do not experience discrimination. Is it not racist to be stereotyped and labeled "studious and passive"?

On several occasions over my career, I have heard my coworkers laugh and comment at my software and math skills. I have heard phrases like, "Can you fix this computer issue? It should be easy for you," alluding to the tech support stereotype. Or when I use the calculator app on my phone, "Should you not be able to calculate that in your head? Why are you using a calculator?" During the height of the Iraq War, a visibly concerned bar patron came over to my friend and chastised him for fraternizing with the enemy (he thought I was Iraqi because I was brown). He then proceeded to tell me to get out of this country and go back to my bomb-ridden hellhole. Sadly, some insecure individuals cannot reconcile with the universal truth that different kinds of people make up this world.

Two Personal Anecdotes

I am an Indian who came to the United States for my doctoral studies. I got a job in Midwest America and my wife and I moved to the heartland of the United States for a while. We spent the first month exploring the place—shopping malls, grocery stores, restaurants—you get the idea. Our first experience was pretty scary. On our way back from a lake that our friends said we had to check out, we decided to stop at a Walmart Supercenter for groceries. Our first sign was the greeter, who stared at us funnily as if we were not meant to be there. We continued to get stares in the aisles. People seemed visibly uncomfortable around us. My wife and I quickly checked out and loaded up our car. We had a pickup truck follow us from the grocery store pretty close to us. I tried to shake the truck off, but the driver continued to tailgate us aggressively. I finally pulled over to the side to allow the truck to pass me. The truck pulled up beside me, and the occupants of the pickup flipped me off and yelled, "Go back to where you came from. America is for Americans. We don't want your kind here." The passenger side occupant then threw a beer can at our car and sped off. That was our first taste of racial intimidation.

The second experience that I would like to share happened in a corporate office and highlights stereotyping. I had met a friend for lunch, and we decided to continue our conversation at his office. In this building, like many organizations, each floor was dedicated to a specific business function. Floors 3 and

4 were dedicated to IT while the executives were assigned the top floor (Floor 8). The post-lunch crowd was returning to work, and the elevator was crowded. Since my friend's office was on the top floor, we maneuvered ourselves to the back of the elevator. We stopped at the IT floors, and several people got out. As we resumed our ride, I heard an executive breathe a deep sigh and state, "The elevator smells like curry now!" I heard laughter from the others in the elevator. My friend looked at me and gave an apologetic smile, but it astounded me how comfortable others felt around that statement. We reached the top floor, and I got out, and the executive who had made that disgusting remark was shocked to see a non-white person enter one of the executive offices. My friend then told me that several executives were pretty "conservative" and had a different view of the world. Indeed!

Black Lives Matter Demonstrations

Since 2013, the Black Lives Matter (BLM) movement has spotlighted the debate about police brutality in the United States. However, the tangible impact of the demonstrations became visible only after the death of George Floyd in May 2020. In a widespread show of solidarity, individuals of all races came together to extend their support to the victims of racial violence. States across the country have approved or pledged to adopt measures, in various capacities, to confront the permeating racism within police departments decisively.

Although the BLM movement has its roots in the United States, it has garnered widespread international support with local demonstrations in at least 60 countries globally[37] because racism and discrimination are found in almost every society.

The historical background underlying contemporary racial inequalities are unique to each country, but there are certain commonalities. The EU Agency for Fundamental Rights reports[38] how pervasive racism thrives within the European continent. It highlights how the racial minorities are often reduced to the color of their skin. For example, in terms of employment, Austria, Luxembourg, and Italy reported the highest number of cases where the prospective employees faced discrimination due to their racial background. Racial discrimination is also visible in Brussels, which houses significant EU institutions. Several French and international human rights organizations have taken the issue of racial discrimination to court. Reportedly, law enforcement officials have mocked the gravity of hate crimes by downplaying the racial factor behind them.

The United Kingdom has witnessed waves of protests across cities like Manchester, London, and Bristol. The UK has a longstanding legacy of police brutality being committed against the black community members. Along with France, it remains one of the worst-affected countries by racial profiling.[39] The marginalized community accounts for 8 percent of the total custodial deaths. In comparison, their population count is only 3 percent of the entire population of the United Kingdom.[40]

Cultural violence is prevalent in these societies. It occurs when certain beliefs become so deeply embedded within the fabric of a society that they are uncritically reproduced throughout generations. The perception that nonwhites are primitive and intellectually inferior to Caucasians has carried well into the twenty-first century. The systematic forms of racism are embedded deep within our societies. Being black or Latino triggers images of racism, poor housing, crime, and poor jobs with many privileged or elite members of society.

In additional to cultural violence, structural violence enforces the marginalization of a given section of the population. It is done through ratification of laws or through a cultural mandate that legitimizes the perpetuation of such acts. Direct violence, on the other hand, instills emotions such as despair and humiliation among the marginalized community. It is a direct result of structural violence.

This section of the society has borne the overwhelming impact of this kind of violence. Although each of the previously mentioned countries does operate according to the democratic principle of "right to equality," they, however, choose to apply it selectively. Victims of discriminatory policies suffer mainly on the grounds that they frequently experience the struggle of living within a fractured system that denies them justice.

BLM Resources

It is extremely tough to pick a few examples of racial injustice, prejudice, or discrimination against the black community. Each story, each encounter, each experience is saddening, infuriating, and insightful in its own unique way. I have enclosed a few organizations that are fighting against racial injustice, violence, and racial hatred. I have also included a short list of books that have been insightful, thought-provoking, and beneficial in expanding my mind on this critical topic.

- **Black Lives Matter.** Founded in 2013 in response to the acquittal of George Zimmerman, who killed Trayvon Martin. It is a global foundation and has the mission of eradicating white supremacy and intervene in violence on black communities by the state and vigilantes. https://blacklivesmatter.com/

(continues)

The Toll on Humanity

(continued)

- **Reclaim the Block.** Started in 2018 to organize Minneapolis to defund the police and instead fund other areas that promote community health and safety.
https://www.reclaimtheblock.org/

- **TMI Project.** Founded by Eva Tenuto and Julie Novak, TMI Project has a mission to amplify radically true stories to ignite human connection, challenge the status quo, and enable people to take action for positive social change.
https://www.tmiproject.org/

- **NAACP Legal Defense and Educational Fund (NAACP LDF).** A nonprofit organization, NAACP LDF is the US premier legal organization fighting for racial justice since 1940. LDF has been fighting to transform society to achieve racial justice, equality, and inclusivity.
https://mnfreedomfund.org/

- **Black Visions Collective.** An organization that believes in uplifting the inherent worth of all black people, build collective power to address racial injustice and influence global movements, celebrate black heritage and history, and strive for a better future for the black community.
https://www.blackvisionsmn.org/

- **Minnesota Freedom Fund.** An organization that envisions a world where justice restores humanity and dignity of all people. This organization pays criminal bail and immigration bonds for those who cannot afford it and seeks to bring systemic change to Minnesota's criminal justice system and eradicate it of discriminatory, coercive, and oppressive jailing.
https://mnfreedomfund.org/

Books

- *Between the World and Me,* Ta-Nehisi Coates
- *The New Jim Crow,* Michelle Alexander
- *Women, Race, & Class,* Angela Y. Davis
- *When They Call You a Terrorist,* Patrisse Khan-Cullors, asha bandele
- *How to Be an Antiracist,* Ibram X. Kendi
- *They Can't Kill Us All,* Wesley Lowery
- *So You Want to Talk about Race,* Ijeoma Oluo
- *White Fragility,* Robin DiAngelo
- *One Person, No Vote,* Carol Anderson
- *Why I'm No Longer Talking to White People about Race,* Reni Eddo-Lodge
- *Born a Crime,* Trevor Noah

There are thousands of stories online and several books on this topic. I encourage you to read some of them and help bring racial justice, equality, diversity, inclusivity, and equity into our society.

Gender Inequality and the Pandemic

Throughout history, crises are never gender-neutral, and COVID-19 is no exception. Although society has faced unprecedented challenges, women had an uneven share of adversity and were impacted far more than men.

With childcare centers and schools shutting down, many working mothers of young children were challenged with juggling both work and home. Many mothers left the workforce or reduced their work hours to take care of their families. Several of my friends expressed that they were grateful for their wives leaving their jobs to help their children adapt to virtual schooling or take care of the babies. It is commendable that these mothers prioritized their families over their careers, but it has not been easy for them to return to work post-vaccination. With high unemployment rates, the competition for well-paying jobs has increased. Add to that gender inequality and bias in talent acquisition, and it is harder for women to reclaim their places in the workforce.

Many industries that women traditionally were more prone to be employed in were impacted the most in 2020 and have declined.[41] Industry verticals such as retail, food services, hospitality, education, healthcare, and social work are still reeling from the impact of the global pandemic. They have been struggling to recuperate their losses. These industries have had a high level of unemployment, furloughs, and reduction in force events. These layoffs have negatively impacted women, especially women of color.[42] In many countries, layoffs also mean no unemployment benefits, healthcare benefits, or protection. As a result, more women have been driven to poverty than men.[43]

In the workplace, women have to face not just gender discrimination but also racial discrimination and sexual harassment (or sexual abuse). Even before the pandemic, gender inequality was predominant, and COVID-19 might have set back any hard-won progress on closing this gender wage gap.[44]

The #metoo movement[45] is one of the prominent social justice and empowerment movements, started by sexual harassment survivor and activist Tarana Burke. This movement resulted in the exposure of widespread sexual abuse and harassment across the world. Today, it is an international movement for justice for marginalized people in marginalized communities.[46]

In addition to all these challenges, women have traditionally been handling the burdens of housework and caregiving. I remember how my mother—a doctor and head of the department for a prestigious medical institution in India—would come home, spend a few minutes relaxing and freshening up, and immediately head into the kitchen to prep for dinner, despite being exhausted. Societal expectations of a woman's behavior and the urge to control every aspect of their lives are sadly prevalent throughout the world and add to women's stress and anxiety.

Actions for Impact

What can people who identify as male do to help? Here are a few suggested actions for impact:

- **Increase awareness of the challenges women face.** Be an ally for a women's employee resource group or affinity group in your workplace. Work with your HR group to improve hiring for women and underrepresented minority groups.[47]
- **Respect women, treat them as equals, and empower them.** In the workforce, women have been stereotyped and designated specific roles. Their opinions are disregarded subtly (or blatantly in severely male-dominated organizations). Prejudice and bias are unfortunately rampant in the workplace. Later on in the book, I share an interview where a woman felt double persecution for being a woman and nonwhite. She said that she did not know which was worse.

(continues)

(continued)

It is not enough to celebrate women during International Women's Week and treat them as equal only during the month of March. Respect must come from within and not be mandated.

- **Appreciate everything women do and empathize with them.** Share the workload both at work and at home. Perform all the household chores on occasion and allow your loved one to relax or take some time just for herself. Have a reverse mentor in the workplace to understand a woman's perspective. Refrain from being condescending or mansplaining.[48] Recognize and leverage their strengths. Accept the reality that almost every woman has at least two roles—a professional role in the workplace, and a mother, sister, aunt, daughter, partner (or all of the above) role in her personal life, and sometimes personal life takes precedence. Empathize with them and try to help them by reducing the pressure at work.

Virtual Schooling

Switching to a remote, digital experience for education was a harrowing time for almost everyone. Parents suddenly became substitute teachers and had to be more involved in their child's education and mental development. Working parents had to juggle work and school. They had to help when their children had challenges with distance learning technology, handling disturbances during the workday gracefully, and caring for and feeding their children. With the whole family often occupying the same space day after day, the strain seemed unrelenting. Unemployment or even the fear of being laid off added considerable stress on working parents. What we faced was not a traditional work-from-home situation but what I refer to as *existence from home*.

Teachers and educators also faced similar stress during virtual schooling. They had to change, sometimes within a couple of days, their teaching mode, their management of children, and their technology toolset. They had to learn how to handle an entire classroom through video conferencing and provide individual attention to students remotely. When many schools adapted a hybrid schooling model, teachers had to exert themselves more with a classroom divided between in-person and remote attendees (roomers and zoomers, as my child's school called it). Imagine the amount of stress for a teacher who also had a child attending school!

Despite their sacrifice and anxieties of adapting to digital schooling, some parents failed to empathize with their plight. These parents tried to project their stress and concerns on teachers and felt deceived into being homeschool teachers for their children. Unfortunately, any amount of hard work put in by teachers did not seem to be enough for a section of society that took their children's education within a physical school environment for granted.

The effects of the pandemic on education are yet to be fully comprehended. As schools prepare to have in-person teaching once again, middle school and high school children are excited to interact with their teachers, friends, and peers in a physical setting. Some elementary schoolchildren, including my son, have trepidations because they have not been vaccinated yet (as of writing this book), but hope springs eternal.

Dealing with Your Child's Stress and Fears

After watching the news or overhearing an adult conversation regarding the pandemic and other social unrest, children might feel scared and uncertain. Many of the events of the past few years have been front and center in the news, so it should be a top priority to address your child's fears and reassure their physical and emotional well-being.

Talk at an age-appropriate level. If your child is young, don't volunteer too much information, as this could cause their imagination to run wild. Instead, try to answer any questions they might have. It's okay not to know everything; if your child is older, help them find accurate information from the US Centers for Disease Control and Prevention (CDC), Black Lives Matter, or StopAAPIHate.

Answer questions clearly and honestly. If your child has questions, know that honesty is always the best policy. Although you don't want to frighten young children, there's nothing wrong with talking about complex topics such as racial injustice, gender inequality, xenophobia, or racial profiling. *A word of caution:* Children are impressionable but not yet corrupted, so be careful not to promote your biases, views, or prejudices on them. Try to be fair and share different perspectives.

Give extra love and affection. The last few years have been a stressful time for all of us, and we could all benefit from extra affection. Your child will appreciate extra hugs and kisses.

Designate special one-on-one time. If everyone is at home with each other all the time, having one-on-one time with each child is a great way to forge a closer bond. Have your child choose an activity for the two of you to participate in together.

Find things to be grateful about. Each evening, share with your children one fun or positive thing you experienced that day and encourage them to do the same. It could be a work or school accomplishment, a home repair, or something as simple as witnessing a beautiful sunset. It may sound cliched, but acknowledging gratitude and positive experiences can provide a respite from negative thinking and really boost your family's mood.

Financial Impact on Industries

With the announcement of lockdown in many cities and safety protocols for COVID-19, many businesses were forced to close, and the economy has suffered a downturn in GDP, major borrowing costs related to the furlough scheme and other central government incentives, and increased unemployment. Coronavirus has had a devastating impact on a wide range of industries, although some have thrived in the new world ushered in by measures taken to stop the spread of the virus. With the enforced changes to our lifestyles, we've had to adapt. For example, we have been more reliant than ever before on services such as online ordering and home deliveries of groceries and other essential household items.

The pandemic affected the arts sector as well. The nature of this sector, in which audiences gather at close quarters, has meant theatre shows and live performances could not take place safely during the pandemic. Many museums have had to lay off workers and close down as they did not qualify as essential establishments. Gyms and community centers have suffered similarly. Lockdown protocols and social distancing guidelines prevented these establishments from opening, causing some gyms to go out of business or declare bankruptcy.

On the flip side of this, some industries saw a significant increase in sales or demand for their services.

Our reliance on technology and more specifically communications technology has never been greater. Businesses that previously never had employees working from home now need to ensure that they can maintain productivity and that their teams can keep in contact with one another. This, coupled with the increase in online socializing to keep in touch with family and friends, has seen video-conferencing software soar in popularity. Zoom saw a thirtyfold jump in use in April 2020, and at its peak counted more than 300 million daily participants in virtual meetings.[49]

Online retail has benefited immensely since February 2020. With the shutting of many physical stores during the full lockdown, consumers had no alternative but to shop online. Although stores have reopened, online retail sales have been over 46 percent higher than at February's prepandemic levels,[50] suggesting that many people prefer the comfort and convenience of shopping online to visiting a physical store. This change in behavior may be a long-lasting one, now that so many people have got used to online shopping as the default option. The world has shifted to a contactless, digital, remote economy.

Household goods saw an increase in sales,[51] which were 9.9 percent higher in August than in February 2020, coming mainly from the increased sales for home improvement items. With much more of their time now spent at home, consumers decided to improve and update their living and working-from-home spaces, with considerable building work taking place to extend and enhance that space.

In addition, because lockdown protocols forced people to stay at home, remodeling and home improvement projects also surged. Backyard improvements such as play areas for children, patios, kitchen gardens, pantries, decks, redesigning basements, and attics as office work areas or landscaping are some of the popular home improvement projects brought on by the pandemic. Houzz, an online home modeling site, listed a 58 percent increase in home improvement projects just for the month of June 2020.[52] IHS Markit, a leading information analytics global firm, reported upward of $440 billion for home improvement products alone.[53] A global lumber shortage has resulted in backorders of home building, renovation, and furniture, coupled with skyrocketing prices.[54]

One positive thing that came out of 2020 is the way communities came together and supported each other through times of hardship using an empathetic approach. There is debate over whether our behaviors and habits will be changed permanently, but our reliance on certain social habits and comforts we had taken for granted has certainly been jolted, as we continue to adapt to new circumstances.

The Negative Impact on Healthcare

COVID-19 turned healthcare systems throughout the world upside down in just a few months. The current discourse focuses mainly on the health consequences of the virus and its socioeconomic consequences. The rapid deployment of forces dedicated to managing patients with the virus and culling its spread was seismic. However, emergencies and patients who have chronic health conditions have not simply vanished.

Over 28.4 million procedures had been postponed during the peak 12 weeks of the pandemic due to canceled or postponed surgical procedures, and 2.3 million cancer surgeries were expected to be postponed.[55] Estimates projected that 72.3 percent of all surgical procedures would be canceled and that benign disease and orthopaedics would be the most affected procedures. On the other hand, a study published by the same group could show that postoperative pulmonary complications and mortality were significantly elevated in operated patients with COVID-19. To minimize the risk for COVID-19 related complications after hospital procedures, some healthcare facilities have introduced clinical pathways and care processes to decrease exposure to convalescing patients.

Kudos to Our Healthcare Workers

COVID-19 overwhelmed healthcare workers, paramedics, first responders, and medical researchers. Despite challenging situations, these heroes have responded with immense empathy and have gone above and beyond the call of duty, risking their lives—and the lives of their loved ones—to help humanity. They have selflessly endured long hours and strenuous shifts, assisting strangers to feel better, providing extra care in these trying times to alleviate patients' anxieties. It can be exhausting at times, and the personal cost is high, but the resolve and grit that these heroes have demonstrated are commendable indeed.

"Every day is a different kind of battle with no idea of what we will encounter," said a California hospital nurse in October 2020. "There is always the fear of accidentally being exposed to the virus and contracting it, or worse, transmitting it to my family. We try to take as many precautions as possible, but there is always the risk of exposure.[...] I could never forgive myself if I was the reason my family got infected." Some nurses confessed that some COVID-19 patients treated them as bad omens and angels of death when they came to check on them. "I decided to become a nurse to help people and comfort them in their times of suffering, but instead, I am being treated like an evil presence, waiting to disconnect the ventilator," said a nurse almost in tears.

It is unquestionably a difficult situation. Adding to this misery, for a few months there was a shortage of hospital and medical supplies—nitrile gloves, personal protective equipment (PPE), hand sanitizer, or cleaning supplies. "We had to use our personal gloves and masks for a while, increasing the risk of infection to our families," reported a pharmacist. "How can people be so greedy when the whole world is suffering?" a first responder said, referring to the many news reports of excessive hoarding and inflated prices for these items.

The challenges do not stop in their lines of work, either. Many have reported that they have been denied access to certain services such as regular dental or vision checkups because they work in COVID units. Close friends and relatives consciously shun them and their families because they could carry the virus. "It is tough for me to arrange a playdate for my child," said a paramedic. "Everyone is scared right now, and I can understand that, but my child is suffering extra from this pandemic. First because of virtual schooling and second because of being shunned on account of me. And she did nothing wrong. I am very concerned for her mental and emotional development."

It is hard to see these wonderful, selfless human beings going above and beyond what they need to do. On the other hand, people refused to wear a mask in public, threw parties, and mingled openly in public areas, openly flaunting lockdown protocols as a defiance to the "system." One can get a sense of despair, gloom, and hopelessness looking at how inconsiderate some people can be. At the same time, we see hope for humanity through the actions of a few empathic people who have chosen to lead and elevate the human quality of life.

The Negative Impact on Retail

The retail industry is customer-obsessed as it is designed to cater to consumer needs. Customers, however, are highly demanding, and their needs shift constantly. With the proliferation of smartphones, tablets, 5G connectivity, and ubiquitous computing, the retail industry had started to explore omnichannel and personalized experiences before the pandemic. The global pandemic disrupted the entire industry, forcing retail companies to rethink their business models, market strategies, and delivery mechanisms.

The impacts on the economy have been hard enough that some retailers say that recovery could extend several more years. Staying at home and not going out to the store made online purchasing spread widely among those who had not used it before, and retailers have responded by decreasing in-store inventory while carrying more products online. Due to the change in workstyles resulting from people being forced to work remotely from home, life via online channels has become normal. The digital technology that supports the online lifestyle has been popular for some time, but its spread has accelerated explosively since the onset of the pandemic.

Due to the government's request for essential business continuity, retail businesses that handle food and daily necessities such as supermarkets, drugs stores, and convenience stores (excluding stores located in office districts) have remained in good condition as consumers wait in long lines at cash registers to buy products, many of which have even sold out. On the other hand, retailers of shopping goods and luxury items deemed nonessential, such as apparel and home appliances, have stagnated.

Let's focus on the changes in the business processes of the retail industry that were particularly affected by COVID-19. In retail businesses handling food and daily necessities, some examples of quick action taken include the application of floor stickers to indicate appropriate social distancing positions for customers waiting in check-out lines. Vinyl curtains were also installed at cashier check-out counters, in part to protect employees. In addition, actions such as disinfection of shopping carts and individual packaging of products to prevent droplet infection were added to everyday routines in response to customer demand for safety, which have added to employee fatigue. Some tried to induce customers to use electronic commerce by placing orders online for in-store pickup. The aim was to disperse in-store customer visits, but the capacity of pre-order systems were too small to achieve the anticipated outcome.

Fear for Her Life

Mary was a cashier at a grocery chain. When the pandemic hit, she was scared to go into work but had no choice since she was the sole breadwinner of her family. Her husband lost his job when the restaurant he worked in was forced to shut down. She witnessed the panic when canned goods, toiletries, and disinfectants disappeared off the shelves. "Customers were frustrated, irate, and panicking. It was very stressful working at the store, not just because of the pandemic but also because I was scared of being assaulted by an angry customer. They seem to target us as the reason for them not finding toilet paper or disinfectant wipes." Mary shared her coworkers' recounts of how one customer filled two grocery carts full of toilet paper, hand sanitizer, gloves, and disinfectant wipes. At the same time, his wife loaded up another grocery cart full of canned goods. "It felt like people were shopping for a zombie apocalypse or the end of the world. It felt unreal. People jostled each other;

(continues)

(continued)

there were fights in the aisles, people stealing from each other carts, yelling and shouting at the checkout lines demanding faster service. It was like an explosion waiting to happen."

Several grocery chains raised worker wages temporarily to entice their attendance at work, and those measures helped a bit. However, due to supply chain challenges and shortages of items, prices rose, offsetting any benefit workers could derive from the temporary wage increases. "I had to spend extra money on disinfecting my work clothes regularly—laundry detergent, disinfectant wipes, hand soap. Our water and electricity bills increased."

Sanitation protocols and deep-cleaning practices were rolled out, adding to their workload. "I was exhausted by the end of my shift. Being a cashier, I had to wipe my hands, the conveyor belt, payment pad, and my station for every customer. I had to be quick about it, but at the same time ensure proper cleanliness. People have lost their patience, and it has been a long time since anyone has treated me like a human," Mary confided. "It is a miracle that I have not gotten infected so far, knock on wood."

As stores started demanding customers wear a mask at all times in the store, things started heating up again. Many people considered this an affront to their freedom. There were numerous reports of customers screaming obscenities and shouting at workers who tried to enforce the mask mandate at store entrances. Some of Mary's coworkers were physically abused. "One lady even spat on my coworker," Mary recalls. "We were terrified. How can people be so selfish and think only about themselves? All we are doing is asking them to wear a mask to reduce the risk of airborne transmission. Do they question the TSA when they are asked to remove their shoes and jackets at airport security? Some people are insecure and they try to demonstrate their privilege through these petty ways."

There are numerous reports of vicious attacks on grocery store workers by these so-called "maskholes." Spurious organizations such as the fictitious "Freedom to Breathe Agency" provide an avenue for selfish and inconsiderate people by legitimizing their disregard for communal safety. Mary said that she and her coworkers continually hear misguided people claim that there is no legal obligation to wear a mask and that mandating them to comply violates their civil liberties.

"We are putting ourselves and our families at risk because we want to provide essential service to the community. We have older people who come into stores or people who cannot afford to shop online. All we are asking is for people to be considerate, and well, human."

Company headquarters, meanwhile, were forced to act urgently to achieve business continuity while responding to the sudden shift to remote workstyles. They had to implement changes such as granting authority to their employees to allow them to use company PCs at home, and to arrange for paper documents to be taken off company premises. Another example is the rotation systems they created for employees. One characteristic of the retail business is that when storefronts are fully operating, the headquarters that support them can't stop operating either, so they were forced to make big changes in their conventional working methods. In addition, because they were unable to receive stable supplies of products from business partners, stores had to come up with new operations to deal with stockout issues, such as limiting purchases to one per customer for certain products.

In this way, business processes throughout all areas of the retail industry have felt the impact, and have been dealing with these countermeasures for several months now.

The Negative Impact on Travel and Hospitality

In the past decades, travel and tourism experienced continued growth and became one of the fastest-growing economic sectors globally. The sector witnessed a 59 percent growth over the decade in international tourists' arrivals from 1.5 billion 2019 compared to 880 million in 2009.[56] Tourism is also a key driver for socioeconomic progress, with tourism specific developments in an increasing number of national and international destinations.

Globally, the tourism industry contributed to $8.9 trillion to the global GDP in 2019 equaling a contribution of 10.3 percent. It is also to note that 1 in 4 of all new jobs around the world is in tourism, equaling 334 million jobs.[57]

However, the strong historical growth has been halted in 2020 amid the global COVID-19 pandemic. With airplanes on the ground, hotels closed, and travel restrictions implemented, travel and tourism became one of the most affected sectors since the very start of the virus spread. The pandemic cut international tourist arrivals in the first quarter of 2020 to a fraction of what they were a year ago.

The aviation industry's revenue totaled only $328 billion, over 60 percent lesser than 2019. In fact, 2020's revenue was similar to what it was two decades ago.[58] The travel industry, in particular, had to incur considerable costs due to the pandemic. Hygiene, sanitization, and safety standards had to be maintained. Several countries restricted travel both internationally and domestic to contain the spread of the virus.

As more people are getting vaccinated every day, travel and tourism have started booming again. After months of being confined to homes, there is a global desire for people to travel once again, take those vacations that they had put off for over a year, and celebrate life and their newfound sense of freedom. Business travel is slowly picking up. Countries are slowly opening their borders for travel and tourism to capitalize on leisure trips that people are longing to take.

However, travelers will need to prepare themselves for changes that the industry has started rolling out:

- The frequency and flexibility of flights out of certain areas will be low for a while as airlines cautiously reevaluate their flight economic. As business travel ramps up, this might change, but tourist hotspots will be the priority for most airlines for now.
- During the pandemic, many airlines had to incur debt to stay solvent. They will inevitably target passengers to recoup these costs. Ticket prices will increase and will remain high for a while. I foresee a minimum of 3–7 percent hike in ticket prices for the rest of 2021 and into 2022. The cost of jet fuel and changes in flight patterns due to atmospheric and climate changes could increase ticket prices further.
- Service levels of airlines and their performance will drop initially. Flight crews will be more stringent for a while, adhering to strict safety guidelines. Food and drink service will be limited on domestic flights for a bit.
- Immigration lines will be longer and more complex as each country will implement stringent requirements, checks, and validation to prevent the spread of COVID-19 variants and other infections. Some countries might require a short quarantine even if tested negative. Proof of vaccinations might become mandatory and enforced, similar to the requirement of passports and visas.

Furthermore, the impacts of the crisis have affected hospitality and tourism in a massive way. Many hotels found themselves empty and looking to fill the once-full lobbies and rooms. In the United States, hotels experienced unprecedented booking cancelations due to the pandemic, eliminating up to 4 million jobs (this accounted for 50 percent of all hotel jobs in America).[59]

In India, the hospitality industry was hit hard. With the rampant rise of COVID-19 cases[60] in 2021, tourism and travel came to a standstill.[61] In Europe, industry experts estimated a profit decline of 11–29 percent. The KHN, which represents bars, cafés, and hotels, said that the emergency measures to limit the spread of the virus caused a serious impact, with cancellations at almost 50 percent. The average occupancy in Italy was down by 96 percent; the United Kingdom down by 67 percent. In China, compared to 2019 figures, occupancy in 2020 was down by as much as 68 percent, but as it was the first market to deal with the coronavirus, it was also the first to show signs of stabilization. As per data, 87 percent of the country's hotels are now open and occupancy is beginning to rise.

Nevertheless, the grave situation has given space for worldwide solidarity with many hotels around the world providing their premises to house medical staff, first responders, or hospital patients not suffering from coronavirus.

In the United States, several breweries and distilleries stopped producing spirits and beer. They switched over to making hand sanitizers to help the community.[62] Many of these businesses donated hand sanitizer batches to hospitals, assisted healthcare facilities, and healthcare workers. It was heartwarming to see and hear about many food drives and meal initiatives pop up worldwide. Diverse communities got together to cook and deliver meals to people impacted by the pandemic, homeless, and underprivileged schoolchildren who received their food through free school meal programs. Restaurants converted into meal kitchens to support struggling households, assisted healthcare facilities, and care homes. Food service teams and chefs worldwide mobilized in order to arrange free meals to the medical staff while putting themselves at risk in order to battle the crisis.

Entities such as bed & breakfast, hostels, pubs and clubs, cafés, restaurants, bistros, and beach bars, to name a few, being small family businesses, felt the crisis more acutely than other actors in the private sector due to being intrinsically vulnerable to change. They were heavily affected by the change in the supply chain and the lesser demand, and sadly, many went out of business.

It will take a few years for the travel and hospitality industries to recover from the aftermath of the global pandemic. Airlines will continue to find ways to cut costs and recuperate their lost cash reserves, sometimes at the expense of traveler convenience, which can be unfortunate for us customers. However, in the short term, people will not mind these inconveniences, as they are raring to travel again. The tourism and hospitality sectors will thrive once again and evolve to accommodate a more contactless, digital interaction with tourists and travelers. Hopefully, the changes make for a better customer experience and happier memories, and not just financial gains for the industry.

What Can You Do to Help?

Trust and empathy have become precious assets in these trying times. People do not trust media, public officials, or systems anymore. It is hard to blame them when there are so many reports of injustice, greed, self-indulgence, and exploitation all around them. But that does not mean that we should give up. We need to rally around trust and work toward elevating the level of trust in our communities. The best way to build trust is to say what you will do and do what you say you would do. It takes hard work, but if you keep your "Say to

Do" ratio as close to 1 as possible, you can build trust. And if what you say reduces the pain and anxiety of the people you are addressing, you demonstrate empathy and build trust quicker.

People who peddle in fear mongering and posting false information on social media should be held accountable for the damage they are causing to society. We should increase transparency in systems. The technology firm, Apple, has been making some great strides in user privacy and transparency by informing users of how applications are using their information and data and if they are actively listening.

Public officials should continue to talk about the measures introduced to make the system fair for all demographics openly. As more people are vaccinated and see the vaccine's safety, people will begin trusting the vaccine more. As individuals share their true stories of how they are being treated by the government and vaccine distributors, I hope that people who are currently hesitant will be more likely to become vaccinated for the greater good of society.

Summary

The last few years have been challenging for all of us. The world has seen immense adversity in a short time frame. *Apocalypse bingo* was a reality, and it has impacted humanity on many levels—a global pandemic, racial inequality and injustice, natural disasters, economic instability, and unemployment. People lost their livelihood, source of income, sense of security, and their social constructs overnight. The personal cost of this pandemic has been inordinate.

It sometimes feels like we had not just one bur five pandemics raging at the same time:

- The COVID-19 global pandemic
- Racial injustice (black, Asian, Hispanic)
- Economic inequality

- Privilege and elitism (white, politically connected, male)
- Anti-intellectualism (anti-vaxxers, flat earthers, conspiracy theorists, deniers)

Almost every facet of our life was impacted, fundamentally disrupting and debilitating various industry sectors such as travel, hospitality, retail, and healthcare in many areas. Unemployment skyrocketed, world economies weakened and destabilized, and companies had to close down or declare bankruptcy. Schools and universities had to shut down overnight, disrupting education for generations. Hospitals and healthcare facilities were overwhelmed and strained beyond capacity. The global pandemic has forced society to reimagine and reinvent business processes, engagement models, and interactions.

These drastic changes introduced a substantial contrast to how we live, work, and interact with our fellow humans and generate significant stress, anxiety, and insecurity. And we are just now beginning to feel the long-term effects of all of these disruptions. Going forward with empathy and compassion for all involved is our best bet in mitigating the adverse effects of the pandemic.

Reflections

- What are the top three ways in which COVID-19 has impacted you and your loved ones?
- What stories of adversity have you heard in your community? Have you identified an action plan to address this adversity?
- Have you been a victim of racial injustice, gender inequality, or sexual violence? How did that affect you and your loved ones? What actions did you take to overcome this?

(continues)

(continued)

- What are some of the things that you and your loved ones are grateful for during the pandemic?
- What was your most memorable staycation (at-home vacation) experience in 2020?
- Can you estimate how much carbon footprint you have reduced by not traveling during the pandemic?

Chapter 3

Overcoming Stress and Anxiety

When you are having a bad day, ask yourself, "Was it truly a bad day, or did a few bad minutes hijack my entire day?"

S tress and anxiety have been childhood friends of mine, and we were inseparable for many years. Growing up, I was two years younger than everyone in my class. I remember having to work harder to catch up with children that were more mature than me. We had recently returned to India from the United Kingdom, and I had to go through cultural, educational, and emotional readjustment. The Indian education system has three languages as part of its curriculum—a first language which is the primary mode of teaching, the national language (Hindi), and the regional state language. My first language was English, the second was Hindi, and Kannada, the regional language of Karnataka (the state), was my third language. I was at a disadvantage and did not know Hindi or Kannada, and I vividly remember learning these languages with my mother. We spent many late nights together, with my mother patiently teaching me pronunciation, grammar, and sentence construction.

I failed in Hindi and Kannada in my first test. It was the first time I had failed at anything and the first time I experienced the feeling of disappointment. I was anxious to redeem myself in my parents' and teachers' eyes and put more effort into my studies. I barely passed in Hindi in the next round of tests but flunked Kannada again. It took two more attempts to consistently scrape through the examinations and an additional year and a half for me to catch up with my classmates. I had considerable anxiety about tests and picked up overeating as a coping mechanism.

I struggled with stress, anxiety, and pressure to perform throughout middle and high school. It impacted my sleep patterns, and I started sleeping only four to five hours a day to keep up with the competition. Coffee was my companion, and I was liberally dosing myself with caffeine to keep me awake. My mother was herself studying for her Doctor of Medicine, and she had significant stress with working, studying, and taking care of the family. She was my accountability partner and used to wake me up early in the morning. I am by no means a morning person, but I have fond memories of drinking coffee with my mother and discussing how much of our syllabus we had completed the previous day and what we were going to target for the current day. I did not know it at that time, but this ritual was our daily standup.

I started developing tension headaches in high school due to my stress and anxiety issues. These episodes were unbearable at times and felt like someone was jackhammering the insides and periphery of my skull. I had trouble focusing due to these headaches, which increased my stress, and in turn, increased my episodes. In my mind, slowing down and not pushing myself to the limit was not an option. Call it an Asian stereotype, but having highly qualified parents (a doctor and a doctorate), studying in one of the top schools in the state, and trying to meet parents and teachers' expectations can be notably stressful. Being underage and continuously struggling to keep up with your classmates that are more mature than you— physically, mentally, emotionally—wears you down rapidly. I was prescribed medication for my tension headaches and continued to consume them through my high school years. My stress levels finally dropped when I entered university, and I was able to stop my prescription.

Looking back, I could have handled my stress and anxiety better and not suffered through my formative years with terrible headaches, overeating, and sleep deprivation. Hindsight, as they say, is 20/20. It is impossible to rue my decisions or think of what might have been if I chose otherwise.

These life events are what have shaped me and made me who I am. I have intimate experience dealing with stress and anxiety, and I believe that these experiences, however painful they might have been, make me more empathic to people undergoing similar pain and motivate me to share my experiences and techniques to understand and manage my stress and anxiety.

Understanding Stress

At this point, you might be thinking, "Why is it important to understand and mitigate stress in a book about empathy?" Well, stress is ubiquitous and affects everyone. It has spread its roots in almost every aspect of human life and can adversely influence one's energy, mood, relationships, interactions, behavior, and work performance. In *The Art of War,* renowned Chinese general, military strategist, and philosopher Sun Tzu said that if you know your enemies and know yourself, you will not be imperiled in a hundred battles.[1] Therefore, it is imperative that we understand stress, how it affects us, and how we can mitigate it.

Stress is your body's way of responding to any kind of demand or threat. When you sense danger—whether it's real or imagined—the body's defenses kick into high gear in a rapid, automatic process known as the "fight-or-flight" reaction or the "stress response."

This stress response is the body's way of protecting you. When working properly, it helps you stay focused, energetic, and alert. In emergency situations, stress can save your life—giving you extra strength to defend yourself, for example, or spurring you to slam on the brakes to avoid a car accident.

Stress can also help you rise to meet challenges. It's what keeps you on your toes during a presentation at work, sharpens your concentration when you're attempting the game-winning free throw, drives you to study for an exam when you'd rather be streaming a show on Netflix. But stress is not just a manifestation of our modern lifestyle. It has been a critical part of human evolution. It was stress that saved your ancestors from that saber-toothed tiger that was chasing them, so it has essentially helped ensure you're here today. Beyond a certain point, though, stress stops being helpful and starts causing major damage to your health, mood, productivity, relationships, and your quality of life.

If you frequently find yourself feeling frazzled and overwhelmed, it's time to take action to bring your nervous system back into balance. You can protect yourself—and improve how you think and feel—by learning how to recognize the signs and symptoms of chronic stress and taking steps to reduce its harmful effects. Positively managing your stress levels will help you be kinder, gentler, and more compassionate-to yourself and others.

The Three Major Stress Hormones

Our body's nervous system consists of two main parts—the central nervous system and the peripheral nervous system. Our central nervous system includes the brain and spinal cord, while the peripheral nervous system contains the nerves that connect the central nervous system to every part of our body. This is how we sense, feel, and interact with our surroundings. The autonomic nervous system plays a prominent role in managing feedback from our environment and is made up of parasympathetic, sympathetic, and enteric nervous systems. The parasympathetic nervous system stimulates activities that occur when the body is relaxed, such as salivation, lacrimation, digestion, or sexual arousal. The enteric nervous system focuses on managing the gastrointestinal tract and can act independently to the other two functions of the autonomous nervous system. On the other hand, the sympathetic nervous system has the primary purpose of stimulating the body's fight or flight response. It is contrary to the parasympathetic nervous system and is constantly in an active state to maintain homeostasis in living beings.

When the sympathetic nervous system senses a situation threatening survival, it primes our body for action by suppressing activities managed by the parasympathetic nervous system. In other words, when it feels that there is a threat for survival, the stress level within our body goes up, all nonessential functions of our body are slowed down, and our body prepares for fight-or-flight through the release of the following hormones.

Adrenaline

Adrenaline, also known as epinephrine, is produced both by the adrenal glands and a small group of neurons in the medulla oblongata of our brain. It plays a crucial role in the fight-or-flight response by controlling the blood flow to muscles, increasing heart rate, dilating pupils for increased focus, and increasing blood sugar levels within the body for quick access to energy should the muscles need it in a survival situation. As a result, it is commonly referred to as the *fight-or-flight hormone.*

Adrenaline is also responsible for knee-jerk or immediate responses that we perform when we are in stressful situations. For instance, that sudden fear and pounding of your heart that you feel when an aggressive dog comes barking at you, or that rush of fear that you experience when you try to change lanes on the interstate but don't see a car in your blind spot, causing you to swerve back into your lane are all attributed to an adrenaline rush.

The release of adrenaline is not limited to physical events. When one is stressed and has undergone an emotional or traumatic

79

experience, adrenaline is released along with other stress-related hormones when contemplating or reliving those events. The brain perceives these events as stressful, blood vessels are constricted, nonessential systems are shut down, and sleep is impacted. One feels exhausted, irritable, and restless, and this adversely affects one's health.

Norepinephrine

Norepinephrine, also called noradrenaline, is a hormone released by the body to prepare the brain and body for quick response and action during a fight-or-flight situation. Alertness and vigilance are increased, attention and focus are improved, and memory of the current event is stored if the knowledge of circumstances needs to be utilized later. Heart rate and blood pressure are elevated, blood flow is increased to skeletal muscles in case of rapid response, and glucose level in the blood is also increased for quick bursts of energy. Norepinephrine also reduces blood flow to the gastrointestinal system and limits the body's urge to urinate or excrete, allowing for a quick escape from a life-threatening situation or a stressful event.

While it might seem that norepinephrine is redundant in our body, there are slight differences in how the hormones help in stressful or life-threatening situations. Epinephrine has more of an effect on the heart, while norepinephrine affects blood vessels more. Epinephrine is mainly produced by the adrenal glands, although small amounts are generated in the nerves. On the other hand, norepinephrine is produced primarily in the nerves, although small amounts are also produced in the adrenal glands.

Cortisol

Cortisol is another hormone secreted by the adrenal glands and released in response to stressful situations and conditions where blood sugar levels drop. Cortisol is also called the stress hormone and performs the essential functions of suppressing the immune system, increasing blood sugar levels, and facilitating the metabolism of fat, carbohydrates, and protein to increase energy levels in the body. In situations requiring survival skills, cortisol suppresses noncritical body functions such as growth, digestion, and immunity. However, the prolonged presence of cortisol in the body can lead to adverse effects such as obesity, reduced libido, and suppressed immunity.

Do You Really Need That Stress?

Nathan was an IT operations manager at a financial organization. His team was in charge of an aging, legacy platform that handled customer transactions. Due to its age, technical debt, and the organization's unwillingness to modernize the platform, it was not uncommon for the team to spend three to four nights per week on incident resolution calls, frantically trying to resolve severe or critical issues that regularly popped up. As an IT manager, it was Nathan's job to lead these troubleshooting incidents with multiple teams, drive the teams to resolve the issues that popped up quickly, while at the same time managing the executives that kept asking for updates and why the incident had not been resolved yet. Every minute of outage cost the organization considerable money, so Nathan and his team's stress level was tremendously high. As the team manager, Nathan was that "one throat to choke" for executives when incidents occurred, and failure was not acceptable in the organization. The organizational culture was toxic, and Nathan was sleep-deprived, unsupported, undervalued, verbally abused by his executives, and overall under considerable stress.

(continues)

(*continued*)

Nathan suffered a heart attack at 35 on December 30. A stroke paralyzed the entire left side of his face and left arm. His wife, Beth, a stay-at-home mother, was seven months pregnant with their second child at that time. They were saving up for the baby and moving to a new house in the summer. Overnight, those plans were secondary to Nathan and Beth. The family struggled to cope with this catastrophe but was resolute and determined to stay strong through the hardship. Nathan and Beth ushered in the new year in the hospital, their first child spending the night in a friend's place.

On January 1, the legacy platform that Nathan was responsible for suffered an outage. Nathan was paged but did not join the call. Per escalation procedures, the incident bridge paged Nathan's supervisor Brad to get hold of him. Nathan had not yet notified him about his condition, and Beth had been too preoccupied trying to bring sanity into her upturned world to tell Brad, either. Brad hopped onto the incident bridge and helped resolve the incident. Several executives asked Brad to take severe action against Nathan for shirking his duty and ignoring incident pages. Not one executive stopped to think that something unfortunate could have occurred.

Beth finally responded to Brad's texts and voicemails on January 2, informing him of Nathan's conditions. To his credit, Brad was understanding and told Beth that they both needed to focus on Nathan getting better and the baby. He stopped over that day to check on them and to drop off paperwork for medical leave approval. He managed the approval process and pushed back against the executives who demanded blood for losing valuable revenue.

Nathan recuperated from his tragedy but still has minor impairment in speech and mobility. He took his doctor's advice and left his job for a less stressful position. He and Beth had a beautiful girl in March, and they continue to be strong as a family. Brad, however, was let go in February. The official reason stated was "performance issues," but everyone knew that Brad was the proverbial pound of flesh offered to the executives to recover lost revenue. Brad now works at another IT organization with a positive culture and is happier than he ever was in his previous role.

Effects of Chronic Stress

Stress has, unfortunately, become an accepted evil in our daily life. Work, relationships, political events, socioeconomic fears, and even watching the news have become stressful and affect us all adversely. A small amount of stress can be beneficial in helping us focus and perform necessary activities or prevent us from hurting ourselves. On the other hand, too much stress is dangerous, and a constant level of stress can be debilitating and wear us down mentally, physically, and emotionally.

As we evolved as a species, actual situations that require fight-or-flight have considerably reduced, and we have started to perceive other situations as stressful. Stress is also very subjective, and what causes stress for someone might not be concerning for others. Also, it feels as if some people are better equipped to handle stress than others, but everyone suffers from the consequences of chronic stress.

When one is stressed, the brain perceives a life-threatening situation and switches into a fight-or-flight response. Our body releases the hormones adrenaline, norepinephrine, and cortisol into our bloodstream. These, in turn, suppress all the nonessential functions in our body and elevate sugar levels in our blood for instant energy if required. Heart rate increases, pupils are dilated, blood vessels are constricted, immunity is suppressed, digestion and growth are stopped.

Prolonged effects of such a state include:

- Headaches, depression, and anxiety
- Heartburn, digestive problems, and ulcers
- Increased risk of heart attack, high blood pressure, and blood sugar levels
- Insomnia and other sleep disorders
- Obesity, autoimmune diseases, and muscular tension
- Loss of libido, gynecological or fertility problems
- Skin conditions such as eczema, hair loss
- Paranoia, loss of trust, and memory problems

Chronic stress is not a state that anyone wants to be in. It severely impacts life span and overall joy and happiness in one's life. However, it is alarming to note that stress is increasing in daily life. High-pressure jobs, fear of unemployment, unrealistic expectations of productivity levels, and office politics are primary reasons for chronic stress in the workplace. Technology, or rather the abuse of technology, is keeping us in a state of chronic stress. Society's "always-on" mode of being on devices constantly and having the need to be connected and plugged in at all times is a significant contributor. The need to check email or the urge to respond to an email has become almost Pavlovian in response, driven by the familiar chime or popup notification on our phones.

These behaviors have impacted our sleep patterns, not allowing our brains and bodies to relax and rest, leaving us irritable, sleepless, and restless during the day. This, in turn, increases stress and paranoia, reduces trust, lowers camaraderie and team relationships, and thus causes a very unpleasant and toxic environment. Chronic stress is the maelstrom in the ocean of life, and we must recognize, understand,

and overcome stress to improve the quality of life for ourselves and our society at large. It's hard to be empathetic to yourself and to others if you are under constant stress and just managing to get by.

Symptoms of Stress Overload

The most dangerous thing about stress is how easily it can creep up on you. You get used to it. It starts to feel familiar, even normal. You don't notice how much it's affecting you, even as it takes a heavy toll. That's why it's important to be aware of the common warning signs and symptoms of stress overload.

Cognitive symptoms:

- Memory problems
- Inability to concentrate
- Poor judgment
- Seeing only the negative
- Anxious or racing thoughts
- Constant worrying

Emotional symptoms:

- Depression or general unhappiness
- Anxiety and agitation
- Moodiness, irritability, or anger
- Feeling overwhelmed
- Loneliness and isolation

Physical symptoms:

- Muscular tension, body aches, and pains
- Diarrhea or constipation, digestive problems
- Nausea, dizziness, tension headaches
- Chest pain, rapid heart rate, irregular breathing
- Loss of sex drive, gynecological or fertility problems
- Frequent colds or flu

Behavioral symptoms:

- Eating more or less
- Sleeping too much or too little
- Withdrawing from others
- Procrastinating or neglecting responsibilities
- Using alcohol, tobacco, or drugs to relax
- Nervous habits (e.g., nail biting, pacing)
- Loss of drive or enthusiasm

Overwhelmed by Pandemic Stress

This is a statement by a 48-year-old woman from California.

I did everything "right": a good job, good healthcare, good retirement plan, emergency savings, living in our means. Then I acquired a disability, and it changed. I could no longer go without insurance because medications are expensive, and I couldn't risk not being covered by insurance. When the World Health Organization declared the pandemic to be a Public Health Emergency on January 30, 2020,[2] I had been unemployed for 14 months. We no longer had the reserves to navigate the uncertainty of a global pandemic, unemployment, let alone make it through a protracted recession, which was a given, despite others wanting to pretend that it wasn't. I work in a field where unusual market forces affect work availability as companies manage their expenses down to weather the storm. My partner was working but not closing the gaps, but then he lost his job. I picked up some work from the Census, which started the day that the Shelter in Place order was announced in the Bay Area. The Census took three days to close as nonessential work, putting me out of work again. That was an unexpected boon, making me eligible for federal pandemic leave and unemployment at the stimulus plan's increased rates. I despaired of finding a new job but soon realized that the shift to remote work would be in my favor for a more accommodating job when three recruiters called me the following week. That was enough to get me to do another round of resumes and searches.

That said, all but my daughter have preexisting conditions that put us at high risk of severe COVID, up to and including death—a chilling thought, to be sure. Add in the general sentiment among some of the healthy population that the elderly and those with preexisting conditions were essentially disposable. That combined with personal unemployment, skyrocketing unemployment across many industries, and the rather high-pitch of survival anxiety that everyone experienced put my stress level high. For scale, the Holmes-Rahe Stress Inventory put me at 571 points. At 150 points on the inventory, you have an increased risk of injury or illness. At 300, you have a high risk of getting seriously ill or injured. I was at almost 600.

How did I get through it? In my case, we did what we could. My generous partner spoke to the local grocer and told him he was happy to help in any way. That was a Wednesday; he was in training on Saturday as a grocery picker, assembling grocery orders for the new world of curb-side and delivery business. The money wasn't great, but that job gave us early access to food in shortages and paid for it, too. It also meant that I could avoid exposure to the virus. With that money, my boosted unemployment, and stimulus checks, we were okay. Not great. We could pay our most critical bills. We qualified for discounts on utilities, including the medical baseline, under a COVID exception. We applied for forbearance on the mortgage

(continues)

(*continued*)

(although we never used it because of the balloon payment) and the car payment. We pieced it together as much as we could.

That said—we were the LUCKY ones. We had resources, information, support, privilege.

In another two weeks, I would not have qualified for unemployment, including the federal assistance which kept us afloat. My partner and son were now both essential workers, bringing in some income. We were not likely to become homeless, although it often felt imminent. We haven't gotten sick or evicted. We had food on the table, electricity, although we went without heat for a while when the heater died.

I was dumbfounded when I got a call from a company I applied to in January. I wrote it off as a dead lead until April when they called me for the HR screen, which seemed to go well. I interviewed a total of three times, each time being told they would get back in a few days, and each time, I wrote them off because I did not hear back for a week. Then they offered me the job. I accepted and started the role remotely during a pandemic, with a modest increase, better healthcare than I had had in a decade, more vacation time, etc. I had been looking for a full-time job for over four years, and I got one during a global crisis on a scale that we could not have imagined. I had my reservations. When I did not have that first flush of new job feeling after starting the job, I worried that I had made a horrible mistake. Friends and family held me steady when I couldn't do it. Thursday was my crying day for months.

In hindsight, my stress level was so high that survival mode was so intense. The fear was so strong that I could not relax. I hadn't been sleeping well before the job started, and that got worse. I was in a constant emotional storm, and anxiety was beyond high. It was months before I could think about planning a financial recovery from joblessness. I was afraid to pay too much of our bills in the event that I suddenly needed cash, or the job fell through, or someone got sick.

I want to tell people that their jobless friends are not okay—treat them to dinner, check on them, send them things, and make them laugh. Employment gaps are not a character flaw and have many varied reasons. Kindness is king. Social programs save lives and build stronger communities. You are not your job. You will be okay if you just keep swimming, even if it feels like you are drowning. Find that one thing that keeps your head above water. Ask for help. Accept help, maybe only because others see what you don't. Sometimes help comes from the most unexpected places and in the most unexpected ways.

Causes of Stress

The situations and pressures that cause stress are known as *stressors*. We usually think of stressors as being negative, such as an exhausting work schedule, a critical production incident, or a strained relationship. However, any situation that puts high demands on you can be stressful. This includes positive events such as getting married, buying a house, planning a child, going to college, or even receiving a promotion.

Of course, not all stress is caused by external factors. Stress can also be internal or self-generated, when you worry excessively about something that may or may not happen, or have irrational, pessimistic thoughts about life. Stress also depends on your perception of it. While some of us are terrified of getting up in front of people to perform or speak, for example, others live for the spotlight. Where one person thrives under pressure and performs best in the face of a tight deadline, another will shut down when work demands escalate.

And while you may enjoy helping to care for your elderly parents, your siblings may find the demands of caretaking overwhelming and stressful (see Table 4.1).

Table 4.1   Common Causes of Stress

External Causes	Internal Causes
Major life changes	Pessimism
Work or school	Lack of self-confidence
Relationship difficulties	Inability to accept uncertainty
Financial problems	Rigid thinking
Being too busy or overwhelmed with activities	Unrealistic expectations/ perfectionism
Children and family	Negative self-talk
Poor emotional support system	All-or-nothing attitude

Top 10 Stressful Life Events

According to the widely validated Holmes and Rahe Stress Scale,[3] these are the top 10 stressful life events for adults that can contribute to illness:

1. Death of a spouse
2. Divorce
3. Marriage separation
4. Imprisonment
5. Death of a close family member
6. Injury or illness
7. Marriage
8. Job loss
9. Marriage reconciliation
10. Retirement

Have you faced any of these life events? If it is not too painful to relive the past, think about how much stress that life
event introduced into your life and how you managed to cope
with stress and anxiety the life event induced.

Write down the coping mechanism that proved beneficial
to you. Have you used this coping technique elsewhere?

What's Stressful to You?

Whatever event or situation is stressing you out, there are ways of
coping with the problem and regaining your balance. Some of life's
most common sources of stress include:

Stress at work. While some workplace stress is normal, excessive stress can interfere with your productivity and performance,
impact your physical and emotional health, and affect your relationships and home life. It can even determine the difference
between success and failure on the job. Whatever your ambitions
or work demands, there are steps you can take to protect yourself from the damaging effects of stress, improve your job satisfaction, and bolster your well-being in and out of the workplace.
Job loss and unemployment stress. Losing a job is one of
life's most stressful experiences. It's normal to feel angry, hurt,
or depressed, grieve for all that you've lost, or feel anxious
about what the future holds. Job loss and unemployment
involve a lot of change all at once, which can rock your sense
of purpose and self-esteem. While the stress can seem overwhelming, there are many steps you can take to come out of
this difficult period stronger, more resilient, and with a renewed
sense of purpose.

Financial stress. Many of us, from all over the world and from all walks of life, are having to deal with financial stress and uncertainty. Whether your problems stem from a loss of work, escalating debt, unexpected expenses, or a combination of factors, financial worry is one of the most common stressors in modern life. But there are ways to get through these tough economic times, ease stress and anxiety, and regain control of your finances. There are several online resources and programs for debt relief or consolidation techniques especially during the pandemic, along with services such as nonobligation financial advisors. *A word of caution:* Research these resources thoroughly as there are many fraudulent sites and scammers.

Caregiver stress. The demands of caregiving can be overwhelming, especially if you feel that you're in over your head or have little control over the situation. If the stress of caregiving is left unchecked, it can take a toll on your health, relationships, and state of mind—eventually leading to burnout. Fortunately, there are plenty of things you can do to rein in the stress of caregiving and regain a sense of balance, joy, and hope in your life.

Grief and loss. Coping with the loss of someone or something you love is one of life's biggest stressors. Often, the pain and stress of loss can feel overwhelming. You may experience all kinds of difficult and unexpected emotions, from shock or anger to disbelief, guilt, and profound sadness. While there is no right or wrong way to grieve, there are healthy ways to cope with the pain that, in time, can ease your sadness and help you come to terms with your loss, find new meaning, and move on with your life.

How Much Stress Is Too Much?

Because of the widespread damage stress can cause, it's important to know your own limit. But just how much stress is "too much" differs from person to person. Some people seem to be able to roll with life's punches, while others tend to crumble in the face of small obstacles or frustrations. Some people even thrive on the excitement of a high-stress lifestyle.

Factors that influence your stress tolerance level include:

- **Your support network.** A strong network of supportive friends and family members is an enormous buffer against stress. On the flip side, the lonelier and more isolated you are, the greater your risk of succumbing to stress.
- **Your sense of control.** If you have confidence in yourself and your ability to influence events and persevere through challenges, it's easier to take stress in stride. On the other hand, if you believe that you have little control over your life— that you're at the mercy of your environment and circum- stances—stress is more likely to knock you off course.
- **Your attitude and outlook.** The way you look at life and its inevitable challenges makes a huge difference in your ability to handle stress. If you're generally hopeful and optimistic, you'll be less vulnerable. Stress-hardy people tend to embrace challenges, have a stronger sense of humor, believe in a higher purpose, and accept change as an inevitable part of life.
- **Your ability to deal with your emotions.** If you don't know how to calm and soothe yourself when you're feeling sad, angry, or troubled, you're more likely to become stressed and agitated. Having the ability to identify and deal appropriately with your emotions can increase your tolerance to stress and help you bounce back from adversity.
- **Your knowledge and preparation.** The more you know about a stressful situation, including how long it will last and what to expect, the easier it is to cope. For example, if you go into surgery with a realistic picture of what to expect

93

Overcoming Stress and Anxiety

post-op, a painful recovery will be less stressful than if you were expecting to bounce back immediately. Knowing that there is a high probability of loss when investing in a risky portfolio would help reduce the stress caused by market volatility.

Maslow's Hierarchy of Needs and the Pandemic

Abraham Maslow (1908–1970) was an American psychologist best known for his theory of the hierarchy of needs. He proposed his theory in 1943 in his paper "A Theory of Human Motivation" in *Psychological Review*.[4] In his theory, Maslow proposed that people's motivations were dependent on seeking fulfillment and individual growth. He further expanded these fundamental needs of a person into a tiered pyramid that we know as "Maslow's Hierarchy of Needs."[5] The psychologist stated that before a person can proceed to higher levels of the hierarchy of needs, the lower level requirements must be fullfilled. (See Figure 3.1.)

If the requirements of lower level are not fully satisfied, reaching to higher levels becomes difficult or sometimes impossible.

Pandemic Stress

The coronavirus pandemic turned our lives upside down. It affected every facet of our lives. Going to school, offices, meeting with friends and family, going out to dinners, cinema, and concerts and traveling; these are the things we mostly took for granted before. The definition of a stable lifestyle has been shaken. What was considered normal in the past might seem alien to us now.

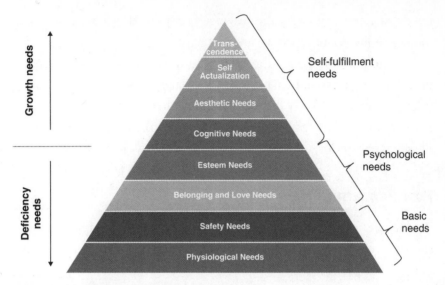

Figure 3.1   Maslow's hierarchy of needs.

Meeting the fundamental physiological and growth needs was not such a great challenge before the pandemic. During the pandemic, we struggled to meet the ends and the lower lower tiers of Maslow's pyramid were eroded. Physiological and safety needs of people were impacted. There was fear of breathing normally when surrounded by other people due to an invisible enemy. When the shelter-in-place and social distancing guidelines were introduced, it further stressed people. They were not allowed into their offices, losing that sense of professional belonging. The workforce had to switch to a remote working setting overnight. Many people had never had the luxury of working from home in the past and were not equipped to spend long hours online.

Schools were closed and they had to not only maintain their prior productivity but also help their children adapt to distance learning. Challenges with new technologies and drop on productivity impacted people's esteem needs. As a result of all these events, the deficiency

Overcoming Stress and Anxiety

needs of many people were adversely impacted, severely stressing them and increasing anxiety levels.

As the pandemic raged, economic and social impacts also manifested. Retail, hospitality, and travel industries were hit pretty hard—unemployment was on the rise, resulting in an existential crisis for many people. Many popular brands declared bankruptcy, small businesses went under, and no one knew when it would end.

Post-Pandemic Stress

People are getting vaccinated and can venture out again. As we started seeing the light at the end of the tunnel, new stressors have emerged to plague us.

Agoraphobia

Agoraphobia[6] is a type of anxiety disorder characterized by a fear of performing an activity or being in an environment in which people feel they cannot leave or escape. People who have agoraphobia feel panic-like symptoms or severe anxiety, and may even have panic attacks. They are unable to feel safe in public spaces, especially around crowds, sometimes so crippling that they may be unable to leave the safety of their home.

Does this sound familiar? Many of us had to be cooped up in our homes during shelter-in-place and lockdown protocols for long periods. Visiting a grocery store or a hospital made us anxious. Even when governments reduced restrictions, many of us were hesitant to step outside. We were afraid of crowds and limited our social interactions to our close relatives and pandemic bubble. COVID-19 might have induced varied levels of agoraphobia in our communities due to our social isolation and safety protocols.

I had to visit the hospital in October 2020 due to a foot injury, and the anxiety that I felt was palpable. I did not want to leave the comfort of my home even though I was in considerable pain. I finally gave in and went to the hospital. However, I still vividly remember my wife sanitizing the wheelchair and that I vigorously sanitized my hands each time I came across a hand sanitizer dispenser. Getting on a subway or a plane at that time would have increased my stress levels considerably, and I am sure that many of you would have undergone similar experiences. I can only imagine how much worse it has been for people who had agoraphobia before the pandemic.

Post-Pandemic Stress Disorders

According to the WHO Director-General, COVID-19 has caused more mass trauma than World War II, and he said that the mental health toll from the pandemic would last for many years to come.[7] Almost every human on earth has been affected in some way, and this will have a lasting effect on communities. Some of the symptoms of post-pandemic stress disorders are similar to post-traumatic stress disorder (PTSD).[8] A few of my friends reported reliving traumatic experiences, such as being isolated in the hospital with a ventilator and not seeing their loved ones. They said that they kept having nightmares about dying alone and having vivid experiences of reliving their hospital stays. Others said that they are scared to go grocery shopping without masks and nitrile gloves anymore. They have become germophobes and feel the need to obsessively clean any surface they come in contact with and sanitize their hands regularly. I once was walking with a friend, and as we approached the end of the road, I asked her to press the button for pedestrian crossing. I was appalled to see her visible consternation and anxiety to press the button. I spared her the pain by pressing the button with my elbow but used my shirt as a protective layer. The way we analyze events and act has changed considerably.

The Stress of Not Having a Vaccine

If you reside in the United States, you have the opportunity to get the vaccine. However, other countries and regions still struggle with getting access to reliable vaccines. It may be a long while before the entire world has equal access to the various COVID-19 vaccines.

In addition, lack of vaccinations still remains stressful for children 11 years and younger. My son, who is 7 years old, still needs to wear a mask when he goes out. He feels sad when he sees middle and high schoolers without that limitation and has expressed how unfair it is on multiple occasions. We are hesitant to go on vacations and, as with many other parents of elementary schoolchildren, are concerned about sending kids to school physically.

The Impact on Our Hierarchy of Needs

In the context of COVID-19 pandemic, Maslow's theory of hierarchy of needs seems to fit well. Lockdown, social distancing, working from home, closing of educational institutes, and online education were the immediate responses imposed by the governments to contain the spread of virus.

Situations like a pandemic are always stressful. Social isolation, fear of getting infected with this deadly virus, financial crisis, and fear of not being able to meet subsistence needs all have triggered the negative emotions. Mental health issues rose and were a burden to an already overburdened healthcare system. In the middle of a pandemic, the global population faced new challenges that it was not prepared to face. The majority of the population was pushed to lower levels of the pyramid as the psychological needs became the utmost priority for all. Thus, Maslow's theory proves precisely relevant to the COVID-19 pandemic. The following sections discuss how Maslow's Hierarchy of Needs pyramid was impacted adversely.

Physiological Needs

The bottom tier of Maslow's pyramid enlists the fundamental needs for an individual's survival such as food, shelter, clothing, air, sleep, and so on. Perhaps the greatest challenge for many of us during the pandemic was to fulfill these basic needs. People started hoarding food items, toilet papers, sanitizers, and things that were necessary for survival. Initially, even the supermarkets could not keep up with the huge demands. Likewise, getting a peaceful sleep is not easy in such traumatic and stressful times. The daily routine was also disturbed, which affected the normal sleeping pattern. In a nutshell, the first level of the pyramid was hardly fulfilled, making it difficult to reach the next levels of the pyramid.

Safety Needs

The second tier of the pyramid addresses the safety needs that become important once one's physiological needs are met. It includes stability, emotional security, education, financial stability, and so forth.

Financial instability was a real challenge during the pandemic. Many small businesses were shut down, unemployment increased as companies had to cut short their budgets, and many people had to work for minimal wages. According to the reports of the International Monetary Fund (IMF), the economic recession during the pandemic shrank the global GDP by 3 percent in 2020.[9]

Personal security is another challenge. In the beginning, no strategy was working against coronavirus infection. The frontline workers were at greater risk due to insufficiency of personal protective equipments and related facilities. The healthcare workers are particularly affected by pandemic-related stress. Psychological health issues, such as post-traumatic stress disorder, burnout syndrome, physical and emotional exhaustion, dissociation, isolation, and fear of being stigmatized for being in direct contact with the COVID patients, were more prevalent in frontline workers.

Overcoming Stress and Anxiety

Numerous reports of mutated strains and the overall efficacy of the new-developed vaccines on large populations continue to be significant stressors.

Belonging and Love Needs

Humans are not designed to be isolated for long periods. The real challenge was for those living alone. Though the use of technology is helpful to make us feel connected, we still missed the face-to-face conversations, a hug from parents and siblings, and going out with friends. This situation adversely affected the mental health of many.

Studies reveal that quarantine and social isolation may lead to prolonged and adverse effects on psychological health. In young adults, social isolation and loneliness, especially after the educational institutes are closed, decreased physical activity, more screen time, irregular sleep patterns, and unhealthy diet all contribute to onset of psychiatric disorders. Various studies reveal drastic increase in quarantine-related psychological health issues including PTSD symp-toms, anxiety, confusion, rage, anger, and depression.[10] There is a direct correlation of financial instability or economical crisis to increased cases of suicides, mental health issues, addiction disorders, domestic disturbance, altercations, and less life satisfaction in adults.[11]

As reported by the Centers for Disease Control and Prevention (CDC), the mental health issues and depressive disorders increased considerably in the United States during April–June of 2020.[12] In the 18–40 age group, about 40 percent of respondents were found to suffer from one major psychiatric disorder related to the pandemic, and more than 10.7 percent of the respondents revealed suicidal ten-dency. The prevalence of depressive disorder (24.3 percent to 6.5 percent) was approximately four times that reported in the second quarter of 2019.

Self-Esteem

Per Maslow, there are two categories of self esteem; one is the acknowledgment of our achievements and dignity and the second is the desire of respect from others.

Taking into account the educational system, with the closing of most of the educational institutes, online teaching was introduced. Many students and teaching staff were not adequately equipped to handle long hours of online learning. The learning curve to adapt to newer methods of communication stressed them. Many were frustrated as a result of this. Failure to adapt quickly also impacted their self-esteem. Another major issue was the lack of training both for students and teachers. The data reported by the School Education Gateway survey, conducted from April–May 2020, including the participants from more than 40 countries, reveal that approximately 66.9 percent of the respondents had to teach online for the very first time.[13] For teachers with no experience of teaching online, their performance is usually not the same as in the classroom. The same goes for the students. It affects the self-esteem, performance, and confidence of the person.

There is also a lot of social judgment about what we are doing. During the lockdown, people spend more time using social media apps. Social media keeps us connected, but at the same time, it introduces challenges, such as an unhealthy obsession with likes, fans, trends, or hashtags, an obsession of the self, easy access to misinformation, and a hesitation to interact in the real world.

Self-Actualization

The topmost levels of Maslow's pyramid refer to becoming the "the ideal version" of ourselves, through the achievements of our desires and dreams. This level was difficult to achieve during the pandemic. Self-actualization can vary from person to person. For instance, for a student, self-actualization is to achieve a post-grad degree or distinction. For an entrepreneur, becoming the successful businessman is self-actualization.

An encouraging environment and face-to-face conversations have positive impacts on a person's performance and self-esteem. Similarly, a student's interaction with fellow students and teachers is found to be essential for positive self-esteem, confidence, and a sense of identity. Moreover, such interactions along with creative classroom activities boost the cognitive skills, performance, and school achievement. According to the reports of UNESCO, educational institutes were shut down in 186 countries by April 2020, affecting approximately 74 percent of total enrolled students.[14] A huge number of students of developing and poor countries may still not be able to rejoin their schools. Thus, the goal of self-actualization has almost gone astray.

We are only now beginning to understand how different tiers of society have been impacted mentally and psychologically by the events of the last few years. It will take time for us to fully gauge how the events of the previous few years have affected humanity.

Happy Chemicals

Stress releases adrenaline, norepinephrine, and cortisol in our body and switches it into a fight-or-flight situation. In a society undergoing social, physical, and emotional anxiety, these hormones trigger aggression, self-preservation, and fear, leading to paranoia and loss of self-esteem, thereby eroding trust and empathy in fellow human beings. (See Figure 3.2.)

Luckily for us, the human body usually knows how to heal itself. There are four chemical hormones that help combat stress and increase happiness within us. These happy chemicals are then released into the bloodstream to be distributed within the body and regulate mood and emotions:

- **Dopamine.** The *happy chemical*. More than a hormone, it is a neurotransmitter and induces the feeling of being rewarded. All pleasant sensations due to the mere anticipation of an achievement are due to the effect of this hormone. This chemical is capable of regulating all motor functions, even memory and learning.

- **Oxytocin.** The *love chemical*. Oxytocin creates intimacy, trust, and builds healthy relationships. It is usually generated through physical interactions—a hug, a high five in the hallway, a pat on the back, and so on. This chemical increases empathy and helps us feel closer and bonded to others.

- **Serotonin.** The *leadership chemical*. This hormone and neurotransmitter regulates the mood along with dopamine. The hormone also regulates sleep, memory, and activities related to learning. This provides a sense of pride and importance when someone praises us, along with a sense of accomplishment.

- **Endorphins.** The *runner's high*. Act as a natural pain reliever of the body. This ability makes this hormone important in stressful cases when someone may also be suffering from some sort of physical pain. This chemical motivates people to push themselves (power through) and achieve their goals.

These natural mood-boosters help promote positive emotions and reduce stress and anxiety. It helps people be happier, less stressed, more energetic, and feel good about themselves overall.

How to Combat Stress

Stress and anxiety are widespread in our society. A Global Burden of Disease study conducted in 2017[15] reported that at least 1 in 10 people—at least 792 million people—suffer from at least one mental disorder worldwide.[16] Mental illnesses have been identified as one of the most prevalent forms of disability, and anxiety tops the list.

Even before the pandemic, over 20 percent of adults in the United States experienced mental illness.[17] Suicide was the second-leading cause of death among people aged 10–34 in the United States and the tenth leading cause of death worldwide. The global pandemic amplified stress and anxiety for all and made things worse for everyone. In fact, anxiety disorders affect over 40 million adults in the United States alone, and over 68 percent of adults said they feel stress or anxiety daily.[18]

These numbers are appalling and need to be addressed through proper treatment, education, and awareness. Stress is a significant contributor to anxiety, so let's discuss a few effective ways to combat stress—through sensory relaxation, physical relaxation, and mental relaxation.

Relaxing Your Senses

- **Sight (vision).** Visualization or guided imagery are techniques that involve creating a detailed mental image of a peaceful environment to promote stress reduction. These methods have shown progressive muscle relaxation, reduced anxiety, improved self-confidence, and an increased ability to cope with stressful situations. Similar to guided meditation, the more one is absorbed in the imagery, the deeper the state of relaxation.[19]

- **Hearing (auditory).** Significant positive changes in the stress-inducing hormone cortisol were reported when listening to music before and during stressful situations. Either listening to or playing music promotes stress relief as it provides mental distraction and releases muscle tension. Your favorite artist, soothing music, or nature sounds require your mind to focus and provide a distraction from stress.[20]
- **Smell (olfactory).** The smell receptors in our nose are stimulated by natural essential oils, sending messages to our nervous system to relieve anxiety and stress and regulate mood. This aromatherapy employs aromatic substances extracted from plants. There are several essential oils to choose from depending on personal preference, like valerian, jatamansi, lavender, jasmine, holy basil, bergamot, and chamomile, to name a few.[21]
- **Taste (gustatory).** Mindful eating and drinking help with stress management and anxiety. It has been reported that including stress relief foods like brazil nuts (high in selenium), fatty fish (high in omega-3), pumpkin seeds (high in zinc), or dark chocolate (high in tryptophan) in our diet promotes mood enhancement and relieves stress or anxiety.[22] Consequently, reducing the consumption of stimulants like coffee or alcohol to moderate amounts leads to stress relief. In the long run, caffiene boosts the immune system.[23] In general, limit yourself to 400 milligrams, or four or fewer cups (8 oz), of brewed coffee per day.[24]
- **Touch (tactile).** Physical touch triggers the release of the hormone oxytocin, which helps us form a positive emotional connection that fosters well-being and happiness. This behavior is also evident among primates who touch each other to ease tensions in social settings. Hugging or cuddling reduces social anxiety and blood pressure.[25]

105

Overcoming Stress and Anxiety

Relaxation Techniques

Consider some or all of these relaxation techniques:

- **Be active.** Any form of physical activity can act as a stress reliever. Physical exertion in any form (walking, jogging, biking, house cleaning, or gardening) lowers the stress hormone cortisol and helps release feel-good endorphins that uplift mood and general well-being. Regular physical activity has immediate benefits in sleep quality, reduced anxiety, and long-term benefits in heart health, brain health, and bone strength.[26] Performing these physical activities with a loved one has the added benefit of releasing oxytocin and strengthening relationships.

- **Deep breathing.** Of the two types of breathing—chest and diaphragmatic—we find ourselves involuntarily resorting to chest breathing. Chest breathing uses the secondary muscles in the upper chest and is designed to be used in situations that involve exertion, such as a sprint or race. During stressful situations, we inadvertently resort to chest breathing. A direct consequence of this kind of breathing leads to tight shoulder and neck muscles and sometimes even headaches multiplying the already existing stress. Diaphragmatic breathing, or belly breathing, uses the body's dominant breathing muscle—the diaphragm. This type of breathing is more effective and efficient. It can lead to feelings of relaxation instead of tightness. Sustained diaphragmatic breathing relieves anxiety, general stress, depression, and PTSD.[27]

- **Yoga.** In its purest essence, yoga is the union of the body and the mind. It involves a series of postures and controlled breathing exercises that relieve stress and invigorate the body. With varying levels of hardness to suit personal preference, it has become a popular technique to manage stress and anxiety. A research study found that participants who practiced yoga three times a week for four weeks—or 12 sessions overall—reported lower levels of depression, anxiety, and stress, compared to those levels before starting their yoga practice.[28]

- **Meditation.** A part of yoga, meditation has been practiced to achieve a sense of calm, peace, and balance that can benefit both emotional well-being and overall health.[29]

- **Spend time with friends, family, and pets.** Over time, our human instinctive reaction to stress and anxiety is social isolation leading to loneliness, especially chronic stress. Research has shown that social contact promotes good stress relief, as it provides support to face stressful situations.[30] Taking a coffee break with a friend or having a family dinner distracts the underlying stress. Volunteering is another great way of socializing and helping others.

  Interaction with animals has been shown to decrease cortisol, release oxytocin, and lower blood pressure. In addition, physical interaction and bonding with animals reduce loneliness and foster feelings of social support.[31] Laugh. Have fun with your loved ones and friends. Watch a comedy show or movie.

- **Maintain a journal.** Journaling involves the practice of having a diary or journal and expressing your thoughts and feelings that occur throughout the day. Journaling is an excellent therapeutic tool to record your thoughts and reflect upon them later. It is also an excellent method to document your gratitude toward positive events in your life and serves as a reminder that life is not as bad as you may think.[32]

- **Set boundaries.** Being mindful and self-aware of our boundaries helps avoid long-term stressful situations and boosts self-confidence.[33] We might not want to assert ourselves to prevent conflicts or to keep the peace. However, setting boundaries is critical for healthy relationships, even though it might feel like you are putting yourself first. A relationship is bidirectional, working both ways equally. One side should not have the upper hand on the other. If it does, it could lead to subservience, unhappiness, and strife. Sometimes, it is okay to say no.

- **Prioritize and manage time.** Any given day, we are racing to finish more tasks than we have time for. Setting priorities and staying on top of them avoids anxiety and stress that negatively affects health and sleep quality. Listing tasks, setting realistic deadlines, avoiding procrastination, and assigning uninterrupted time to achieve these tasks are all strategies for preventing work-related stress.[34]

- **Express gratitude.** We experience many emotions and thoughts throughout the day, whether it was a joyous one or an unpleasant day. A good exercise is to write down these lingering thoughts (preferably in your diary or journal) to count your blessings and release otherwise pent-up emotions that lead to stress and anxiety. This act of expressing your gratitude shifts your focus from stress to a more positive state of mind.

- **Seek professional help.** Professional counselors or therapists can help identify sources of stress and share new coping tools.

Activities for a Healthy DOSE of Happy Chemicals

You can stimulate more happy chemicals with fewer side effects when you leverage the job Dopamine, Oxytocin, Serotonin, and Endorphins (DOSE) were evolved to do. The following sections discuss a few ways to stimulate each, and how to avoid unhappy chemicals.

Dopamine: Embrace a New Goal

Approaching a reward triggers dopamine, and this release was essential to the survival of the species. Our ancestors released dopamine when they found a water hole or when they succeeded in hunting a wildebeast. The expectation of a reward triggers a good feeling in the mammalian brain and releases the energy one needs to achieve the reward.

Dopamine motivates you to strive for a reward, whether you're seeking a coveted promotion or a parking spot near the donut shop. Dopamine motivates persistence in the pursuit of things that meet your needs, whether it's a bar that's open late, the next level in a video game, or a way to feed children. You can stimulate the good feeling of dopamine without behaviors that hurt your best interests. Embrace a new goal and take small steps toward it every day. Your brain will reward you with dopamine each time you take a step. The repetition will build a new dopamine pathway until it's big enough to compete with the dopamine habit that you're better off without.

Oxytocin: Build Trust Consciously

Trust triggers oxytocin. Mammals stick with a herd because they inherited a brain that releases oxytocin when they do. Social bonds help mammals protect their young from predators, and natural selection built a brain that rewards us with a good feeling when we strengthen those bonds.

Sometimes your trust is betrayed. Trusting someone who is not trustworthy is bad for your survival. Your brain releases unhappy chemicals when your trust is betrayed. That paves neural pathways that tell you when to withhold trust in the future. But if you withhold trust all the time, you deprive yourself of oxytocin. You can stimulate it by building trust consciously. Create realistic expectations that both parties can meet. Each time your expectations are met, your brain rewards you with a good feeling. Continual small steps will build your oxytocin circuits. Trust, verify, and repeat. You will grow to trust yourself as well as others.

Serotonin: Believe in Yourself

Confidence triggers serotonin. Monkeys try to one-up each other because it stimulates their serotonin. People often do the same. This brain we've inherited rewards social dominance because that promotes your genes in the state of nature. As much as you may dislike this, you enjoy the good feeling of serotonin when you feel respected by others. Your brain seeks more of that feeling by repeating behaviors that triggered it in your past. The respect you got in your youth paved neural pathways that tell your brain how to get respect today. Sometimes people seek it in ways that undermine their long-term well-being. The solution is not to dismiss your natural urge for status or fame, because you need the serotonin. Instead, you can develop your belief in your own worth. People are probably respecting you behind your back right now. Focus on that instead of scanning for disrespect. Everyone has wins and losses. If you focus on your losses you will depress your serotonin, even if you're a rock star or a CEO.

Endorphins: Make Time to Stretch and Laugh

Pain triggers the release of endorphins. That's not what you expect when you hear about the *endorphin high*. But runners don't get that high unless they push past their limits to the point of distress. Endorphin causes a brief euphoria that masks pain. In the state of nature, it helps an injured animal escape from a predator. It helped our ancestors run for help when injured. Endorphin evolved for survival, not for partying. If you were high on endorphin all the time, you would touch hot stoves and walk on broken legs. Endorphin was meant for emergencies. Inflicting harm on yourself to stimulate endorphin is a bad survival strategy. Fortunately, there are better ways: laughing and stretching. Both of these jiggle your innards in irregular ways, causing moderate wear and tear and moderate endorphin flow. This strategy has its limits. A genuine laugh cannot be produced on demand. A genuine stretch requires a little skill. But when you believe in the power of laughing and stretching, you create opportunities to trigger your endorphin in these ways.

Cortisol: Survive, Then Thrive

Cortisol alerts animals to urgent survival threats. Our advanced brain alerts us to subtle threats as well as urgent ones. Cortisol especially grabs your attention when it's not being masked by happy chemicals. You might have a sudden bad feeling when your happy chemicals dip, even though there's no predator at your door. If you can't get comfortable with that, you might rush to mask it with any happy-chemical stimulant you're familiar with. Your well-being will suffer. You will lose the information the cortisol is trying to give you, and your happy habit will have side effects. More cortisol will flow, thus increasing the temptation to overstimulate your happy chemicals. This vicious cycle can be avoided if you learn to accept the bad feeling you get when a happy chemical surge is over. It doesn't mean something is wrong. Cortisol is part of your mammalian steering mechanism, which motivates an organism to approach rewards and avoid threats. If you learn to accept your cortisol, you will be free from the rush to mask it in ways that don't serve you. You will make better decisions and end up with more happy chemicals.

Building New Happy Habits

Happiness is just one thing that hormones are responsible for. Your hormones are affected throughout the day, every day. Metabolism, response to injury, stress levels, energy, reproduction—our endocrine system, the system of glands that produce hormones, regulates all these things. Essentially, hormones are the messengers that control many of our bodily functions. They regulate our physical health and our mood.

There are some things we can do to help our bodies ensure that these processes operate efficiently. Our brain gets wired from past experience. Each time our neurochemicals surge, neurons build connections. Experiences wire us to turn on our brain chemicals in the ways they turned on in the past, making them repetitive, memorable, and habit-forming.

So pick a new happy habit and start repeating it. Over time, those new happy habits will feel as natural as your old ones, and you won't have the unfortunate side effects.

Eat Healthy

Eating healthy is an easy happy habit to form. Here are some foods you can eat and habits and activities you can start adding to your day to naturally boost the happy hormones in your body: serotonin, dopamine, and endorphins.

Snack on nuts and seeds. Serotonin is the hormone that regulates mood, perception, memory, and attention. Because the endocrine system is linked with the gastrointestinal system, foods that might complement hormone production are a good way to promote the release of those hormones. Think about this: Your brain has to breathe in order to help you think. Oxidative stress makes it difficult for your brain to breathe. As we age, damage from free radicals—imbalanced atoms that scavenge our bodies—causes oxidative stress on our cells. Vitamin E, which can be found in nuts and seeds, for example, protects cells from this oxidative stress and thus boosts brain function.

Incorporate salmon into your diet. Good fats in your diet provide energy for your body. The omega-3 fatty acids in fish have been proven to reduce inflammation and may lower your risk of depression.[35] It's important to get this through your diet because omega-3 is considered an essential fatty acid, meaning the human body can't produce it. The research on the connection between lower levels of depression and consuming fish is growing, and some researchers think it has to do with omega-3 fatty acids boosting the levels of dopamine and serotonin circulating through your body.

Munch on blueberries. Improved blood flow to your brain helps support endocrine activity, making it easier for your body to circulate dopamine and serotonin. Blueberries are rich in antioxidants, simple carbs, and fiber. Like in seeds and nuts, the antioxidants in blueberries prevent free radical damage as well as reduce inflammation. There is also a possible connection between the flavonoids (plant chemicals with strong health benefits) in blueberries and their interaction with serotonin and dopamine receptors.

Indulge in dark chocolate. An excuse to eat chocolate? Yes, please. The caffeine in dark chocolate blocks adenosine, a substance in the brain that increases sleepiness. As a result, you might notice that you're more focused due to the stimulant. Dark chocolate is also rich in antioxidants, so it might provide similar mood-boosting effects to that of blueberries.

Add avocados. Monounsaturated fats are healthy fats found in avocados. You still need fats for healthy body functions. They help to provide you with energy. It is the monounsaturated fats that don't clog your arteries, allowing blood to move more freely through your circulatory system and thus better able to circulate dopamine and serotonin throughout your body. Better circulation also means better blood flow to your brain, allowing for more production of these hormones. Half an avocado is a serving size, and that will provide 7 percent of your daily fat intake.[36]

Infuse citrus. The brain needs constant blood flow. Cerebral circulation provides the organ with the oxygen and nutrients it needs for healthy brain function—like sending the right messages to the right receptors. Citrus fruits are high in antioxidants and work as natural blood thinners while preventing plaque buildup at the same time. This reduces your risk of poor circulation or clotting, and your brain will get the blood flow it needs to keep you energized and happy. An easy way to get your citrus in is by eating an orange or grapefruit, or by infusing your water with lemons and limes.

Eating healthy requires discipline and restraint. Having an accountability partner helps keep you motivated and engaged. The sheer act of sharing a healthy habit increases oxytocin and serotonin between you and your accountability partner. Set achievable goals for both of you. Encouraging each other to achieve these goals releases endorphins. Consequently, when set goals are achieved, dopamine is released.

Exercise and Meditate

The "runner's high" is no joke. Consistent, focused workouts can release endorphins that will quickly alleviate feelings of distress and reduce feelings of pain. You don't need to go on a run to feel the effects of endorphins; take a walk, go ice-skating, lift weights, or sign up for a spin class.

Studies have shown that there is a link between meditation and increased dopamine levels.[37] Meditation can have a quieting effect on a wandering mind. Take a few minutes to close your eyes, take some deep breaths, and exhale. Allowing yourself a few minutes of peace by regulating your breath can help soothe nerves and lower symptoms of depression.

Take Time to Show Gratitude

Maybe your friend showed up at your door with your favorite coffee. Maybe your grandma called to catch up. Maybe your husband tidied the house up while you ran errands. Maybe your manager thanked you for your work. Whatever it was that made you smile, take time to really appreciate it. Showing gratitude is a positive emotion. Dopamine, serotonin, and endorphins are released when you smile.[38]

Achieve a Goal

Positive feelings are also attached to accomplishing a goal. Did you run an extra mile this week? Did you get the kids to school on time today? Did you make it through the month without going over your budget? A sense of pride and happiness comes with accomplishing something, and you might find yourself smiling, which releases all three of those feel-good hormones. Take some time to dwell on the excitement, and feel your mood improve as you do. Celebrate your achievement with a happy dance or a symbolic gesture such as ripping up your stickie note that held the task. *Note: Do not routinely celebrate with food or drink, as that will act as negative reinforcement and make you unhealthy.*

Do Something You've Never Done Before

Kind of like achieving a goal, do something new. Whether it's going to a new restaurant you've been wanting to try or going on a helicopter tour over your city or skiing a new mountain, do it. Dopamine is released when the brain experiences something new because there is pleasure in accomplishing—or trying to accomplish—things.

Ask for a Hug

Have you ever hugged someone and felt angry? Chances of that happening are low, and that's because hugging people results in feelings of comfort and positivity from a release of dopamine. Hugging also releases serotonin, and studies have shown that continuous hugging of around 20 seconds releases oxytocin as well.[39]

Go Outside

Seasonal depression is a condition that affects your mood when the seasons change. A common one is the "winter blues," which might result from lack of sun. Though the exact cause has not been found, theories suggest it is because our biological clocks are imbalanced, causing hormones to shift.[40] It is suggested that exposure to sunlight can boost serotonin levels, so hop on a bike, go for a walk, or simply sit in the sun for a mood-booster.

Think about a Happy Memory

Do you ever find yourself feeling sad, so you go through old pictures or hold something nostalgic like your old Little League baseball glove or a necklace you got for your birthday years ago? Thinking about happy memories does the same thing as feeling thankful for something. It causes you to smile, and thus those happiness hormones course through your bloodstream and elevate your mood.

Remedy with Tea

Lemon tea has similar effects to citrus-infused water with its antioxidant benefits. Turmeric tea reduces inflammation. Chamomile tea is used to ease insomnia and invoke calmness. Buy some tea bags or, in the case of turmeric, make the mixture at home, steep in boiling water, and enjoy.

Get a Massage

Loosened muscles can lead to increased circulation, and the serene atmosphere of the spa itself can reduce fatigue and stress. Serotonin and dopamine will rise, and cortisol—the hormone released when you're stressed—will decrease.

Sleep

Sleeping is crucial for concentration, quick response times, and healthy brain functions. Reducing fatigue through quality sleep will help your brain regulate the endocrine system and reduce symptoms of depression and anxiety.

Pick Up Some Lavender Sprigs or Essential Oils

Aromatherapy releases dopamine and serotonin. This happens because the smell receptors in your nose send messages to your nervous and limbic systems, which are the parts of your brain related to emotions. Lavender has been shown to lower distress and anxiety.[41]

Summary

The global pandemic in many ways profoundly affected our sense of love, caring, intimacy, and belonging. It disrupted our support system along with our identities and self-worth and impacted our physiological and psychological safety. There was a deficiency of basic needs and safety, resulting in increased stress levels and anxiety worldwide. Even as we slowly return to pre-pandemic conditions, we still find stressful the new situations we find ourselves in and must name and address these stressors as part of our recovery.

When we are stressed, our brain switches into a fight-or-flight mode and our body releases adrenaline, norepinephrine, and cortisol to prepare our bodies for quick responses in life-threatening situations. However, we are not built to handle prolonged stints of stress, and chronic stress has had debilitating effects on our health. Luckily for us, nature has provided us with happy chemicals—dopamine, oxytocin, serotonin, and endorphins—to counter the effects of stress within our bodies, and we need to embrace ways to dose ourselves and the people around us with these happy chemicals through thoughful interaction and actions. Positive emotions such as compassion, kindness, and caring for others are influential in the healing process. The world needs empathy right now to get better.

Reflections

- What techniques have you employed to manage your pandemic stress?
- Share one of these techniques on your social media or with your close circle. Use #leadwithempathy or #empathicleadership to tag your posts.
- What kind of activities have you introduced into your team or organization to DOSE your teammates or workforce?
- What new habits did you develop during the pandemic? Which are healthy and which are unhealthy? How can you eliminate any unhealthy habits as you work toward a post-pandemic existence?

Part II

Empathy and Leadership

Chapter 4

The Power of Empathy

There is a profound difference between reducing pain and building happiness. Reducing pain is momentary; building happiness is persistent.

M y mother was a strong and compassionate woman. She decided to become a doctor to help people, heal their pain, and make a difference in the world. She went above and beyond to help people and always said that she felt joy every time they felt relief from their pain or suffering. Her constant desire to give did take a toll on her personal life. She developed chronic rheumatoid arthritis early in her life, which flared up pretty badly at times. Her fingers and joints swelled up during those episodes, but she endured that pain with grit and tenacity. She did an excellent job of hiding her pain from us and always presented a cheerful exterior.

I was a teenager when her condition started worsening, and naturally rebelled at my mother's requests for help with household chores and assisting her with shopping. In my teenage mind, it was impacting my social time, my bonding with my friends, music, or my precious reading time. I am embarrassed to admit that I had many arguments with her on how she was diminishing my freedom and curtailing my social interactions. At that time, I did not try to understand why she was asking for help. It was all about me, and I felt like a victim.

Until one day, I walked into the kitchen and heard her softly sobbing while prepping for dinner. Alarmed, I asked her what was wrong.

She quickly wiped her tears but did not say anything. As I observed her chopping vegetables, I could see her wince every so often. Her wrists and fingers were inflamed, and she was obviously masking her pain. That moment is burnt into my memory, and I can recollect her facial expression, her grit, and my emotions even to this day.

A wave of guilt and shame washed over me. I had been so self-absorbed and selfish, I had been apathetic to my mother's condition. I was wallowing in self-pity, while my mother had been silently suffering throughout—preparing breakfast and lunch for us before she left for work in the morning, coming back home after a long day and preparing dinner, helping my brother with his homework, cleaning the house—with stoicism.

At that moment, I resolved to do something to alleviate my mother's pain. I was experiencing compassionate empathy toward my mother. I told her that I would cook dinner that night if she could guide me. I cooked my first two-course meal with her direction, and cooking dinner with my mother became a regular event in our household. Our emotional bond strengthened, my emotional intelligence increased, my mother shared her work stories and anecdotes, and cooking became the shared experience that brought us closer together.

Emotional Intelligence

When one usually thinks of good leadership, a few common traits come to mind—charisma, vision, effective communication, strategic thinking, courage, and emotional intelligence. People expect their leaders to be understanding, compassionate, control their emotions, be approachable, and listen to their teams before they make strategic decisions that transform their organizations. These are qualities of emotional intelligence, and as the social aspect of human interaction is vital for successful organizations, emotional intelligence has become a critical component of good leadership.

Emotional intelligence or *emotional quotient* (EQ) is the ability to understand and manage one's emotions and be sensitive to people's emotions around oneself. When one has a high level of emotional intelligence, they have a good understanding of their feelings; they understand what their emotions mean and how these emotions impact others around them. These people can positively manage their emotions and channel their energy to relieve stress, resolve conflict, and communicate effectively to overcome challenges. More importantly, people with a high EQ can easily empathize with others, making them much more relatable and personable.

Daniel Goleman, an American psychologist who popularized emotional intelligence, attributed five critical components: self-awareness, self-regulation, motivation, social skills, and empathy. In leaders, self-awareness and self-regulation promote inflection, reflection, and confidence in their ability to assess complex situations, view them from different perspectives, and evaluate the optimal course of action that will benefit not just the organization or themselves, but the workforce as well. Social skills and motivation are crucial for leadership, especially in organizations undergoing a business transformation as a result of the pandemic or other change or stressor. The ability to precisely communicate why the organization has to undergo radical change, how it will impact the workforce and its identity, and the assurance that everyone is in it together provides a level of comfort that the workforce seeks. It helps leaders endear themselves to the employees and increases the willingness and drive to strive for success at the end of an arduous journey. The proper motivation and social skills can release dopamine, serotonin, and endorphins and increase the throughput of value within the organization. When people see that their leaders are not just talking and pontificating from their ivory tower, but instead are actually in the trenches with them, transforming the organization, understanding their pain, and working to improve their quality of life, their trust in their leaders increases, and thereby their oxytocin levels also improve. Team bonding strengthens, and people are willing to take more risks. The organization embraces a positive culture and the stress levels of the workforce decrease.

When an organization that works together and has low levels of stress is combined with a strong vision and plan for transformation, it's much more likely the organization can successfully endure any business transformation. Therefore, emotional intelligence is essential for successful leaders, and demonstrating empathy is imperative in these adverse situations.

Empathy

Think about how you felt during the pandemic. Did you wish for someone that you could talk to and express how you were feeling? A friend that you could confide in, someone who would really get you and commiserate with? An avenue to vent or just let your hair down without any judgement? If you answered yes to any or all of these questions, then you were craving interaction with someone who was empathic.

On the other hand, have you been the friend in these situations and helped someone else with their pain or lent a shoulder to cry on? Do you feel a strange pain when you hear tragic events on the news or when someone narrates them to you? Does your mind immediately put yourself in other people's shoes and you feel what it might have felt like in those situations? Or probably you feel overwhelmed or drained of energy when someone shares their pain with you. If any of these conditions are true, you might be highly empathic.

Empathy is the ability to sense and understand what other people feel, see things from their point of view, and experience emotions that others might have gone through by putting oneself in their place. In the book *Dare to Lead*,[1] Dr. Brené Brown, a research professor at the University of Houston, said that empathy is a powerful way to connect to the other person's emotion and make them realize that they are not alone when they struggle. She refers to four qualities of empathy:[2]

- To be able to see the world as others see it
- To be nonjudgmental
- To understand another's feelings
- To communicate your understanding of that person's feelings

Empathy is the ability to truly be present. It's the ability to hold a safe space for others to feel their own emotions completely and to be able to understand their experiences. It is a way to put yourself in someone else's shoes, feel their stress and pain, and do something about their pain.

Empathy is also love and understanding for your fellow humans, a way to reach out to people and make sure that we are collectively working together as a community and are happy. It could be as simple as having a solid connection with your significant other or your loved ones as part of a family or being the leader of a large enterprise and striving to keep your workforce happy and less stressed.

Empathy is deeply rooted within our evolutionary history. In prehistoric times, men were the hunters while the womenfolk were foragers and caregivers. Anthropologist studies have revealed that injured men were cared for and tended to by the tribe. Archeologists have also found remains of deformed children cared for by the tribe even though there was no intrinsic value being contributed by the child. We are social beings, and years of evolutionary programming still exist in us. By understanding others, we develop closer relationships, strengthening our bonding within our family, social circle, community—in essence, our tribe.

Empathy is not purely a human trait, either. Animals demonstrate a considerable amount of empathy to their fellow creatures and other animals. Several studies have shown how household pets are impacted by emotional responses of pain, stress, or anxiety of family members.[3] Further studies on primates documented consistent empathy among monkeys, bonobos, chimpanzees, and other apes. Many studies also captured how these primates showed empathy to humans and other animals, such as injured birds.[4]

How Do You Know if You Are Empathic?

These signs show that you tend to be an empathic person:

- You care deeply about other people and feel pain when they tell you about their problems. Sometimes, you do not stop there. You try to help reduce their pain induced by those problems or help them eliminate the problem.
- You are an active listener and can pick up small, nonverbal cues when the speaker narrates their story or tells you about their problems.
- You put yourself in the other person's shoes and try to experience what they might have gone through in that situation. You may experience pangs of pain when you do this.
- You can detect when people are being disingenuous or are trying to exploit you.
- You sometimes feel overwhelmed or drained of energy by tragic events or when you interact with people and help them reduce their pain.
- You care deeply about others and sometimes find it difficult to set definite boundaries in your relationships. This could get you into trouble sometimes, but you feel that this is a part of being empathic.

Having a great deal of empathy makes you concerned for the well-being and happiness of others. It also means, however, that you can sometimes get overwhelmed, burned out, or even over-stimulated from always thinking about other people's emotions.

How often does that happen to you?

The word *empathy* is derived from the ancient Greek word *empatheia*, which means physical affection or passion (*pathos* can mean passion or suffering). German philosophers Hermann Lotze and Robert Vischer used this term to create the German *Einfühlung* ("feeling into"). Edward B. Titchener translated *Einfühlung* into English as "empathy" in 1909.[5] The word *empathetic* first appeared in 1927[6] and has been used interchangeably with empathic, as both of them having the same root, empathy. Empathic is typically preferred in scientific writing, while empathetic is used in others forms of literary works. I prefer empathic when explaining a concept or relating temptation to emotions or actions, and empathetic when used as an adjective. But I have also used these two words interchangeably in this book.

Types of Empathy

There are different types of empathy that a person may experience. The three most common types of empathy are cognitive, emotional, and compassionate.

Cognitive Empathy

Cognitive empathy is the ability to put oneself in the other person's shoes and rationally experience what the other person is going through. It involves being able to understand another person's mental state and what they might be thinking in response to the situation. This is related to what psychologists refer to as theory of mind, or thinking about what other people are thinking. Cognitive empathy is contrived, willful, and does not require any emotional investment.

Team leaders find cognitive empathy useful in understanding how their team members are feeling and how they can help them succeed. Negotiators use cognitive empathy to quickly assess their counterpart's emotional state, actively listen, encourage their counterpart to open up, and establish common ground through reinforcement of any emotional connection that they tactically built during the negotiation. Sales executives use these effectively to measure their prospective client or customer's mood, which helps them quickly assess the most effective approach to reach out to the client.

Since cognitive empathy is a rational and intelligent approach and devoid of emotional connection, there is a possibility of people using this for negative outcomes or for their own purposes.

Emotional Empathy

This is the ability to share feelings of another person and have a deeper understanding with the person. This is also called *affective empathy* because it affects or modifies the way the observer feels. It involves the ability to understand another person's emotions and respond appropriately. Such emotional understanding may lead to someone feeling concerned for another person's well-being, or it may lead to feelings of personal distress. This is a method of creating a genuine connection with someone.

Emotional empathy can be exhausting and energy draining. People with this kind of empathy can get overwhelmed or involved in other people's problems at the expense of their own emotional state or well-being. This can be detrimental to people. However, it is beneficial for a leader to express some level of emotional empathy with people that they interact with on a regular basis. It increases trust and helps develop transparency and candor in the relationship.

Compassionate Empathy

This is the most active form of empathy. It involves not only being concerned about another person and experiencing their emotional pain, it also involves taking effective actions to help reduce the pain or origin of suffering. Compassionate empathy is wholesome—it considers an overall view of the person and their situation, and tries to drive action.

Have you ever had a situation where you observed one of your team members or close friends showing signs of stress or anxiety that was out of the ordinary? What did you do in that situation? Did you ignore the situation and walk away? Did you ask the person what was upsetting them and lend them a patient ear and felt the pain they were going through? Or did you listen and then work with the person to resolve their predicament and eliminate their pain?

Ignoring the situation and walking away is an example of *apathy*. Acknowledging the person's pain and stress is valuable, and affirming their reaction by showing signs of those feelings yourself is an illustration of emotional or affective empathy. Dedicating quality time to work through the situation and providing guidance through this collaboration is demonstrating compassionate empathy.

While sympathy and compassion and are related to empathy, there are important differences. Compassion and sympathy are often thought to involve more of a passive connection, while empathy generally involves a much more active attempt to understand another person.

The Difference Between Empathy and Sympathy

The difference between empathy and sympathy can be confusing at first because both of these emotions start from good intentions. Dr. Brown said, "Empathy fuels connection. Sympathy drives disconnection."[7] She also says that empathy is a trait that bonds people and makes them feel included. On the other hand, sympathy introduces a level of disconnection and distance by creating a complex power dynamic where the sympathizer is better positioned than the recipient, even though it is not intended to be that way.

131

People often confuse sympathy with empathy because they feel sorry for that person and assume that they are experiencing similar pain as the other party. Dr. Brown gives a great example of how someone uses the word "at least" when exhibiting sympathy, highlighting the core difference that sympathy is based on comparison. When someone is sympathetic to the other, they are showing that they are sorry for the other person and even demonstrating pity for them. They feel sad that the individual is suffering and try to respond comfortably. This usually translates into finding a silver lining for the unfortunate situation that the other person is going. And hence the usage of "at least." The problem with this phrase is that it could be construed as condescending or introduces a power dynamic between the two parties. The sympathizer is not really trying to understand and connect with the other party at an emotional level but instead trying to rationalize the suffering and weirdly focus on themselves in this interaction. For instance, one can feel sympathy for homeless people, someone crying on the street, or painfully hobbling along with crutches on an icy footpath.

On the other hand, empathy is the ability to create a safe space for others to feel their own emotions completely and to be able to understand their experience. It is a way to put yourself in someone else's shoes, feel their stress and pain, and do something about their pain.

These critical components are not as easy as they would seem. Our own past experiences can interfere with connecting to another person. Once an emotion is triggered, it can be difficult to show empathy or be present in a genuine way.

Empathy creates connection while sympathy creates separation and disconnection. With empathy, there is a resonance between people; a bridge of understanding is built between them that strengthens trust and connection. However, with sympathy, there is a fixation on one person's experience rather than understanding and connection.

My Guiding Principle for Empathy

My mother used to tell me, "If you do not make a positive impact in someone's life, what is the point of living?" That stuck with me, and I adapted it as part of my philosophy. She was a big believer in the concept of karma and went out of her way to help others. Her actions encouraged me to be compassionate, empathic, and kind to people. I am fortunate to have had her as my role model and have channeled her approach into my guiding principle for empathy, which is:

When you can look at a human being and put yourself in their shoes, understand the pain and stress they are undergoing, value their happiness above your own, AND do something about their pain, then you are genuinely empathic.

This principle has been my North Star for empathy, and I recognize and embrace the reality that I lean more toward compassionate empathy. On my leadership journey, this guiding principle has also aided me in developing two fundamental beliefs:

1. Happy people are productive people.
2. Strategic disruption leads to progress.

My two beliefs have helped me be an empathic leader and focus on being a servant leader to my people, be it in the workplace or community, with an additional lens of empathy.

The Benefits of Empathy

Human beings are certainly capable of selfish, even cruel, behavior. A quick scan of any daily news feed quickly reveals numerous unkind, selfish, and heinous actions. Occasionally, we read some phenomenal stories of how people were empathic and went above and beyond to help others in need. These heartwarming stories of empathy are what make enduring adversity worthwhile.

There are several benefits of being able to experience and demonstrate empathy. Empathy enables people to build social connections. By understanding what people are thinking and feeling, people are able to respond appropriately in social situations. Research has shown that having social connections is important for both physical and psychological well-being. Empathizing with others helps people learn to regulate their own emotions. Emotional regulation is important in that it allows people to manage what they are experiencing, even in times of great stress, without becoming overwhelmed.

When a community or culture has an abundance of empathy, trust, and respect increase among the community members. Collaboration and communication improve; there is increased serotonin and dopamine from helping and solving the community's pain and suffering. These behaviors, in turn, increase oxytocin, which enables stronger bonds within the community.

When a community has trust and respect, there is considerable psychological safety among its members. People feel enabled and empowered and know that they can rely on others to help them in times of need. Stress levels reduce, and if the community is an organization, the workforce is happier, and there is lower attrition in such organizations.

Communities with high psychological safeties are more willing to take risks and innovate. They are more comfortable experimenting and are not afraid to fail as they know that the community is nonjudgmental and supportive of their aspirations. The culture of such a community blooms and becomes positive. Knowledge is no longer a commodity to be hoarded but is instead shared freely. People are happy and embrace continuous learning and improvement.

Leading with Empathy

Empathy promotes helping behaviors. Not only are people more likely to engage in helpful behaviors when they feel empathy for other people, but other people are also more likely to help them when they experience empathy.

Empathy Is on the Rise

Over the last few years, Google trends[8] reported that searches for the phrases "what does empathy mean" and "examples of empathy in the workplace" increased over 3,200 percent and 1,500 percent, respectively, compared to before the pandemic. We can gain several insights from this data point:

- The usage of the word *empathy* has increased considerably, making it a mainstream trait for humanity.
- People are genuinely trying to understand what empathy is and how to use it.
- Many people are striving hard to introduce empathy in the workplace and make it part of organizational culture.
- While there are truly horrific stories of how people have exploited the unfortunate, desperate, or gullible in times of adversity, a considerable population has stepped up and is looking for ways to lead with empathy to counterbalance negativity in the world.

These statistics are positive indications of empathy being recognized as one of the most important psychological traits essential for humanity's emotional well-being.

What Impedes Empathy

If empathy is so important and valuable to humanity, why do we not have an abundance of empathy in our communities? As part of our evolution, why have we not made it a core value? The reality is that demonstrating empathy requires putting other people's needs above our own, which is hard for many people. History has proven that a majority of humans are inherently self-centered and focus on their needs before thinking of others. Some may argue that this is a consequence of capitalism and social media, emphasizing hedonistic pleasures and suppressing eudemonism. However, this nature has existed in us even in ancient times.

It is hard for many humans to think of other people's needs before our own. But, there is no reason to feel shameful or disappointed in ourselves. This behavior is not limited to humans alone. There is evidence that even animals and plants demonstrate these behaviors. At its base level, the focus on self is the need to protect oneself and their interests. This drive is a vital trait for survival, and evolution has amplified this need. Without this urge to defend oneself, species would go extinct.

But there is a profound difference between focusing on one's needs for survival and being self-obsessed. Understanding this difference and acting on it is what differentiates higher forms of intelligence from the rest. As humans, we have the capability to not only sympathize with the pain of others but also are able to perceive how the other person could be feeling, comfort them, and in some cases, collaborate with them to reduce the pain that they are undergoing.

Empathy is a trait available for us to demonstrate if we choose to. After all, women have been demonstrating high levels of empathy since prehistoric times. I have personally seen and experienced high levels of empathy shown by my mother, who went out of her way to help others in need. And I am confident that you are probably thinking of situations where your own mother, sister, or mother figure in your life demonstrated strong levels of empathy. So, should we not have benefited from these collective experiences and evolved into a highly empathic society? The fact that empathy is still a parsimonious trait in our civilization underscores that this has not occurred yet. It is not a simple nature versus nurture argument. Let's explore what is impeding the spread of empathy.

Psychological and Emotional Composition

Several kinds of research[9] have confirmed a significant correlation between gender and how empathy is experienced or manifested. People who exhibited higher levels of feminine traits are more disposed to demonstrating empathy. These studies also showed that children who grew up in a matriarchal family or with a strong maternal figure had a higher probability of being empathic. Similarly, people who are more comfortable with themselves and have embraced their feminine energy are more prone to being empathic.

Surroundings and Culture

Upbringing and culture play a prominent role in one's conditioning. Individuals suffering from adverse surroundings such as poverty, racial discrimination, abuse, or fear of living operate in a constant state of anxiety and chronic stress, with heightened survival instincts. Naturally, they are focused on their physiological needs and safety over others' psychological needs. They, therefore, are less prone to demonstrating empathy to people who are not in their immediate circle or have not earned their trust. Clans are a powerful representation of trust in many cultures, and empathy is usually limited to clan members.

Bias and Privilege

One of the failings of humans is their propensity to measure themselves relative to others around them. This behavior introduces complexities of bias and privilege. Throughout history, the way people behave with others depends on how they interpret differences between themselves and others.

Bias impacts the way people perceive the world around them consciously or unconsciously. Biases are universal and can severely impact behavior.

Consider the example of a marketing pitch that an employee has to deliver to a potential client. Suppose the employee botched the delivery of the pitch or did not convince the client. In that case, the other team members could be biased that the employee was not prepared or did not have the necessary skills to deliver such an important pitch. They could also think that the employee wasted a chance to impress the higher-ups and probably reconsider if they are really invested in their role. On the other hand, if we consider the same situation but this time, have yourself be the employee delivering the pitch. What would your response or bias be if the pitch did not go well? Typical answers are the complexity of the pitch, that the client is unreasonable, or that the team did not help in critical moments. Is it not uncommon for people to assume character flaws or lack of skill when assessing other people's failures, while deflecting their own failure on external situations out of their control.

Privilege is a situation where a person has an unfair advantage over others and assumes that they are entitled to special benefits due to their privilege. Such people suffer from a bloated sense of self and ego and dehumanize anyone that they perceive as different or beneath them in either class, color, or social status. The pejorative "Karen" is widely used for someone demonstrating privilege (though the Internet is yet to decide on the name for a male Karen—Ken or Kevin being the closest that forums could agree on). There are numerous examples and video footage of privilege lately, from people refusing to wear masks to unrealistic demands of service from essential and restaurant workers. A sad fact is that privilege and entitlement run deep in our society and often rear their ugly heads.

Hedonism

Hedonism is the pursuit of pleasure through physical or material gratification. People driven by hedonistic tendencies believe that amassing wealth or items that bring happiness to them defines who they are, and the more they have, the more important they feel. But how much is enough? Where does it stop? Hedonistic pleasures are addictive. People who aggressively pursue money, prestige, status, or the number of likes on social media are addicted to the temporary feeling of goodness they achieve when they acquire these material-istic items. Earning more money translates to more dopamine release, and since they relate money to pride and importance, serotonin is released as well. A similar concept can be observed with social media. Many youngsters feel that the number of followers they have is a measure of their importance. Each like or comment on their posts delivers dopamine, and one can get quickly addicted to the sensation of pride, reputation, and feeling good. But, similar to other addictive substances, the effectiveness of these releases diminishes over time, driving people to post more or push the envelope, per-forming dangerous acts all for that dopamine and serotonin release that they crave. This self-spiral drives people to become highly self-obsessed and not think about others.

Social media apps and platforms such as Facebook, Instagram, Snapchat, WhatsApp, TikTok, OnlyFans, and others amplify these needs and enable instant gratification. They have made us slaves to our devices. How many of us dare to completely disconnect from our phone or laptop for more than two days? The concept of digital detox did not exist before smartphones became mainstream. The frightening part is that we have just gotten started. Augmented and virtual reality are enhancing our interactions with artificial environments and video games, designed to boost our self-importance in these simulations. After all, what is the appeal in a game where the player does not get rewarded or is not celebrated as a hero by thousands? Facebook recently announced[10] that they have prioritized building a version of Instagram for children under 13, which I believe is not only horrifying but is also a severe threat to society.[11] There are so many implications of this form of photo and information-sharing technology catering to underage children, ranging from privacy and protection concerns (such as child pornography, grooming, trafficking) to severely disrupting child emotional development (self-obsession, narcissism, device addiction) to stress and anxiety (cyberbullying, body shaming, unrealistic expectations).

Personal Story

There are numerous stories and anecdotes where racial prejudice and bias—conscious or unconscious—can influence people to become apathetic to others' suffering, stress, and anxiety. I want to share a personal story that demonstrates this.

Due to a series of events, I was slated to defend my thesis in 2009. In hindsight, the timing was probably not a smart decision on my part, because I had lost my mother recently. Although I had failed at making her proud by seeing me become a doctorate, I wanted to honor her wish by graduating as quickly as I could. Unemployment was high, with companies laying off people to compensate for the economic downturn, resulting in a lot of talent in the market. It was hard to get a job as a graduate with fewer than five years of industry experience. I received a considerable amount of job application rejections, which humbled me further. I was on my student visa at that time and had a short runway to find a full-time job in my field or leave the country. I had already spent five years in the United States, got married, had friends and a life, and as you can imagine, my stress and anxiety levels increased with every rejection.

I had three good leads, but the turnaround time was slow, as the hiring managers had several candidates to evaluate. I had 20 days to get a job or leave the country, and being at my wit's end, I decided to reach out to the HR associate of one of my leads that was taking a considerable amount of time in the interviewing process. I explained my current situation to the associate and impressed upon her the direness of my case. I clearly stated that all I was looking for was an estimated date to reach a decision.

What I heard from the HR associate shocked me. She said that it was tough that I had a limited timeline and probably should start packing and planning on leaving the country. She also noted that it was probably a good thing because I would not be a good fit in an American culture anyway and might find it hard to succeed in the company. The apathy that she demonstrated and the racial prejudice that she exhibited was an indicator of the organization's culture. After I hung up the call, I struck that company off my list. That experience has stuck with me so vividly, and I use it as a constant reminder to promote empathy in our world.

Luckily for me, I started a full-time job with 11 days to spare, but that was a very stressful time for my wife and me— losing my mother, writing and defending my doctoral thesis, getting a full-time job—all on a student visa.

Enabling Empathy

As adversity and stress increase in the world, humans have responded by creating security blankets and safety bubbles around us. Most of these bubbles that we are a part of contain people who look like us, vote like us, earn like us, spend money like us, have educations like us, and worship like us. The result is an *empathy deficit,* and it is at the root of many of our biggest problems. Homogeneity of social circles have amplified groupthink and have converted these circles into echo chambers, quickly introducing unfavorable traits such as elitism, privilege, and biases. Empathy makes people relatable and trustworthy. This trust makes them better family members, managers, coworkers, and leaders. People become more open, transparent, and candid. Having a genuine connection with someone improves oxytocin and serotonin and makes people feel more psychologically and physiologically safe. The following sections discuss some easy ways to practice and enable empathy in your life.

Create New Connections

The first step to improve empathy in your life is by broadening your perspective. To create a heartfelt connection with someone requires having a natural curiosity to get to know the person. Imagining how someone might feel is not viable as your imagination is biased by your experiences and emotional makeup. You should make an effort to get to know the person. It might be intimidating at first, but start small.

Try these simple techniques to begin with:

- Start conversations with fellow attendees in virtual conferences, webinars, other other online gatherings. Invite a colleague or neighbor you don't know well to lunch. Go beyond small talk—ask them how they're doing and what their daily life is like. Show a genuine interest in them. After each interaction, jot down three memorable things about the meeting and two interesting facts that the person shared.

- Follow people on social media with different backgrounds than you have (such as a different race, religion, or political persuasion). Broaden your perspective.

- Electronic devices have pervaded our lives and disrupted healthy conversation and lighthearted banter. Make a rule to put away all electronic devices when you want to have a conversation, even if it is with people you interact with daily. This act enables you to give your full attention to the discussion, allowing you to pick up on nonverbal cues such as facial expressions, gestures, and body language. At our home, we have established the rule that we will not have electronic devices when all of us are having a meal to have an opportunity for conversation as a family. Some people have a device drawer, basket, or charging mat for guests to place their devices when they come over for get-togethers. It seems to work; my personal experience has been that conversations have been more stimulating and involved at such parties.

Experience Someone's Life from Their Perspective

You must have heard of the old idiom, "Don't judge a person until you have walked a mile in their shoes."[12] Experiencing someone's life from their perspective will help broaden your mind and make you understand their point of view, how they think, and why they rationalize events in their unique way. When you do this consistently with people, especially the people you work with, you become more empathic to their pain and try to identify realistic ways to help them. It becomes less about you and more about what works for them.

Attending a spiritual event or place of worship with the other person is a powerful way to experience someone's life. It signals to the other person your willingness to overcome your personal convictions and discomfort and expand your horizons to get to know the other person's guiding principles.

If you are irked by someone's behavior or reaction, rather than stew over it and spoil your mood, try to understand why the person behaved that way. Put yourself in their shoes to understand if they were stressed, upset, angry, or affected by something and lashed out at you instead. Maybe it is a cry for help, and the other person did not know how to handle their emotions. Instead of taking personal affront, try to empathize with the individual.

Join Others in a Shared Cause

Humans are highly clan-oriented and form social bonds around a singular objective or purpose of a clan. This profoundly grounded behavior is one of the reasons why people rally around symbols or mottos, forming a clan with a common goal. There is an intrinsic bond between clan members because they are part of something bigger than themselves.[13] Trust and camaraderie are established easily.

Volunteering is a powerful way to become part of something bigger and better than yourself. It also gives you a sense of accomplishment, pride, and bonding, releasing Dopamine, Oxytocin, and Serotonin (you are DOSing yourself). You could volunteer to build homes, help with a community project, tutor others, work at a homeless shelter, or even in a booth at events. Share your skills to help underprivileged children. Join a school committee. Offer to shop and deliver groceries for the disabled and elderly. If you have experienced grief or loss, join with others who have experienced something similar. Volunteer online if going to a physical location intimidates to you.

I was fortunate to come from an academic family. My father, brother, and I all have PhDs, and my mother had an MD in microbiology. Education for underprivileged communities; uplifting the downtrodden has been my shared cause. I believe that education, coaching, and mentoring will open doors for underprivileged communities and give them a fair chance in an extremely discriminatory world. As a compassionate empath, I mentor, coach, and teach students who have untapped potential.

When my wife and I arrived in the United States, we volunteered at various events to get to know different people, cultures, traditions, and foods. It also allowed us to share our backgrounds with others. We got to know many wonderful people of different ethnicities, backgrounds, and cultures. We shared our pains, grief, and suffering, our feelings of being away from home all by ourselves with no one to help us truly. Being disconnected from our loved ones with no easy way to immediately reach out to them if something dreadful were to happen was hard. But we formed a strong connection within our clan and could empathize with each other.

Empathy in Children

Instilling empathy and empathic values in children helps improve their emotional intelligence. It helps them cope with stress and have better social relationships. Higher EQ increases empathy and helps children be more sensitive to others' feelings and handle conflict better. It also helps them to connect with others at a deeper level and develop stronger friendship bonds.

Have you ever seen a baby mimic your facial expression and attempt to smile back at you? Remember how they coo softly when you are happy and suddenly cry or are upset when you are in a bad mood? Children learn to express emotions and empathy from a very young age. They might not fully comprehend their feelings and cannot express themselves coherently, but they exhibit a range of emotions similar to adults. It takes a while for children to understand other's emotional states and perspectives. One does not have to look further than toddler interactions in a playground or when they have to share their favorite toys at daycare or on a playdate.

As parents, guardians, and childcare givers, it is our responsibility to inculcate empathy in our children. Chapter 9 discusses actions for empathy and specifically discusses how to encourage empathy in children.

Learning Empathy from a Child

Every year, hundreds of thousands of acres of land succumb to wildfires in California. 2020 was no exception; it set a record for the size of destruction. A whopping 4.5 million acres of land was burned in 2020 caused by heat waves, dry vegetation, and complex lightning strikes, making it the largest fire season that California faced since the 1900s. There was even a fire (El Dorado fire in Southern California) started by a smoke-generating explosive used at a gender reveal party. What was meant to be a celebration ended up burning over 10,000 acres of land. The year 2020 truly was chock-full of adversity.

We had the unenviable fortune of experiencing this first-hand. As with other California residents, we suffered from bad air quality for months (even worse than usual). The skies were orange, the gray clouds blotted out the sun on some days, and we even saw red suns, emphasizing an apocalyptic experience. Ash fell from the skies for days on end, coating the ground, cars, roofs, and grills. Compared to other parts of the country and even the world, we were isolated from even our front and backyards due to the wildfires. It was a dystopian future that came alive in 2020. Numerous memes floated on the Internet and social media comparing California skies to science fiction movies like *Blade Runner*, or games such as Half-Life, Journey, or Borderlands. There were comparisons to Martian skies and even to hell on earth. It certainly felt that way for months.

The fires spread quickly despite the heroic efforts of the firefighters. They worked tirelessly around the clock to contain the fires as quickly as possible. It was scary and nerve-wracking. We were in the flight path of the helicopters deployed to provide air assistance and spray fire retardant for containment. The fires came pretty close to where we lived. At one point, we were less than 200 ft from the containment area and were on evacuation alert. We had our bags packed and stored in our car, praying that the winds would not shift and put our house in the path of destruction. It was harrowing to decide what was important in our lives and what we could live without. It was humbling to realize that, of all the worldly possessions, our health and legal documents were what was truly valuable, and everything else didn't mean much in the grand scheme of things.

Our six-year-old son was affected by these events immensely. He is an outdoors kid and loves to spend time in nature. The pandemic had already impacted his interaction with his peers

(continues)

The Power of Empathy

(*continued*)

and friends. Now, with the wildfires, he had to stay cooped up in the house. He felt suffocated, restless—like a caged animal. When we had to pack emergency bags in the event of an evacuation, we told him that he could pack whatever he wanted as long as it fits in his backpack. Also, he was allowed to choose only two toys. I thought that he would fight this and try to sneak in more toys, but I was incredibly proud of how he handled this situation. He packed his essential items—school books, scratch pads, pencils, markers, and crayons, and his two toys. He then took the rest of his toys, put them in trash bags, and asked me if he could put them in the car. I wondered why he wanted to do that, and his response amazed me. He said that he wanted to donate these toys to children who were already evacuated rather than leave them in the house and let them burn. He asked me if we could stop by one of the evacuation centers to hand the toys on our way. I could not have been prouder of my son and was touched by his level of empathy. I remember thinking that was the level of empathy I should aspire to and spread love and compassion to the world. Luckily, due to the fantastic work from our hero firefighters and wildfire response teams, we did not have to evacuate. However, we did end up donating the toys, along with food, water, clothing, and other essentials, to people in need.

The National Parent Teachers' Association (PTA)[14] decided that the Reflections theme for 2020 would be "I matter because..." An apt theme for the adverse times that the world was facing, especially with the increase of racial inequality, hatred, and stories of racial abuse, white privilege, white supremacy, abusive immigration policies, and a concerted effort to dissuade nonwhite populations from entering the United States. My son's entry was a painting of the California wildfires and animals with speech bubbles saying, "We matter, too!" When asked where he derived inspiration for this particular imagery, his simple answer was that everyone thinks about people and why they matter. We cannot understand what animals are saying, so he wanted to draw this picture to increase awareness and help people understand that animals matter too and need help. Once again, I was touched by the level of compassionate empathy in my six-year-old, and I am incredibly proud that my child can be my guide for leading with empathy in a world that is overwhelmed by apathy.

I am sure that you have your favorite story of empathy to share, and I would love to hear about it. I encourage you to share it on your favorite social media forum with the hashtag #leadwithempathy so that we all can hear these wonderful, touching stories, spread cheer around the world, and learn different ways to be empathic.

Summary

Empathy is the ability to truly be present. It's the ability to hold a safe space for others to feel their own emotions completely and to be able to understand their experience.

Empathy is one of the most vital of emotional fitness skills, especially during difficult times for a person or in the face of a crisis. Developing empathy will increase your emotional intelligence overall.

Reflections

- What are some techniques that you have employed to improve your empathy?
- What was the most challenging situation where you had to refrain from sympathizing with someone and instead truly empathize with them?
- What books have you read that have elevated your understanding of empathy?
- Make a list of your biases and reflect on how they impact your interactions with others.

Chapter 5

Leading with Empathy

You do not need to have a leadership title to lead with empathy.

Your actions to improve human quality of life in adverse times makes you a leader.

Start Your Leadership Journey with Emotional Intelligence

Undoubtedly, leadership has been one of the most frequently tested skills during the COVID-19 pandemic. It is effortless to read articles on a leader's behavior during COVID-19 and what they should do and didn't. But in reality, it is a whole different ballgame and requires consistent work and practice.

Emotional intelligence (EQ) is a critical part of behavioral shift essential for powerful empathic leadership. Emotional intelligence sets high performers apart from others having the same technical skills and knowledge. EQ is the ability that refers to the perception, control, and evaluation of emotions. Some researchers claim that emotional intelligence is an inborn characteristic, while others think that you can learn and strengthen it with time.

It is essential to have the ability to express and control your emotions. At the same time, it is vital to know the correct way of understanding, responding, and interpreting others' feelings. Rather than traditional cognitive abilities, EQ provides increased value to a leader's character, achievements, happiness, and success. Leaders with a high EQ have a higher sphere of influence and more considerable followers.

The next sections include suggestions for leaders to increase their EQ.

Label the Emotion

This is a popular technique that psychologists and leadership experts recommend. By labeling your emotion, you are shifting your perspective from an abstract concept to a tangible object. You are starting to define your feeling of fear and increase your awareness of the emotion you are undergoing. Practice by saying that you are feeling an emotion rather than expressing yourself with it. For instance, if you are anxious about a meeting, acknowledge it by saying, "I am feeling anxiety," rather than "I feel anxious." This subtle shift in focus shifts your mindset from being the emotion to experiencing the emotion, making it manageable and allowing you to address it.

Assign Time to Develop Self-Awareness

Many leaders are so involved in the act of leading that they forget to stop and introspect. Some find reflection and introspection unpleasant as such sessions tend to highlight personal areas that they perceive as weaknesses and failings rather than opportunities for improvement. A small portion of leaders considers that spending time thinking about themselves makes them self-absorbed, self-centered, or even egoistic.

The reality is that self-awareness and self-reflection help us be more sensitive to our behaviors, emotions, triggers, and pressure points. We can work more effectively with others by knowing ourselves, our feelings, tendencies, reactions, and, most importantly, our thoughts.

You do not need to invest too much time in self-awareness. At the beginning of every day, take 60 seconds to write down the answer to these two questions:

- What feelings am I experiencing right now?
- What events could prevent me from having a positive day?

Repeat the exercise midday, writing down your feelings up to this point. Write two of the thoughts that keep running through your mind. Are you worried, angry, or fearful? The mere act of acknowledging your emotional state reduces the power that these feelings hold on your mood and behavior.

If some events transpired to prevent the day from being positive, ask yourself what you can do to counter that and shape your day back into a positive one. Finally, retrospect on the entire day's events and identify areas that you can improve upon for the next day. This approach is also called *emotional check-in,* and this powerful technique is not limited to leaders. I use emotional check-ins with my six-year-old to increase his self-awareness and develop his EQ.

Be Vulnerable

This is good advice for anyone, but more so with leadership. Share your concerns, thoughts, and personal worries about the matter. Being vulnerable disassociates your role/title from you as a human and endears you with your teams. This enables your team members to follow your example and overcome their difficulty in expressing themselves and sharing their fears, anxieties, and emotions. It increases trust within teams and improves bonding. Share your fears, anxieties, hopes, and aspirations in addition to your coping strategies. This behavior will encourage

153

and inspire them to do the same, increasing the team's collective EQ and making the team high performing.

Dedicate Some Time for Yourself

We all must have seen the videos or posts of leaders that look exhausted. Many people do not realize how demanding the role of leadership can be and tend to forget that a leader is human. Besides, you cannot help others when you are devoid of energy. Therefore, you need to take care of yourself.

Dedicate some time performing actions that recharge your batteries. A long walk, exercise, or biking with your family are some activities that you can introduce into your daily schedule. Try not to embrace sedentary events during your personal time, such as watching television or relaxing on your couch. Physical activities have a higher rate of reinvigorating you physically, mentally, and emotionally. Your body also gets a burst of happy chemicals with physical activities. Combine this with healthy eating to improve your overall well-being.

To take care of yourself, spare part of your time enjoying something that makes you relax and brings pleasure. Everyone has a fuel through which they generate stress reduction and productivity by rewiring the brain.

There is an intricate connection between our behavior, feelings, and thoughts. Your changing thoughts have a helpful link in shifting your actions to be more productive and impacting your emotion's intensity. These steps help in leading toward a more positive environment and sometimes even bring changes to your neurochemistry.

Empower Positive Emotions

Positive emotions play a vital role in balancing out negativity and pessimism and have some excellent benefits. Unlike negative emotions that narrow your thoughts, positive emotions benefit your memory, awareness, and attention.

When we shift ourselves from negativity to more positivity, we open up new possibilities and improve our learning skills. We are receptive to new ideas, feedback, and suggestions. We tend to be less defensive and can have crucial conversations. We understand the context and origination of people's remarks or statements and evaluate them in the right light. This, in turn, results in overall positivity in our outlook, behavior, energy, collaborations, and communication. Positive people care healthier, happier, and friendlier.

The Benefits of Exhibiting Emotional Intelligence

According to leading researchers,[1] self-awareness makes it easy to have control of emotions. Instead of being stuck in a situation, it helps the leader find an alternative solution.

To make emotional intelligence useful, the first step is to start the evaluation of you. You can never work on the other person's well-being, emotions, and improvements unless you master operating your emotional level. The thing that distinguishes leaders is the emotional intelligence levels that help them create a more effective and prosperous environment.

Here are three benefits of emotional intelligence:

- **Better collaboration.** When people have higher EQ, they are adept at working with others. They know how to value each other, have good communication, and the best thing is they trust each other. The team with emotionally intelligent people responds to a suggestion in a productive and better way.
- **Better adaptability.** Many of us are not fond of changes, but they are part of life, and EQ gives us the tool that helps us deal

with the changes. Many people experience considerable stress and anxiety with changes, and an emotionally intelligent person can inspire other members to feel positive about themselves and improve their state of mind.

- **Better communication.** EQ helps you handle challenging situations, whether it is an upset employee or an angry customer. If you have emotional intelligence, you can find the solution to the problem by connecting with another person even before you arrive at a resolution.

- **Better leadership.** In outstanding leadership, it is essential to understand the people and appreciate their work and know-how to work harder. Emotional intelligence helps you achieve such understanding that it benefits you to become a great leader to guide your team in the right direction.

"You Are Not One of the Boys"

In Chapter 2, we took a look at gender and racial injustice and how it affects nonwhite male personalities in developed worlds, and non-male personalities universally. Here is an example that underscores the challenges that underprivileged people face in the workplace.

Valentina was a sales executive at a reputed software company. She had several years of experience in the IT industry and was a consistent top performer. She prided herself on having a track record of meeting at least 150 percent of her goals and had won many awards over the course of a long and illustrious career. Being Hispanic and a woman, she knew that she faced a double whammy of discrimination and worked extra hard to overcome these "disadvantages" as she shared her stories with me.

When I met Valentina, I found her to be a very empathetic and kind person and was the antithesis of the pushy, obnoxious salesperson stereotype. She told me that she was in sales for her software company because she genuinely believed in her organization's mission of helping clients in their digital transformations. I could feel the pride in her as she talked about what she did and how her company's products help improve her clients' quality of life. Customer empathy seemed to be a big focus for her, and Valentina said that cognitive empathy was essential for her to be successful in her role.

But being a highly empathetic person, she also demonstrated emotional and compassionate empathy. She was a team player and stepping in to help her colleagues in a bind. The word "no" did not seem to exist in her vocabulary and she would selflessly help her team and others in the organization. As a successful leader, she mentored and nurtured other women even though it was taxing on her. "I want to give other women a chance to grow and become powerful. What is the point of having all this knowledge and learning if I do not share it with aspiring women leaders? We need to help one another and bring diversity and inclusion into the workplace," she told me.

Her empathy did work against her many times, she shared. "I was never good enough to be part of the good-old-boy network, even though I consistently crushed the competition with my performance. I didn't know if it was because I was a woman or a Hispanic. Probably both," she narrated, talking about her challenges working in a predominantly white-male-dominated environment. "Being the only woman on the team, guess who had to plan parties, send-offs, birthdays, or purchase

(continues)

Leading with Empathy

(*continued*)

gifts for admin assistants day? Not only was I a sales executive, but I was also an assistant. My team assumed that just because I am a woman, I needed to perform such duties, even in the workplace. It was demeaning, but I smiled and helped because I knew that no one would step up if I declined," she shrugged.

Valentina also talked about how her supervisor always assigned vanity accounts and accounts with a good probability of success to his favorites and how he entrusted her with accounts that were a challenge. "My manager would hand me the account list and say that he had complete faith in me bringing these sales in because I was so good at handling hairy, complex challenges, as if that would justify his actions. It always felt like I was being set up to fail. I had considerable stress and usually ended up burning out within two quarters. But I had to persevere. If I failed, it would not be because I exhausted all my avenues, and the client was inconsiderate and was unwilling. It was because I was a Hispanic woman and not good enough for the game, never mind my previous track record. It is pretty unfair. On the other hand, if the team's golden boy failed, it was a wrong account, and we should not have pursued that company. They always had excuses if one of the men failed, but I was under constant scrutiny. It is very demeaning, condescending, and a serious blow to your confidence when your supervisor assumes that you are incompetent and decides to help by teaching you Sales 101 motions and how to create slides that will engage the customer."

Her manager finally quit the company, and Valentina did arrange the send-off party. This opened up an opportunity for promotion, and she applied for the role, as did her colleague.

She had the experience, leadership skills, coaching and mentoring skills, along with a proven track record of turning bad situations into profitable ones, in addition to an exemplary record. Her colleague did not have the amount of experience or success rate that she had, but he was a white man. In a rational world, she would be an ideal candidate tailor-made for the role. Despite having worked in the organization for over six years, she had to go through the entire interview process like an external candidate. She had seven rounds of interviews, including a panel, where she had to convince people of her skills.

"I had a terrible experience during the panel interview, which was the last round. The body language of one of the panelists showed that he was bored or disengaged. Another was scowling as if this interview had dragged him away from his favorite show. As I was going through my strategy for the team and my 30-60-90 day plan, I glanced around and could acutely see that the majority of the panel was disinterested. The questions asked were all at an operational level, even though the panel interview's purpose was to outline the team's strategy if I were to become the manager. I realized at that moment that I would not get the job. They had already decided whom to offer the role to and that this was just a perfunctory meeting, a checkbox to claim that the interviewers had gone through the process."

Sure enough, there was an announcement of her colleague's promotion, and everyone talked about how he deserved it and that he was the right choice. Valentina reached out to the area managers, one of the panelists, and asked for feedback. "He told me that the team felt I was too empathetic to the customer and might end up compromising with the

(continues)

(*continued*)

clients rather than to the team. He emphasized numerous times that it was not because I was a woman, but I knew otherwise. I was just the wrong race and sex to be leading the team, and in addition to these impediments, I was an empathetic person. It is an unfair system, but that will not prevent me from being who I am—an empathetic woman leader, trying to break the barriers in a male-dominated world."

Reflections

- Have you experienced or heard similar stories in your workplace? What emotions did you feel?
- What actions did you take to prevent such situations from happening again?
- How can you convince others that empathetic leadership is a strength, not a weakness?

Overcome Your Limiting Beliefs for Better Empathy

Everyone experiences setbacks and periods of gloom in life. Negative emotions and thoughts tend to linger in our minds, and we are left feeling sad, depressed, and longing for happiness and motivation. These feelings are amplified as a result of stress from the pandemic, social distancing, long hours of remote work, and reduced physical interaction with others. This can overwhelm us into inaction through fear and anxiety, and the truth is that despair truly is one of the greatest enemies for leadership.

Overcoming these thoughts, however, can be challenging when one is experiencing bouts of disheartenment, as these are situations where some of our beliefs engage actively in sabotaging our state of mind. A belief is acceptance that a statement is true or real. It can be a firmly held opinion or conviction and can be formed from an individual's experiences. In its purest form, a belief is just a thought that one has programmed into their mind as a truth or reality. Some of these beliefs are not helpful and potentially hold one back. These are called *limiting beliefs* and could be about you and your capabilities, other people that you interact with, or even about society overall.

Recognize Your Limiting Beliefs

Many limiting beliefs originate from our childhood when societal and family values were instilled in us. Some may have been imprinted during our education and in our interactions with others. Other limiting beliefs masquerade as adages and continue to impact people negatively, such as "Money is the root of all evil," "No pain, no gain," "Life is hard," "Good things come to those who wait," and "You have to pay your dues." These feel true because they have been etched into our minds through repetition as family values or from people we revere, and sometimes are used as excuses for our actions (or inaction). One of my mentors once called them *mind viruses* because they can be passed from one person to another.

Other limiting beliefs are personal and are created from our experiences as we meander through life. These typically start with "I can't," "I'm not," or "I don't," and focus on preventing us from performing some activity due to perceived lack of skill, will, or talent. For example, "I'm not smart enough to solve this problem," or "I can't handle the pressure if I am promoted." Take a minute to think of some of your own limiting beliefs and how they have affected you or held you back.

Despite the negative influence that limiting beliefs exert over us, there is no need to succumb to them and submit to their debilitating effects. The following sections describe an effortless three-step process to effectively gain control of these limiting beliefs and transform them into powerful motivators.

Step 1: Realize that you have an advantage over others

A common limiting belief is "I shouldn't do it because I'm going to fail." Failure has been stigmatized in our society and culture for years and it is only recently that we have started viewing it in a different light. Clichés such as "Failure is not an option," in addition to disparaging comments and remarks from family, relatives, and other parental figures over the years could have instilled limiting beliefs within us.

However, failing is not the same as being a failure. Failing implies that one has actually attempted, a feat that not many people could have accomplished. Albert Einstein once said that "Failure is success in progress." There is validated learning and data to be gained from the failed attempt, which translates to knowledge that gives one an advantage over others.

Remember: Failing at something is not the same as being a failure.

Step 2: Invalidate your limiting beliefs

The power of a limiting belief lies in how deeply one believes in it. An effective strategy to prevent it from taking over is to introduce doubt in one's mind. Here is a simple exercise to help you. For each limiting belief that you have identified, find at least three pieces of evidence against your belief. For instance, if the limiting belief is "I am not smart enough to solve this problem," think of at least three instances when that was not true. We all have overcome several challenging problems in the past even if we did not acknowledge them as hard at the time. Identifying at least three representative examples where you solved challenging problems will help in two ways.

First, your journey into your past will help you identify several situations where you were successful in overcoming different levels of adversity and your mind will be compelled to relatively rank all these successes, making you realize that you have the necessary skills and fortitude needed to solve hard problems. Second, this helps you analyze how you solved these challenges in the past, and that can help you solve your current problem, or at least put you in the right frame of mind for critical thinking and problem-solving.

Step 3: Transform your limiting belief into a motivator

Once you have enough evidence to invalidate and doubt the legitimacy of your limiting beliefs, practice this simple step to convert it into a motivator for your personal growth.

Add a "**yet**" to the end of any limiting belief that disparages you.

For example, "I don't have enough experience to get that promotion—*yet*" or "I can't solve this hard problem—*yet*."

Performing this simple action helps change your perspective, making "yet" one of the most powerful adverbs in the English language. It helps us reaffirm that we have not yet reached the outcome that we are aspiring for and this is just a temporary setback. People who adopt the technique of adding a "yet" become more mindful and aware of their situation. They can recognize their present situation and acknowledge the fact that the negative result will soon turn into a positive one. This thought process helps them to overcome their limiting beliefs with greater ease and conviction. It also allows them to analyze their failed attempt and use that validated learning to rethink their strategy and try again, thus increasing their chances of success.

Change Your Perspective

Famous coach and motivational speaker Tony Robbins once said, "The only thing that's keeping you from getting what you want is the story that you keep telling yourself."[2] Limiting beliefs, especially ones that form out of adverse experiences in the past, are extremely powerful in denigrating us and our potential, preventing us from achieving our goals.

For any transformation to occur, we need to change our perspective first. People who succeed in transforming their limiting belief into a motivator by the simple act of adding a "yet" at the end of it realize that failing at something is not the same as failure. Instead, they reaffirm that the knowledge that they gained positions them better for success in achieving their desired objectives. Conquering one's limiting beliefs makes them a strong leader.

The Debilitating Effects of Limiting Beliefs

When I met Pat, he was a highly functioning technology manager at a Fortune 500 company. A few years ago, his marriage started falling apart, ending in divorce, and consequently limited interaction with his children. As with most divorces, this stress affected his professional life and his productivity adversely. He started drinking more, became abrasive and anxious, and started building a wall around himself. There was considerable friction in his interactions at the workplace.

Then COVID-19 happened, and shelter-in-place was mandated. Pat was imprisoned in his home, all alone, left with his stress, anxiety, and his thoughts. He started becoming paranoid as a result of his existence at home. His productivity took a nosedive, and his behavior became erratic. His supervisor advised him to take some mental time off to recuperate and resolve his issues. Instead, Pat decided to leave the organization because he felt that was the root of his state. Unfortunately, his stress and paranoia influenced his communication style, and Pat's resignation was less than congenial. He ended up "burning the bridges," so to speak.

Pat started applying for various jobs but could not land anything immediately because of the economy and the pandemic. His self-confidence took a hit. He started feeling more paranoid and thought that his previous colleagues were trying to sabotage his career. He felt that people were spying on him and wanted to destroy his life. He became distrustful of everything. Once, he told me that he had started observing that his Wi-Fi connection would degrade on a video conference when he began expressing his views on politics or racial events.

Not having found employment for a few months, being alone, refusing to get help, and having a large mortgage to pay off took a significant toll on Pat. He started suspecting that his neighbors wanted to drive him out of the community because he was not employed. This stress and paranoia seeped into his interviewing, impacting his self-confidence and self-assurance. On several occasions, he was incapable of articulating the work that he had performed in his previous company—accomplishments that he had strategically executed with phenomenal results, that he, the team, and the organization were immensely proud of. He started second-guessing and devaluing himself, considering entry-level jobs despite having considerable industry experience. Pat's limiting beliefs were causing him to feel worthless and rendering him into a husk of his original self.

Pat finally realized that his stress, anxiety, and paranoia were debilitating, and that he was undergoing a mental breakdown. With the help of his therapist, he recognized how his limiting beliefs had started to hamper his work and life, how stress had affected his performance, behavior, and mental well-being, driving him into paranoia. He realized he needed to change his perspective and rediscover himself. When I spoke to Pat last, he had moved to another city "to recharge his batteries," as he called it. He sounded more relaxed, happier, and less paranoid. He had started a new venture, something that he had always wanted to do but was held back by his limiting beliefs. I wish him all the best and look forward to him growing into his former confident self.

Random Acts of Kindness Increase Empathy

"Be the reason that someone believes in the goodness of people." – Karen Salmansohn.[3]

A random act of kindness is your spontaneous decision to help others. It shows your compassion toward other people and is one of the most selfless ways to make someone smile. Acts of kindness can be big or small, according to the situation. It can be helping an older person with her shopping or maybe paying for someone's cup of tea or coffee. You could help a homeless person with some food or clothes. Even your kind words or a genuine compliment is enough to make someone's day, and these are all random acts of kindness.

Random acts of kindness bring positivity to our life, and it doesn't matter whether you are a receiver or a giver. You must have noticed that when you are having a bad day, someone's slight smile or a small compliment can make your day.

The Science Behind Kindness

The warm feeling that you experience after helping someone isn't in your head, but it is in your brain chemicals. Your every act of kindness produces oxytocin, which not only boosts your mood but your overall health. In addition to oxytocin, acts of kindness produce other feel-good chemicals in your body—dopamine and serotonin. These neurotransmitters are beneficial in boosting your overall mood, besides benefits to your overall health.

According to the research, these chemicals help treat your anxiety, depression, mood swings, and relieve your pain.[4] There are unlimited rewards behind your every act of kindness. Besides, your kindness improves your mood and health, and you can play a vital role in making this world a beautiful place.

Your small act of kindness can make a positive change in this stressful life. In pre-COVID times, I had visited a local deli to grab a quick lunch. The person before me was frantically searching in her purse for her wallet. She probably had left it at home, in her car, or at her desk when she stepped out in a hurry. She was flustered and apologized many times to us for holding up the line. Finally realizing that she did not have any money on her, she asked the cashier to cancel her order. I could feel dejection and sadness in her voice. I told the cashier that I would pay for her sandwich, to which the woman was shocked. She could not believe that a random stranger would do something like that. She asked for my information to pay it back to me later, and I told her that she could perform the same act of kindness to someone else in need instead of repaying me. Her eyes lit up, and she agreed to do so. I am sure that the person would have performed a similar act of kindness to a random stranger and brightened that person's day. And maybe, that act of kindness has now been passed on to someone else. A small act of kindness can go a long way and impact many people positively.

The Benefits of Random Acts of Kindness

It is not a big deal to give your seat to an older person or a woman with a baby. The recipient appreciates these simple acts of kindness;

instead of all these, courtesy is becoming uncommon. But by doing little things and playing our role, we can make the world a bit better place for us.

It can make someone's day. You never know what the next person is going through, but your little act of kindness can make someone's day. Even sharing a smile with someone is among the best things you can do every time you want. We all have gone through hard times due to the COVID-19 pandemic. Every little help or even your precious smile can mean a lot to someone and is enough to motivate them to struggle for the good times.

Make the world a better place. We can make the world a way better and more inviting place by being a little kinder to the people around us. Sometimes people are waiting for the reminder to tell them the world still has friendly people, which is enough to inspire them to be kind and good to others and themselves.

Be a role model to your kids. Not only your kids, but there can be some other person who is taking inspiration from your side. You never know whom you are inspiring. But most importantly, every parent is a role model for their kids, and your kindness will help make your kids more courteous and kind toward others.

It is inspiring. Random acts of kindness are always inspiring. A few days back, I read a story of a nursing student on social media. This student went to a bookstore to buy a second-hand medical textbook, and when she opened the book at home, there was a gift card to a coffee shop from the old owner to enjoy drinking coffee while studying. This simple gesture meant a lot to the nursing student, as drinking a hot cup of coffee while reading was one of her favorite ways of learning. She shared this story on social media to encourage others to do the same.

It makes you a happier person. When we perform a random act of kindness, we feel inner satisfaction. It inspires and motivates us to do something beneficial to others. You get oxytocin, serotonin, and dopamine. You experience a surge of pride when a stranger thanks you or expresses gratitude. The positive vibes you are trying to spread makes your life better, elevates your mood, and makes you overall a happier person.

Examples of Random Acts of Kindness

Random acts of kindness do not have to be huge gestures or require us to go out of our way to help others. Here are a few examples of random acts of kindness that we may have observed. These acts of kindness will take you a few seconds or even a minute, but can make someone's whole day.

- Hold the door open for the person behind you.
- Never forget to appreciate others.
- Pay a genuine compliment to someone.
- Surprise someone with a care package or a meal delivered to their home.
- Let the person who is in a hurry pass you in the grocery line. (Returning a shopping cart to the designated area is not a random act of kindness. It is a basic courtesy.)
- Gift a stranger a cup of coffee or tea, maybe buy someone's lunch.
- Call someone you have not interacted with in a while. Ask them how they are doing and genuinely listen.
- Send someone a motivational text or a picture of a cute animal.
- Support a cause, a nonprofit, or a crowdfunded project. (You performed this when you purchased this book!)

Don't Think, Just Do

One of the essential elements of random acts of kindness is unpredictability. The joy of performing these acts stems from not knowing when an opportunity could arise. Planning to commit an act of kindness when you get up or have it as an entry in your daily task list saps the fun out of it and makes it a chore. It will also dilute the act's authenticity, and you could catch yourself forced to perform an action that could be construed as kind merely to tick off a box on your task list, defeating the purpose of the activity altogether. Don't overthink it. If an opportunity presents itself for you to perform a kind deed in the course of your day, embrace it in the spur of the moment. Do not go out of your way or put yourself in harm's way, either. Keep it simple. Just do a random act of kindness.

Acts of Kindness During COVID-19

Throughout the pandemic, we saw some great examples of kindness and demonstration of how people, businesses, and communities can help each other in adverse times. Here are a few notable demonstrations of empathy and empathic leadership:

- Community groups sprung up during lockdown to help people with essentials, provide emotional support for people suffering from being isolated, entertaining people, and keeping people happy.
- Zoom provided unlimited minutes and meetings for K–12 schools affected by COVID-19 through July 31, 2021, transforming virtual schooling overnight.
- Many people dressed up as Santa and offered virtual visitations to keep children engaged and happy during the holiday seasons.

- Many conferences and workshops arranged entertainers, magicians, DJs, and mixologists to appreciate attendees and spread fun and cheer to the entire family.
- During the hand sanitizer shortage in the early stages of shelter-in-place and lockdown, several breweries and distilleries stopped producing spirits and beer. They switched over to making hand sanitizers to help the community. Many of these businesses donated hand sanitizer batches to hospitals, assisted healthcare facilities and healthcare workers.
- It was heartwarming to see and hear about the many food drives and meal initiatives that popped up all around the world. Diverse communities got together to cook and deliver meals to people impacted by the pandemic, homeless, and underprivileged school children who received their food through free school meal programs. Restaurants converted into meal kitchens to support struggling households, assisted healthcare facilities, and care homes.
- Educational businesses provided free access to many parents and educators to supplement children's education at home.
- Business owners, athletes, and sports organizations donated or financially supported low-wage workers, healthcare workers, and people impacted by the pandemic. For example, the National Football League in the United States offered all 30 of its stadiums for vaccination sites.
- Many organizations delivered face masks, PPEs, ventilators, and gloves to hospitals and first responders and distributed care packages for the military, veterans, disabled and elderly, and first responders.
- In many countries, people gather at their balconies and show their love and respect for the healthcare workers' heroic work by roaring applause, singing, and performing.

Leading with Empathy

Despite the adverse times, COVID-19 helped us rekindle our compassion and enabled many kind-hearted people to step up and help the community at large. These empathic leaders set many great examples and positively impacted so many lives.

Empathy is the connection that links everyone together and strengthens our bonds within the families, neighbors, and community. So let's keep spreading love, kindness, compassion, and empathy to our fellow human beings.

Emotional Hijacking

My six-year-old once had a play date with his friend. They both are into Beyblades, and they usually have a great time. I had bought my son a few new Beyblades, and he had mixed different parts to assemble what he called a superBey. Naturally, he was explaining how he created this to his friend with much passion. It is very amusing to hear two first graders talk about their understanding of stamina, strength, tension, angular momentum, and mechanics learned from watching the cartoon series.

As luck would have it, my son beat his friend at several Beyblade battles, which his friend did not expect. He started accusing my son of cheating, that the only reason he won was that he mixed different parts and made a nonstandard artifact that had an unfair advantage. For a while, this went on, and I could see my son getting visibly upset each time his friend called him a cheat. I stepped in and asked them to pack up their Beys and watch something on TV, as it was clear that they could not play nicely. Unfortunately, they both were triggered and could not agree on anything to watch. We ended the play date early and dropped off his friend.

On the way back, I asked my son how his day was, and he burst into tears, saying that it was the worst day ever, that of all his friends, how could his best friend call him a cheat. He reiterated that he did not cheat and that he won the battle fair and square. After consoling him and affirming that I did not believe he cheated, rather he used his ingenuity to create a strong Beyblade and that I was proud of his engineering talent, I decided that it was time for a teachable moment.

I asked him, keeping that episode aside, how was his day. He took a while to answer and said that it was not too bad and that he had an opportunity to have a play date and play with Beyblades. We talked about runaway emotions and emotional hijacking (or amygdala hijacking that Daniel Goleman wrote in his book *Emotional Intelligence*).[5] We also discussed how we should not let a few bad moments spoil our entire day or spoil the memory of the fun that we had.

The next time you feel that you had a terrible day, ask yourself, "Was it truly a terrible day, or did a terrible few minutes hijack the rest of your day?"

Sometimes, we may not wake up in the best moods or feel the most understanding and empathetic on certain days. Maybe we did not get a good night's sleep or had something on our minds. Perhaps it was just one of those days. You need an emotional picker-upper on those days, and the best way to achieve that is to DOSE yourself with happy chemicals.

- Perform a random act of kindness to a stranger. This is one of the quickest ways to get out of that bad mood. The thought that you did something to make a stranger smile or feel kindness is powerful.

(continues)

(*continued*)

- Physical exercise helps. Go for a walk, or swim, hit the treadmill or your bike.
- If you have a pet, play with it for a while or take it for a walk.
- Talk to people who are usually positive or who cheer you up. Ping someone and ask them how they are doing.
- Watch something uplifting or motivational. Look at photos of your favorite memories with your loved ones and friends.

Instilling Empathy and Emotional Intelligence in Children

In previous chapters, we explored Maslov's hierarchy of needs and how the global pandemic impacted us all as adults in the workforce. This effect was equally valid with children.

When our physiological needs were affected by COVID-19 (fear of breathing, essentials shortage, toilet paper scare, fear of illness and death, to name a few), adults underwent various levels of stress. Children, and even pets, are highly empathic, and they picked up on these emotions, especially when we started spending copious amounts of time together in the same physical location.

When schools closed and switched to distance learning, children lost their sense of familiarity and identity. They had to learn in a virtual setting, and that was a daunting experience for many. We can relate this loss to the same emotional impact that we had when prevented from visiting our physical offices for work. The children also lost physical interactions with their peers overnight, along with love, sympathy, and emotional exchanges with not only their cliques but, more importantly, with their teachers who have been critical parental figures outside of their homes. This is a widely researched topic,[6] and the younger the child, the more impacted they are. And as a result of this, many children lose their self-esteem and self-actualization. This feeling is amplified with helicopter, tiger, or other forms of overparenting.

Thankfully, children are very adaptive, and many of them have adjusted to remote schooling quicker than many adults have to remote work. They have discovered virtual cafeteria sessions, virtual breaks, and also virtual playdates. They get their dopamine and serotonin fixes through their assignment grading, classroom interactions, and class projects. Maybe even some virtual oxytocin, but it does not feel that they are receiving the same levels as when they were in physical proximity in school.

Several friends and I mulled over this and agreed to the following two points:

- Children have not yet evolved sufficiently to experience the same highs of happy chemicals as adults.
- As long-term technologists and empathic leaders, it was our responsibility to use our practices and supplement our children's needs.

We ran several experiments over six months and shared our notes. My six-year-old was a happy participant in these experiments, and we both had much fun. Overall we identified four practices that have helped in my child's EQ development. All four of these practices are rooted in Lean, Agile, and DevOps methodologies, but deep knowledge of those methods is not essential to implement these practices. (Chapter 5 does discuss these methodologies a bit.)

Practice 1: Iteration Planning

Schooling has a consistent schedule for the most part, and we know what to expect on a daily and sometimes weekly basis. Routine can become tedious, and iteration planning introduces relatable goals weekly that children can aspire for. These goals focus on fun activities that can be expected at the end of the week if they demonstrate good behavior and a list of daily and weekly rewards.

My son and I agreed that a program increment (PI) would be four weeks, and each iteration would be one week. Daily behavior would be measured and would account for daily and weekly rewards.

We used a star chart (see Figure 5.1) for this experiment and deployed three types of star colors. We reserved gold stars for long-term behaviors that we wanted to instill. Gold stars excite children. It is a matter of honor to have gold stars. These stars are representative of activities that required commitment, courage, and resolve. The child has to strive hard to achieve these gold stars. The act of receiving gold stars helps release endorphins to achieve their goals, dopamine when they see the gold star added to the task, and serotonin when they see those gold stars on the chart.

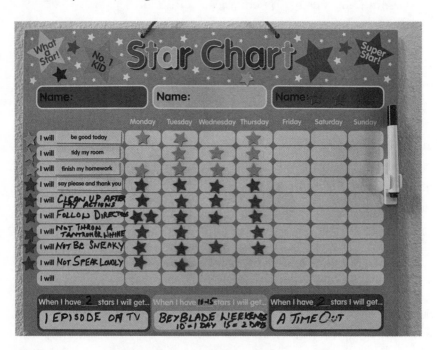

Figure 5.1   Star Chart for measuring daily progress.

Leading with Empathy

Blue stars are achievement stars and help release dopamine. You could use other colors that your child prefers; we chose blue because my child chose it. These tasks are behaviors that are not as intensive as those that earn gold stars and are focused on good habits that you want to inculcate in your child.

But it is not just about instilling a sense of accomplishment. We also want to make our children increase their self-awareness and self-actualization. Children also need to understand that actions have repercussions, so we introduced red stars and time outs. It's not fool-proof, but at least it is habit-forming.

As an example, here are the rewards that my son and I came up with for a sample PI:

Daily rewards. If the behavior was good for the day, the reward is an episode of his favorite TV show in the evening (only when all schoolwork has been completed).

Weekly rewards. My son is into Beyblades, and gold stars account for playing with them. He can get a maximum of three gold stars in a day. Ten gold stars earned in a week can be cashed out for one day of Beytime, while 15 gold stars translate into two days of Beytime (Beytime is only on weekends).

Daily and weekly risks. Two stars in one day result in a time out. More than two red stars, and he loses TV privileges for a day. More than four red stars in a week trigger a grounding, where my son is sent to his room to reflect on his actions and write about how he will make better choices in the future (similar to commit-ment letters in team building). In another PI, we introduced a new rule that if even one red star appears on the star chart, he cannot earn a gold star for overall good behavior. After some shrewd negotiation from my son, I agreed to award him a gold star for good behavior on weekends to earn enough stars for his Beytime.

Practice 2: Spindowns

We conduct a spindown at the end of every day, roughly at the same time every day (also part of habit-forming). We review each activity on the star chart and discuss the positives and the wins that helped win the star. We provide kudos to the child for good behavior and a shoutout when the child has gone above and beyond what was expected (for instance, the art supplies were replaced and cleaned as soon as he completed). Spindowns release maximum dopamine and serotonin in your child's brain and are a very positive affirming event.

A spindown also plays a critical role in winding down at the end of the day. It psychologically signals that the day has ended and allows people (parents and children alike) to relax and spend time in other family bonding activities. This event is significant in a contactless, remote world where everyone is physically co-located and move from one virtual conference into the next, with minimal cues that highlight the start and end of a working day.

Practice 3: Emotional Check-Ins

Staying at home can be challenging for kids. While they can quickly adapt to virtual media and distance learning, they could be struggling emotionally with isolation, lack of physical interaction, and even difficulty with long hours of screen time. Emotional check-ins are an excellent technique to quickly assess their current state and introduce activities to improve their it.

There are many ways to perform emotional check-ins. Parents that work in organizations that practice some form of agility would have been exposed to internal weather reporting to express how they feel with the help of weather. Other methods allow you to express how you feel using a feeling scale (1–10) or through more complex activities based on pop culture, such as, "If you were to use a movie or a song to represent your emotional state, what would it be?"

With children, however, we want to keep it simple. Internal weather reporting is a powerful mechanism to perform emotional check-ins. The goal is to assess your child's emotional state regularly and evaluate trends. A few of my friends have used mood planner apps (see Figure 5.2) to track their children's emotional states over time and have had much success. A mood planner also helps with discussing being mindful, being in the moment, and developing self-awareness. It also helps the child not obsess over their current state but instead look forward to being empowered to change their current emotional state into something better, which can be a potent tool.

Figure 5.2   A Mood Tracker app.[7]

Leading with Empathy

The number of emotional check-ins depends on your child's disposition and how quickly they move from a negative state into a positive one. Some people have found that performing an emotional check-in four times during the day (before school, during the first break, just before the post-lunch session, at the end of the day) works well for their children. Multiple emotional check-ins help the children get more opportunities to improve their overall emotional state.

We tried two check-ins each day with my son and then ended up with only one check-in at the end of the day. We conduct the emotional check-in as part of our spindown activity and have our son assess his entire day and rate it (see Figure 5.3). We also use a simpler scale and use emojis instead of a mood planner.

That last emotional check-in at the end of the day also serves two additional purposes:

- It helps educate the child that every day will have good moments and bad moments and provides awareness to the child about runaway emotions and how they can hijack one's entire day.
- At the beginning of each day, the ultimate goal is to focus on having one joyous day at a time and celebrate it. It will accumulate into a happy week and eventually becomes the norm.

Figure 5.3 Emotional check-in with emojis.

Practice 4: Root Cause Analysis

Life is all about continuous learning, and events do not usually progress how we would like them to. A *root cause analysis* (RCA) is a systematic tool that organizations regularly use to:

- Identify the root cause of problems and events.
- Develop approaches or countermeasures to prevent the problem or failure from occurring in the future.

Performing a good RCA also reduces the tendency to address the symptoms or put out the "fire" instead of focusing on the real causes for the failure or deviation from expected results.

5-Whys Analysis is a straightforward method of RCA. It has its roots in Lean manufacturing and has become the de facto approach for incident analysis in several organizations. This method involves looking at the failure or problem and asking "why" enough times (five, in most cases) so that we reach the real reason why something failed.

Table 5.1 shows a real exchange between my son and me, where I used the 5-Whys Analysis:

We then had a good discussion about being polite, using words instead of emotions, and convincing instead of demanding.

An RCA is a powerful tool in helping the child introspect their behavior and reflect on their actions. It is also a calming time for the child and helps stabilize any runaway emotions that might still be lingering. Once you conduct your 5-Whys Analysis, discuss how you can prevent this incident in the future. You could also have additional conversations around how to observe repetition and repercussions if it repeats.

Leading with Empathy

Table 5.1 Applying 5-Whys Analysis to a Problem: You threw a tantrum.

My 5 Questions	My Son's Answers
"So why did you throw a tantrum?"	"Because I wanted to do X, and you did not let me."
"Why did I not let you?"	"Because you don't understand why I wanted to do X."
"Why do you think that is?"	"Because you don't listen to me when I ask for something."
"Why do you think that?"	"Because I did not use please and I shouted."
"And why do you think that happened?"	"I forgot, but I really wanted to do X." (tears ensued)

Children Are Our Future

It is a good thing that our children are more resilient and adaptive than many of us. They quickly embraced virtual schooling and online education. They learned to log in to a video conference, be on mute unless called upon, and keep their cameras on at all times. They adapted to virtual playdates, field trips, lunches, and even birthdays. They have become proficient with electronic devices and contactless interactions. They accepted wearing marks in public, maintaining safe distances, sanitizing themselves, and recognizing the need to isolate themselves if they had a cold, cough, or fever.

It is up to us as parents and caregivers to provide the necessary guidance, tools, and techniques to instill empathy and emotional intelligence in our children. Supplementing practices that introduce these traits into their daily routine will not only enrich children's emotional intelligence; it will also prepare them for a world where change is the only constant. Be sure to check out Chapter 9, which discusses some specific ways to encourage empathy in children.

Summary

There is a dire need for collaboration, compassion, kindness, and empathy in these challenging times. Empathy is the ability to emotionally understand what other people feel, see things from their perspective, and imagine yourself in their place. It is a skill and not a trait. One's upbringing, environment, life experiences, and interactions with other empathic people strongly influence empathy. Empathy is a scarce resource in our organizations today. You do not need permission to lead with empathy. Anyone can be an empathic leader.

Your actions to improve human quality of life in adverse times make you a leader.

When you lead with empathy, you can empower humanity in the face of adversity.

Reflections

- What steps have you taken that have improved your emotional intelligence?
- What are some of your limiting beliefs and how have they held you back? What would your life be like if you did not have those limiting beliefs? How can you achieve that life?
- What random acts of kindness have you performed over the last 30 days?
- How have you tried to enable emotional development of your child(ren)?

Part III

Empowerment

Chapter 6

Enterprise Empathy

Do not second guess your team's how *if you have clearly articulated the organization's* why. *Empower your teams and empathize with them as they create value.*

As discussed in the previous chapters, empathy can be distilled into the ability to step into a person's shoes, to understand where they are coming from, and to understand their needs. Extending this to a workplace, empathy can be defined as the ability to step into someone's role, look at things from their point of view, and understand the rationale behind why they performed a particular action or had a particular ask from others in the organization. A workforce that does not feel safe, trusted, or cared for tends to suffer from stress and anxiety, impacting their productivity, innovation, and motivation. Empathy is, therefore, crucial in the workplace and it is critical for organizations to promote empathy and make it part of their organizational culture.

Empathy Improves Productivity

Whether you're a manager overseeing a team of employees, the president of your company, an employee in a large organization, or an independent contractor, one truth is persistent across the board. Every one of us has to work with others. We are all in a relationship of some kind and interact with other people every day.

Much of what we are used to experiencing in the workplace is a consistent push for greater productivity and throughput. Unrealistic deadlines stress us, the constant push for delivering faster causes mistakes, miscalculations, or failures that affect results and increase our anxiety. And sadly, this rush to complete the job often creates an unsafe environment, susceptible to physical accidents or emotional strain.

Have you noticed that when people are compelled to act rather than encouraged, mandated rather than challenged, belittled rather than encouraged, and not treated with kindness and respect, the results are never what was aspired or expected? Empathy is crucial for high-performing teams to deliver business value consistently.

Empathy and Kindness

Having empathy for another person means that we are using our ability to understand their feelings. When we put ourselves in their place, we become more compassionate and patient. No matter what situation we are facing, we can treat others with kindness and accomplish more. For example, are you more likely to work harder, push your limits, and help your team achieve the desired results when your team and supervisor are assisting you, being collaborative, and encouraging you?

We all desire to be treated as human beings. And just as we want to be praised and appreciated, we need to give the same treatment to our coworkers and employees. Raising one's voice or threatening someone with consequences, however thinly veiled, is not a characteristic of a leader. Instead, such behavior signals insecurity and weakness. Insecurity is loud and vapid. Self-confidence is poised and inspiring.

Leadership Sets the Example

Leadership sets the example and is who the team looks to for guidance. Leadership has an important role to show by example how to handle challenges and the best way to achieve results. When managers and supervisors are eager to assist their employees, when they encourage the team to share ideas, and when they treat their employees with kindness, their employees will follow suit. If you do not lead by example, you are signaling that you are not of the same tribe as your teams. When that happens, there is no opportunity for the tribe to build trust and bond with you, and a lack of trust implies that they will not follow up. If you do not have people following you toward aspired outcomes, you are not leading. You are just going out for a walk.

No One Comes to Work Planning to Do a Bad Job

However hard we try, our personal lives seep into our professional work environment. This axiom is especially true for those of us who work from home. Children need to be fed and watched over, pets need to be walked and fed, and the house needs to be cleaned daily, with everyone coexisting in the house. This is not just work from home but instead, existence from home, and as a result of that, people are suffering from long bouts of stress and anxiety. Some people might also be a caregiver, adding to their levels of stress.

In short, life happens. People need to recognize that no one wakes up one day and thinks, "I should probably do a terrible job at work today." If someone demonstrates a lack of productivity or engagement, ensure that your first reaction is not to admonish them or point out their failures. Pause and try to think of why the person is not their usual self. Instead of judging them, empathize with them. Do not sympathize with them, instead reach out and ask if there is something you can do to help. Compassionate empathy goes a long way in these situations.

Empathic Leadership

Empathetic leadership focuses on understanding the need of team members, being sensitive to their deficiency and growth needs, and selflessly striving to provide them for the team members. An empathetic leadership style increases psychological safety within the organization. It makes everyone realize that they are important parts of the same team trying to accomplish the same purpose. It increases productivity, team morale, and loyalty. Empathy is one of the essential traits of a good leader.

When leaders understand the organization and team dynamics, they have a better idea of potential challenges or impediments ahead of them from a cultural or value stream perspective. Empathy is deeply rooted within our evolutionary history and is usually defined as the ability to sense and experience a wide range of emotions in fellow human beings. Empathy for leaders is defined as the following:

> *When a leader can look at a fellow workforce member and put themselves in their shoes, understand the pain and stress they are undergoing, and value their happiness above their own, they are genuinely empathic.*

As humans, we have that urge to relate to people, demonstrate our sympathy/empathy, and try to meet them where they are. For instance, workforce managers in industries familiar with remote working might be under the assumption that what their team members are undergoing is something similar, far from the truth.

They should try to embrace the fact that everyone's living conditions are unique, and even if they are part of the same workforce, other factors influence people's lives. For instance, someone might have to be a caregiver to a parent or a loved one, requiring them to spend long hours of the night tending to their needs. It might be a sick child or someone with special needs that require additional attention. Or it could just be a sick pet. Whether we like it or not, personal lives do influence professional work, and it is tough to isolate each of these as different parts. Empathic leaders embrace this reality and are sensitive to other people's pain and stress.

Once, on a supermarket run, I ran into Adam, an IT manager at a large software company. Adam had four children and two dogs, and his wife worked in a hospital. He always had an interesting anecdote or two to share with me. However, this time, he looked sad, drained of energy, and it looked like he had not slept in a while. I asked him how the family was and how he was doing. He shared that it had been hard with his children in virtual schooling, taking care of the dogs, and juggling his work duties. He talked about how hard it was on his wife to avoid everyone until she had thoroughly sanitized herself and the constant fear of exposing her loved ones inadvertently. One of his children had contracted a cold, and he had been awake taking care of her while his wife was working nightshifts that week at the hospital.

He then proceeded to tell me that they had a software release that night and that he had approached his director to see if someone else could fill in for him. He had explained his situation with the director and was confident that someone else on the team could fill in. Unfortunately, things did not go as expected. He was shocked to hear his director curtly inform him that the software release was critical and that he had to be there to ensure that it was deployed smoothly. He was told that he could be online and take care of the child if needed and then had a conversation with the director about how one had to separate personal and professional life and that he needed to step up his game.

Listening to this made me very sad. I asked if he needed any help or if he wanted to drop the other two children at our house, but he politely declined. After he left, I thought about the IT director's response, and it underscored the reality that we have a shortage of empathic leaders in our workplace.

Why We Have a Dearth of Empathic Leaders

With so many benefits of empathy and the value that it provides, it feels obvious that we need to be empathetic in the workplace. However, we do not see an abundance of empathetic leaders in the workplace. Demonstrating empathy also takes a lot of time and effort and is emotionally draining. Here are a few reasons why empathic leadership is so rare in the workplace:

Empathy is considered a sign of weakness. Throughout history, we have been told that we need to be professional in a workplace—calm, composed, not demonstrating outbursts of emotions, stoic. The stereotype of a leader has been military in nature and no leeway for human emotions. This behavior suppresses any dredge of emotion in the workplace and people are hesitant to demonstrate emotion lest they be judged weak and ineffective. This association with weakness might be a deterrent to ambitious leaders.

Empathy requires focusing on others. This is challenging for many people because they have to stop focusing on themselves and give importance to other people's feelings and emotions. This can be hard for people, especially if they are Type A personalities. The current social media culture also makes this harder, with their constant drive for self-promotion, and deriving prestige and validation through likes and comments about their staged events and life. Being empathetic means putting others ahead of oneself, and this can also be extra challenging in today's hypercompetitive world.

Organizational goals do not permit people to be empathetic. Many organizations are focused on performance goals that drive excellence in people at the cost of others. Other organizations pit one team against another in the spirit of competition to make the organization more productive and make it more aggressive and toxic.

Sabotaging a Promising Career

I firmly believe that management can set their teams up for success or failure. An individual contributor shared his personal story of how his management structure sabotaged his career. He shared with me his rollercoaster emotions on his path of failure.

Bobby was an aspiring and hardworking individual. A fresh graduate, he had applied for a position in a reputed company and was thrilled to be offered the position.

Onboarding was memorable and warm, and Bobby felt like a valued member of the organization. The company was accommodating and filed Bobby's H1B application (work permit) just within a week of joining—an activity that organizations perform typically after a year of continuous employment. Bobby was granted his work permit six months later, making him a very lucky and fortunate individual.

His experience with the team, however, was a different story. On Monday after the onboarding week, Bobby was raring to meet the team he would work with. He was inspired to make a good impression and be a positive collaborator, having

(continues)

(*continued*)

heard about the organizational culture's great stories during onboarding. The reality, however, was far from his expectations.

Bobby met his team lead and manager at the reception desk. They escorted him to his work area and introduced him to the other team members—the scrum master and an engineer. The interaction took no more than 15 minutes. Bobby's manager then led him back to his work desk, where his laptop and phone were docked and plugged in. He handed Bobby a printout on how to configure his system, set up his accounts, and walked off to his office. Bobby spent the next 30 minutes setting up his access.

At the top of the hour, Bobby's team lead came over to his cube and asked him to attend a routine meeting in lieu of him to get plugged into the project. Unbeknownst to him, the expectation was that Bobby's team would drive this meeting to resolve a critical issue. The teams waited for someone from Bobby's team to arrive for 10 minutes, after which the project manager said that they could not conduct the meeting without the data team leading. Bobby announced that he was a member of the data team, to which the project manager berated him for not starting the meeting and wasting everyone's time. Bobby could feel ugly stares and said that he was not aware of the meeting's criticality. A partner team lead snorted and, using derogatory language, asked Bobby if this was a joke and if he understood the severity of the situation. He went on to say that he would be having a discussion with Bobby's supervisor about his incompetence and lack of respect for other people's time. Shocked at the derogatory language and accusatory tone,

Bobby blurted out that he was a new member of the team and that this was his first day on the job.

The meeting adjourned early, and not surprisingly, the partner team lead had a conversation with Bobby's manager and team lead. In the afternoon, Bobby got a message to meet the manager. He was met by a scowling manager and a furious team lead. The manager said that he was very disappointed in Bobby's performance and unsure if he made the right hire. The team lead said that Bobby needed to step up if he wanted to survive in this organization and said that this was strike one on Bobby's record.

Bobby returned deflated and went home, wondering if he made a mistake accepting the job offer. The next day, at team standup, Bobby was horrified to see that the scrum master had assigned the incident solution's user story to him. The sprint was under way, and he only had four days to complete the user story. The immense pressure to perform, apathy from the scrum master, and lack of support from the team exacerbated Bobby's stress. As an immigrant on an H1B visa, he had to maintain a full-time work status, but that was a challenging task considering that he had no support within the team and no psychological safety.

Other team members did not come to his aid; they ignored him and didn't include him when they went for coffee breaks or lunches, making Bobby feel unwelcome. Depression, anxiety, and paranoia set in, impacting his performance further.

Eventually, Bobby managed to secure a role in another organization and resigned from a horrible job that made him

(continues)

(*continued*)

cringe and hate going into work. But the damage was already done. This traumatic experience had shattered Bobby's self-confidence and self-assurance. He felt ill-equipped to succeed in his new role, continually reading between the lines, jumping at shadows, and viewing team actions with suspicion. It has been five years since that experience, but Bobby has not yet gained back his confidence, even though his current organization provides extensive resources for employee enablement.

Reflection

- Emotional check-in: What emotions did you go through as you read Bobby's experience?
- Why do you think the manager and team lead behaved this way toward Bobby? Could bias be involved?
- What actions would you perform if a team member approached you with a similar experience?

How to Be an Empathic Leader

Being empathic is not a fixed trait. One can learn to be empathic through coaching and developmental opportunities. Empathy predominantly requires three things: listening to the person, being open, and understanding their needs. This section discusses important ways to be empathic at work.

Be Authentic

Leaders really should want to make people happy. When you ask someone to tell you more about something that is clearly impacting them, mean it. Give them your full attention so that they know you are meaning what you say. Also, when you ask, "How can I help?" realize that you are signing up for something, usually hard. Trying to slide out of the ask or backtracking your offer of help can not only affect your credibility, it will damage your relationship with the person and others when this interaction is recounted. This does not mean that you should avoid asking how you can help. It just means that you need to be prepared to walk the hard path.

Leaders will also need to genuinely be interested in the dreams, aspirations, and hopes of others.

Be Vulnerable

Leaders cannot really exude empathy when they are stiff and stand-offish. They need to demonstrate that they are comfortable enough to wear their heart on their sleeve. Many leaders have been trained to have a stiff upper lip and not show emotions in the workplace. This is unfortunate and forces them to try to put on a façade when they are at work. Instead, learn to be sensitive and share personal aspects of life. When you are having a bring-your-pet-to-work day (or a virtual meeting), don't appear without a pet. When the teams are showing off their spirit, join them. It not only improves bonding with the team, it makes them recognize you as one of the team as well, thus increasing the social bond.

Be Approachable

Gemba is a Japanese term that means "the actual place." A Gemba walk was a practice popularized by Lean manufacturing and developed by Taiichi Ohno, an executive at Toyota. Similar to the concept of Management By Walking Around (MBWA), a Gemba walk instructs management to walk the factory floor or the front lines to familiarize themselves with their organizational processes and continually look for waste and opportunities to improve existing processes. Gemba walks help keep a pulse on the organization and give a firsthand experience of how people are feeling. A quick hallway discussion with teams can provide way more information than a project status meeting. Try to attend your team's standup as a silent bystander to listen in and pick up on team dynamic, social undercurrents, any impediments that will need addressing. Do it on a rotating basic. Check in every now and then to see how teams are doing. Digital versions of Gemba walks include skip-level meetings, Ask Me Anything (AMA) sessions, and lean coffee with teams.

Be Attentive

When a team member reaches out to you and asks for your time, it is imperative that you are attentive and actively listen to the person. They need to be the sole focus for the duration of the discussion. Do not rush them or be impatient. As a leader, you want to spend more time listening to the person talking because you want to understand what the problem is, why it came about, and how it is affecting them. Pay extra attention to verbal and nonverbal cues that might be demonstrated. Ask clarifying questions but try not to ask "why" multiple times. It might come off as you questioning their behavior. Instead ask something like, "How did you come to that decision?" Try not to use words that are interrogative. Another probing question to get more information about the situation is, "What alternative options did you have to evaluate before performing the action?" Remember, you create the space for someone to express themselves. They fill the void with their emotions.

Be Appreciative

Encourage people; appreciate what they are doing and how much they are doing. Appreciate in public. Give feedback in private. Don't be overcritical or emotional when giving feedback. Consider whether there were extrinsic factors involved that resulted in poor performance. Sometimes a colic baby or duress at home could be a factor. Try to remember that no one comes in to work planning to do a bad job.

Be Helpful

Actually try to do the things that you say that you would do. Build trust. Be on the lookout for signs of overwork or burnout and try to alleviate employee stress by slowing down delivery or extending timelines.

Pitfalls of Empathetic Leadership

Being an empathetic leader does also have some pitfalls:

- **Impeding good decision-making:** Sometimes empathy can impact reasoning and cognition and distort judgment by being influenced by situational emotions.
- **Empathy can introduce unconscious bias:** Because leaders feel more empathy for people who are similar to them, there could be some unconscious bias that could enter the workplace. Leaders might give these people preferential treatment, hire, and even promote these people unknowingly. This can reduce diversity within the organization as a result of empathy.

- **Empathy can be limited:** Being empathetic to many people at the same time is hard. It takes a lot of energy to be empathetic to even more than one person. A leader might have to consider many perspectives and apprehensions of many people at the same time, which will not only be taxing, it will limit the number of perspectives that will be considered.

- **Excess empathy can devolve into apathy or burnout:** When leaders constantly demonstrate empathy in the workplace, they can become emotionally drained and this could cause apathy in their own personal lives. As time goes on, this could also result in burnout.

Improving Psychological Safety

Psychological safety is the ability to be oneself and show emotions without fear of any adverse consequence to one's persona, brand, career, status, or social standing.[1] Families with high psychological safety have stronger bonds and treat one another with respect. Psychological safety is critical for people to feel trust in a relationship—personal or professional. People feel included, learn better, are more productive, and challenge the status quo without the fear of embarrassment or punitive actions. Psychological safety focuses on eliminating fear in interactions and introducing respect, permission, and acceptance.

Psychological safety at work describes an environment where one believes that one can freely speak up about any idea, concern, question, and mistake without being humiliated or getting oneself in any trouble. It is concerned with the interpersonal relationships in a workplace, the extent to which individuals feel comfortable in taking positive risks, and the quality of support they get from each other in the working environment. The acceptance of each individual as a valuable member of the organization makes the workplace psychologically safe. Teams with high psychological safety become high performing, take higher risks, and innovate better as the team members know that they have each other's backs and do not have to worry about failing.

Why Do People Feel Unsafe?

Humans have a deep-rooted desire to fit into a group. Even in prehistoric times, members of the tribe aligned with the social norms and standards of the tribe lest they be ostracized or removed from the group. Societies, communities, and families are modern tribes, and the mechanics remain the same. Interpersonal fear contributes to people feeling unsafe. They worry about what others will think of them if they say something, be it an idea or question or any information that needs to be shared.

An organization is also a modern tribe with its beliefs, rules, regulations, norms, and behavior. Naturally, the irrational fear of not being able to fit in extends to the workforce. People try to conform and abide by expectations in the workplace. They fear retribution, punitive action, and rejection. In organizations with toxic or power-oriented cultures, people are afraid to question the status quo, challenge the system, or be tagged as rebellious. What if they upset their higher-ups, got their supervisors in trouble for not conforming, asked the wrong questions in a town hall that was meant to be open, but not really? What if people's impression of them changed because of the way executives thought of them? Nobody wants to get stuck in such a situation.

Individuals sometimes ignore the part they could have played by sharing their ideas or showing their concern just because of their lack of psychological safety in the work environment. Empathic leaders must strive to create an environment where the workforce feels comfortable discussing their problems, challenges, and ideas. They should feel comfortable with failing, knowing that they will not have repercussions when they do so, allowing them to take considerable risks, and sharing their learnings from failure.

The Importance of Psychological Safety

Organizations that promote psychological safety are successful and productive. A successful organization is learning-oriented, agile, engaged, and achieves its goals effortlessly. To guarantee success throughout the organization, we need to ensure the entire workforce's participation to its fullest extent.[2] For that purpose, the people who are part of that organization must feel safe to come, work, and speak up; about what they know, what they don't know, what they see, and what they are worried about. Psychologically safe environments also promote diversity and inclusion, reducing homogeneity and echo chambers.

Empathic leaders cannot instill psychological safety by themselves. They need to bring like-minded people and cultural change agents into their fold. They have to engage the right people motivated to improve the organization's conditions and make the workforce feel safe. They have to coordinate and collaborate with people across teams, departments, silos, functional boundaries, and hierarchies.

Benefits of Psychological Safety

I firmly believe that happy people are productive people. When the workforce has psychological safety, they have more trust with their coworkers, lesser stress and anxiety at work, and better self-confidence and motivation. They are open, collaborative, and dynamic.

Self-Confidence

A psychologically safe environment provides a sense of self-confidence to individuals. They then trust their intuition and fearlessly share their thoughts or ideas over necessary things. Whereas in an environment that is not safe, we have anxious individuals because of the strained atmosphere. There will be many unresolved conflicts because the people there will not be genuinely honest with each other. They will feel comfortable taking risks, run experiments, and innovate faster. They know that failing does not mean that they are a failure and are willing to try different things. Work environments affect team productivity. Encouragement and appreciation provide the individuals the confidence to give their fullest.

Motivated Individuals

In psychologically safe environments, people are more prone to take risks, innovate, make mistakes, accept their failures, and learn from their mistakes. To improve your skills, you need to know where you are going wrong and what needs to be corrected. And it only happens when you accept that you have failed and have an opportunity to course-correct without any consequences. Sharing validated learning from failures is a significant source of knowledge within the organization.

Openness

A psychologically safe workplace allows people to discuss anything openly without worrying about getting criticized for giving some unintelligent idea. Transparency and radical candor become part of the organization's culture. People start to share ideas, which results in better decision-making. They accept failure and know that they can ask for help from each other and not receive flak for making mistakes, which leads to a higher degree of collaboration, thereby a better solution. The blame game will no more be a part of the organization, and people feel free to communicate about the problems they individually face in the assigned tasks.

Positive Energy

In a psychologically safe environment, the workforce will spend their energy and time on valuable activities and tasks. They do not have to exhaust their energy on thinking about the consequences of their actions. They do not have to spend time performing a pros vs. cons exercise for suggestions that they want to propagate up the chain or think of ways in which executives might misconstrue their questions as challenging the status quo. They do not have to brown nose or placate higher-ups as part of their roles, even if they despise them.

Instead, they can spend their energy on high-value activities, productive tasks, innovation, and ways to stimulate their intellect. They do not have to groan thinking of coming into work. Instead, they can feel invigorated and excited to work on tasks that will make them feel productive and valued.

Increased Productivity

It is only in a psychologically safe environment that one feels that the work he is doing has some meaning, and only then can he put all of his efforts into his job because the more engaged we are, the more we perform well. A psychologically safe workplace allows risk-taking, speaking, creativity, and fearlessness, ultimately boosting the organization's success rate. So for high performance and productivity, you need psychological safety.

Failure of one team is validated learning for the entire organization.

When we feel safe inside the organization, we will naturally combine our strengths and work tirelessly to face the dangers outside and seize the opportunities when presented.

How Can Leaders Make Workplaces Psychologically Safe?

In these adverse times, providing a psychologically safe work environment is notably significant. Empathic leaders should acknowledge that workforce stress and anxiety are at an all-time high due to long periods of working from home, the events of the last few years, loss of familiarity, and media-induced fears of COVID-19 variants. These events are not in the employee's or leadership's control for the most part, and the only variables within their control are the organization's environment, behaviors, and actions. Remarkable things happen when leaders put the people in the organization first, sacrifice their comfort, offer tangible results to make people safe, and make them feel that they belong and are valued.

Provide Empathic Leadership

An empathic leader is like a parent who wishes to give her children the best education in the world, discipline, help them grow, provide them with the best opportunity, and enhance their self-confidence. Empathic leaders demonstrate similar love toward their teams, support them through failure, guide them toward their outcomes, and protect them from unfavorable situations to the best of their abilities.

They treat their workforce as humans instead of numbers and head-count. A good leader's attitude is what unites the team by encouraging trust and vulnerability. They are humble and are willing to ask forgiveness. It can be compelling when a leader openly apologizes for impacting psychological safety in the past and takes responsibility for their actions. It humanizes leaders and makes them more trustworthy. People are willing to give others a second chance when they see that leaders acknowledge their mistakes and learn from them. However, they can sense if leaders are disingenuous and are providing lip service. Make sure that your "say-to-do" ratio is as close to 1 as possible. That is the only way you can build trust within your workforce.

Embrace Failure

We are all human, and being human means that mistakes will occur, and we will fail. Limiting beliefs such as "Failure is not an option," or "Act as if it is impossible to fail," or "If you fail, it is your fault" must be eradicated from an organization's lexicon. Leaders should abolish requirements such as 100 percent defect-free or 100 percent uptime for software, systems, or products.

Assure teams that you know things will go wrong and that you are all in it together. You will learn from the failures, figure out the faults, and learn from them. Embrace lean experimentation, hypothesis-based development, and rapid prototyping. Ensure that your processes can generate the data necessary to make data-driven decisions. Encourage your teams to calculate the probability of failure for their experiments and factor in those costs.

> *Perfection is like the horizon. You grow when you continually strive for, but never reach it.*

Protect Your People

When you embrace failures, you are taking risks by letting your teams make mistakes and shield them from these failures' repercussions. Being a leader in these adverse times is hard; being an empathic leader is tough. Due to the pandemic's economic downturn, the revenue stream for many organizations has been impacted, and sometimes there are tough decisions that have to be made. Many organizations take the easy route to recuperate their losses by reducing headcount. While this might provide a reprieve in the short term, this decision could prove costly to the company over time.

Even if the layoffs target people with performance issues, they drastically reduce the entire workforce's psychological safety. Stress seeps into the organization, and top performers decide to move to other positive cultures. Attrition increases, and pretty soon, the only people within the organization are people averse to change, people who could not move to a different organization or people who believe that they are too valuable to the company to be laid off. Layoffs decrease morale and spread a culture of fear and hypocrisy. The remaining workforce starts to adopt behaviors that help them align with the executives. People go into self-preservation mode, finger-pointing increases, accountability is shirked or passed around, and the organization devolves into a power-oriented pathological culture.

As an empathic leader, work on spreading positive emotions in the workplace, such as confidence, empathy, and inspiration. These emotions help us become open-minded and motivated. A creative environment prevails when fear, worry, and burden of work do not overpower us, and our minds are free to think of new ideas. Empathy is the most important among these positive emotions, as it is the key to a friendly environment, ultimately helping people feel safe in the workplace and enjoy their work.

Famous Empathic Leaders

Apple's CEO Tim Cook has urged empathy for years. He has been using his position to bring visibility to this important topic. In 2016, he wrote a memo to Apple's employees during a time of political turmoil in the United States, urging them to have empathy for themselves and the customer, and asked them to work together and respect one another despite their political affiliations and differences. He constantly stresses empathy, compassion, and self-awareness in his commencement speeches and is by far one of the most empathic leaders in the business world. He is not afraid to show his empathic side with employees or the world.

Pat Gelsinger, current CEO of Intel and previously of VMware, has said that he always tried to make sure that empathy was an essential part of VMware's culture. He instilled customer empathy as part of the company's EPIC2 values and has demonstrated empathy on numerous occasions.

Jack Dorsey, CEO of Twitter and Square, is another highly empathic leader and has shared his empathic side numerous times. While many leaders have shied from having a discussion or a public opinion of the BLM riots, Jack was livetweeting from Ferguson during the riots. In 2020, Twitter announced that their employees could work from home permanently if they choose to.[3]

Customer Empathy

We would be remiss if we did not explore customer empathy from an enterprise standpoint.

Customer empathy is understanding the underlying emotions, feelings, and needs of customers—users of the product or service and client organizations you work with—and is a priority in business and customer service. Customer empathy is the epitome of success in any industry and is all about taking a step toward deeply understanding the fundamental needs, emotions, and feelings of your customer toward a product or a service. The core concept of customer empathy is to resonate with the customer's necessities, feelings, and problems.

Satya Nadella, the CEO of Microsoft, emphasizes empathy in every business realm and attributes customer service as the key to all. He says, "Empathy is a muscle, so it needs to be exercised."[4] This sentiment underscores the importance of empathy and how customer satisfaction decides the fate of any organization. Empathy and customer care go hand in hand and results in customer empathy. Customer empathy is all about taking a step toward deeply understanding the fundamental needs, emotions, and feelings of your customer toward a product or a service. The core concept of customer empathy is to resonate with the customer's necessities, feelings, and problems.

Southwest Airlines is probably the best example of a company that has embraced customer empathy. Their vision is to be the world's most loved, most efficient, and most profitable airline, and their purpose is to connect people to what's important in their lives through friendly, reliable, low-cost air travel. Their logo is a heart and has a New York Stock Exchange ticker symbol of LUV. Numerous case studies and articles have been conducted and published on Southwest's culture and obsession with customer (and employee) empathy. It has always been about the heart at Southwest Airlines, connecting people, and championing communities because they firmly believe that distance should not keep people from being neighbors. This is a profound testament of their commitment to customer empathy.

Every organization must practice customer empathy, especially when the whole world is going through hard times. It allows organizations to reach beyond providing essential services and puts things into perspective by viewing the customer's outlook. If demonstrated the right way, empathy optimizes the operation and service of any organization. An enterprise practicing empathy is sure to stand out from the competition.

Verizon is another company that demonstrated customer empathy in a very effective way.[5] Verizon realized that academia and student community were adversely affected by COVID-19. The company offered its customers free data during the pandemic, enabling them to access educational resources and not disrupting their learning. It also provided free resources to support free learning opportunities at home for those working in education. This included free learning resources for kids, free access to top online courses, and free premium access to *The New York Times* for university students. This gesture encouraged convenient work from home and safety for all. Verizon taught companies a beautiful lesson that it is not always about profit margins. It is about doing what is right and being a part of something bigger and better. Your products must be designed to improve the overall life quality of your customers to endear them. Customers will never forget companies that went the extra mile to help them in times of crisis.

Customer empathy is the key differentiator between business success and failure. Over 89 percent of the companies compete on the quality of customer service alone.[6] Customer empathy provides that extra touch and enhances customer service to become a personal and compassionate experience. It also shapes the culture of any organization. Earl Nightingale, an American radio speaker and author, famously said that our attitude toward life determines life's attitude toward us.[7] This philosophy holds true with customer success and empathy as well. If we treat our customers with respect and demonstrate empathy for them, our customers will reciprocate with empathy.

In this pandemic, we all need compassion and empathy. A truly empathic customer service representative listens to the customer and utilizes compassionate empathy to address their pain. It allows companies to treat customers as human beings and brand shareholders. This philosophy, in turn, leads to increased revenues, better company profile, brand reputation, and most importantly, customer loyalty. Better features are not a market differentiator anymore. How a product or service improves the customer's experience and quality of life, how it makes them feel, and how they are treated are the critical components for customer retention.

How to Overcome Obstacles to Customer Empathy

When it comes to demonstrating customer empathy, traditional ways of engaging customers have also evolved, especially during the pandemic. Business and sales executives could not meet customers in person to establish a rapport with customers. The engagement model was digitized overnight, introducing new challenges to connect with customers. Here are three ways to overcome these challenges:

1. **Demonstrate customer empathy.** Understand the customer's point of view and value their input. Understand what challenges they are facing and why are they facing them. Respect the customer's input by actively and compassionately listening to them. Customer experience and service are worthless if it does not eliminate the customer's pain.

    Customer empathy is about taking it to the next level and understanding what they are not saying. Always remember that companies who exhibit empathy receive empathy in return.

Employee job satisfaction and well-being also increase as a result of demonstrating customer empathy.

2. **Don't be defensive.** If you determine that, in conversations with the customer, the cause of a problem or inconvenience is your product or service, own up to it. When Apple launched its iPhone 4, there were numerous complaints of dropped calls or losing reception when people gripped the steel bands at the bottom of the phone. Instead of being empathetic to the customer, the late Steve Jobs responded in an email, saying that the customer was holding it wrong. Apple even went to the extent of issuing an official statement claiming, "Gripping any mobile phone will result in some attenuation of its antenna performance, with certain places being worse than others depending on the placement of the antennas."[8] This event blew up and became a meme called the iPhone death grip.

3. **Be in touch with customer needs.** Market conditions, patterns, and trends constantly evolve and change, especially in tumultuous times such as a global pandemic. Conduct customer surveys, case studies, and polls. Social media is rich with information and should be a reliable data source for information and analysis. Understand the psychology of your customers. You can host online sessions and conduct lean experiments with actual customers. It will let you interact empathetically with your customers at a deeper level.

Demonstrating customer empathy is more than an aspiration for your employees. Make it a requirement of your work culture and a way of working. Customer service departments must learn and practice innovation and empathy. Enrich the teams with knowledge about different aspects of human behavior and how to cope with stress, anxiety, anger, frustration, and other negative emotions. Behavior, speech, and communication experts can also help customer service representatives practice cognitive and compassionate empathy to connect with the customer effectively.

How to Demonstrate Customer Empathy

The global pandemic became a compelling event for many organizations to promote digital to the core of their business models. Traditional methods of reaching out to customers through physical engagement did not work anymore, amplifying the need for omnichannel applications for customer retention. Let us look at five core principles for demonstrating customer empathy.

Understanding the Client

You need to understand your customer's business: their history, challenges, how they grew, what kinds of mergers have occurred, their organic and inorganic growth, and what prevented them from going down the transformation path in the past. You want to clearly understand the client's expectations and impact if these are not met.

Empathy is imperative because the client has engaged with you, acknowledging that they do not have the solution to their problem themselves. They are asking for help. You can't be afraid to ask good, challenging questions, but at the same time, you should aim to be respectful and acknowledge that there may be sacred cows and trigger topics within the organization.

Do not patronize or be dismissive of the client. Decisions, principles, or technical information that might seem intuitive to you—or that might seem extremely simple—may not be that way with the client. By patronizing or dismissing a client, you assume that they understand things just as you do, which is unlikely. It is also worth recognizing that your client has probably worked with other consultants in the past, and some may have been top-notch consultants. You may not be the first people that they're interacting with.

Be an active listener and have a professional outlook toward the work. When you go to a doctor, they engage in active listening, have a comforting demeanor, and ask insightful questions. And even though those questions might seem extremely silly or evident to the patient who might have already assumed a prognosis through online searches, the doctor continues down that route because she is the medical expert. Try active listening and asking essential questions to unravel the client's business outcomes and definition of success.

Keep Your Say-to-Do Ratio as Close to 1 as Possible

This means that you precisely *act on what you said or committed to doing, and, vitally, you do it when you said you would.* This action signals to the customer or client that you identify what steps need to be performed, and you have a timeframe and deadline that you're assigning to the task at hand. This is extremely important and necessary when you're building trust and credibility.

If you are setting up meetings or having conversations, you need to ensure that you drive toward actionable outcomes. A meeting without any action planning or purpose does not add value, and it ends up wasting precious time. Recognize that you're a brand ambassador for your organization and need to live up to your organization's ideals and values. This outlook is critical when you strive to keep your say-to-do ratio as close to 1 as possible. Your behavior and how you interact, behave, and perform actions directly reflect your organization's values, principles, and culture.

Be Flexible and Have an Open Mind

Leave your ego at the door. Every time you engage with a customer, you're starting at level one. Your credentials are just going to get you through the door. You need to build and establish your credibility every single time.

214

It is essential to *state your opinions respectfully*. When you are having a conversation with strong views, make sure that you don't become too passionate to ensure that you acknowledge that other people might have strong opinions like you. Compromise is key here. You can't change people and their perceptions overnight. There is lots of work that goes into it, but negotiating helps you have an open mind and find common ground between you and the client.

You will also have to be *open to accepting rejections from clients*. Articulating your ideas and providing logical arguments does not mean that the customer will be swayed. Transformational changes are highly emotive since they target the fundamental beliefs that clients have held for years, and it may be hard for clients to face changes with ease. It will not be easy to persuade clients to change huge parts of themselves.

> *Everyone has a right to speak, but you need to earn the right to be heard.*

Be *respectful* of other people's points of view, cultures, organization, where they have come from, and how they have evolved and grown. Empathize with their organizational culture and processes. Many of them have been in that particular environment for a long time, and just telling them that the organizational culture is wrong or that their processes are not efficient is not going to help them. You have to empathize and engage if you want to help them transform their organization.

Be Persistent

Changing a company's culture requires a substantial amount of energy. Just like a supertanker loaded with oil in the middle of the ocean, a company is a precious asset, and the goal is to move it from one point to another. If certain conditions require the supertanker to change course in the middle of the ocean, it will be notably slow. There will be considerable resistance due to the tremendous amount of inertia that the supertanker has to overcome when changing course. But slowly, it will start moving, and it will head in the right direction.

> *Minor changes to current strategies are better than no changes at all.*

You have to be *consistent, persistent, and stoic.* In fact, you have to be that beacon of hope that the customer can come to. You can tell them that things will get challenging, and it is acceptable to enter the "valley of despair." It begins with anxiety and quickly grows into fear of the unknown and a propensity to embrace defeat or denial. It is on you to help customers gradually accept change and start moving forward.

Be Approachable

The fifth core principle is particularly relevant in today's world of so many more remote workers. You have to make sure that your sphere of influence reaches people in other settings, such as video conferences and phone calls.

Be sociable. Be approachable. Have an open-door principle. Rather than opposing a belief of the customer or being dismissive by using the word *but,* say, "Yeah, we could try this. *And* we could also do this." This way, you can forward your client's thinking better. You've accepted what the client has suggested while at the same time making them think about your suggestion. Ensure that these two things are within the same domain and that your suggestions will further accelerate or improve the processes, learnings, values, or outcomes the customer is looking for. This is the key to successful enablement.

Ands amplify. Buts impede.

Success is ultimately two-sided. You cannot claim success, nor can victory be declared unless the other party acknowledges that they have received something of value. The client needs to recognize that you have helped and delivered value to be considered a successful enterprise consultant. Adhering to the five core principles will increase your value and expand your sphere of influence and your ability to enable the customer effectively.

Shifting to a Remote Workforce Overnight

COVID-19 brought unprecedented human, socioeconomic, and cultural challenges to every industry vertical. Some companies around the world rose to the occasion, acting swiftly to safeguard employees and migrate to a new way of working that even the most extreme business-continuity plans hadn't envisioned. Others were unable to adapt overnight and succumbed to the hurdles or were severely crippled.

Many leaders had to abandon their strategies midway and pivot to new engagement models. Some even had to transform their existing business models overnight to stay relevant. Due to high levels of stress, fear, and anxiety, customer patience and loyalty reduced considerably. Businesses realized that they had to gratify the customer instantly and deliver their orders expediently or lose their business to competitors. Some customers reported that they preferred to switch to a competitor if the search functionality of the web or mobile application did not render results within 35 seconds. It was instant gratification at a whole new level.

Organizations had to also adjust to a remote workforce and learn new ways of delivering value without relying on colocated teams or having the ability to converse with team members. Every aspect of business value creation—people, process, technology, and culture—had to be evaluated, and leaders had to rethink and reimagine the way that value flowed through the organization. Across industry verticals, leaders will use the lessons from this large-scale existence-from-home experiment to reimagine how work is done—and what role offices, technologies, and travel should play—in creative and bold ways.

Changing Attitudes on the Role of the Office

Before the pandemic, the conventional wisdom was that offices were critical to productivity, culture, and winning the war for talent. Companies competed intensely for prime office space in major urban centers around the world, and many focused on solutions that were seen to promote collaboration. Densification (increasing density of people in a space), open-office designs, hoteling, and co-working were the battle cries for improving productivity and efficiency in office spaces.

According to a survey conducted by Gartner, 88 percent of organizations worldwide mandated or encouraged their employees to work from home because of the pandemic. An overwhelming 97 percent of the organizations surveyed stated that they immediately canceled all work-related travel to ensure the safety of their workforce.[9] In the United States, almost 70 percent of full-time workers have been working from home during COVID-19, with over 75 percent of them maintaining the same or higher productivity while working from home. Over 56 percent of companies allow some form of remote work globally, with 16 percent of companies operating in a fully remote model worldwide.[10] This statistic is pretty encouraging considering that, even in the United States, only 33 percent of workers were always working remotely, 25 percent reported that they worked remotely sometimes, and 41 percent said that they never worked remotely or did not have the option to do so.[11]

Several companies have polled their workforce to gauge their willingness to continue working from home. According to a McKinsey survey,[12] an overwhelming 80 percent of people polled reported that they enjoyed working from home as compared to working in an office. Some 41 percent said that they were more productive than they had been before the pandemic, with 28 percent reporting that they were at least as productive as in an office setting. Many employees have expressed happiness at the thought of being liberated from long commutes, not needing to get up early or leave late to avoid rush hour, and not having to stop at a fast-food restaurant on the way to grab an unhealthy breakfast or sugar-laden beverage. People are happy that they can spend more time with their loved ones, feel less stressed overall, and have more flexibility in their schedule.

Some conservative organizations have struggled with this overnight shift to remote work. These organizations believed that employees were productive only in the confines of an office and required constant supervision and oversight from management. Executives told employees that they could either come into the office and work with full pay or work from home and take a pay cut to offset productivity loss. Other companies reduced working hours for hourly employees, stopped benefits such as 401(k) (retirement fund) matches, reimbursements, promotions, mental and wellness resources, pay increases, and bonuses during the pandemic.[13]

There are several other savings that companies are experiencing as a result of a remote workforce:

- Companies save considerable money by shutting down the cafeteria, not restocking breakroom supplies, vending machines, and office supplies.

219

Enterprise Empathy

- The sheer amount of money saved from office toners and printing paper alone could be upward of thousands of dollars per month for large organizations.
- Companies are downsizing their office space footprint, saving money.
- Energy, water, and even toilet paper consumption are minimal or nonexistent.

Luckily, many organizations have embraced remote working as their primary mode of operation and believe they can access new pools of talent with fewer locational constraints, adopt innovative processes to boost productivity, create an even stronger culture, and significantly reduce real estate costs. They have provided their workforce with the flexibility to work from the office, home, or even adapt a hybrid mode of work. These organizations focus on business outcomes and objectives and key results (OKRs) instead of traditional metrics such as showing up on time for a 9–5 schedule.

Technology Adoption

Organizations worldwide had to evaluate their existing technology stack for remote working and quickly implement ways for their remote workforce to collaborate seamlessly and effectively. Remote desktop software, video conferencing solutions, asynchronous and synchronous collaboration tools, digital whiteboarding software, and secure access service edge software became necessities for every organization.

Though employees reported that it was frustrating to adopt videoconferencing and digital collaboration software as part of their daily work, most of them also mentioned that they were surprised by how quickly they could effectively use these technologies. New features were added to make digital collaboration closer to reality, and video meetings became the de facto standard for many organizations. The expressions "You're on mute" and "Sorry, I was on mute" were two of the most common phrases used during the pandemic, but that did not deter people from using video conferencing technology. People have become comfortable being on camera, and several lighting accessories and vanity filters have been paired with these communication channels to improve appearances.

These technologies have become a part of organizational processes and workflows by striving to become digital twins of everyday, physical interactions. Companies that have invested in their digital workforce during the pandemic see reverting to the old normal as a step backward. Additionally, companies that were already distributed to a higher degree before the pandemic will continue to invest in their remote workforce and introduce newer ways of collaboration, communication, and delivery of business value.

Reduced Travel

Lockdown protocols and social distancing guidelines severely impacted business travel. Many companies mandated a no-travel policy and switched all events to a virtual forum. Many countries closed their borders to outsiders as well, impacting international business travel. These restrictions challenged sales and field organizations, which relied on visiting client locations to extend their sphere of influence and persuasion. Sales executives initially struggled with virtual communication methods but quickly adapted and have been able to demonstrate cognitive empathy virtually. Sales motions have been refined to include dynamic content creation through electronic whiteboards, presentation slideware, and digital canvases such as Miro or Mural. However, emotional connections and the ability to demonstrate compassionate empathy still rely heavily on physical interaction—sharing a meal, having drinks, or attending a sporting event. But over time, resourceful sales and field executives will be able to evolve their tactics to expand their sphere of influence.

Conferences, one of the top places to network and interact with peers, were also converted to an online format, impacting travel and hospitality further. Several conferencing portals introduced features mimicking physical venues such as lobbies with information messages, sponsor booths where conference attendees can interact with sponsors and win swag, coffee bars where people can meet up and discuss, and even networking lounges. These digital twins became the standard for conferences, and companies saved considerable marketing, event management, travel, and entertainment budget by going virtual.

A Hybrid Way of Working

How will workplaces look in the foreseeable future? Many organizations have allowed their employees to work entirely from home if they like. Companies have provided a stipend to their employees to set up their home offices to make them more ergonomic and comfortable for long periods of work. Some organizations have gone completely remote and distributed, with no offices. Some companies have rented workspaces on a need-only basis for program increment planning, company events, or team-building exercises, allowing their teams to work remotely for the rest of the time.

Several companies, especially in cities with high real estate costs, downsized their real estate and office space, allowing employees the flexibility to work in an office setting if needed. During the pandemic, these office spaces had to be retrofitted to comply with social distancing policies, and employees were required to wear masks at all times. As more people were vaccinated, these stringent requirements were relaxed. However, it is hard to predict where companies will land on these issues as time goes by—some organizations might require proof of vaccination, others may mandate vaccinations, and yet others may leave that onus upon their employees.

Could corporate cultures and communities erode over time without physical interaction? Will planned and unplanned moments of collaboration become impaired? Will there be less mentorship and talent development? Did working from home succeed only because it was viewed as temporary, not permanent? Every organization and culture is different, and so are the circumstances of every individual employee. Many enjoyed this experience; others were fatigued by it. Some leaders empowered their workforce, while others felt insecure and struggled with their perceived loss of control. Productivity for some employees increased; for others it declined. Many forms of virtual collaboration worked well; others did not. Each individual's experience was unique and depended on their culture, personal life, and their maturity level on the technology continuum. During my interaction with teams across industry verticals—IT and non-IT—I have observed many individuals exhibit high levels of empathy and fill leadership voids that emerged. These individuals became mentors, coaches, counselors, and confidantes in the workplace. They displayed compassionate empathy to their teammates.

As companies around the globe are preparing to open their campuses and offices back up, I do want to address a concerning perspective that keeps coming up. It is the rhetoric of executives that employees are coming "back to work." This thought has entered leadership echo chambers and portrays a wrong assessment of what the workforce has gone through over the last few years. Employees did not take a vacation or time off during that time and are returning from their sojourns back into the office. Many of them never stopped working at least 40 hours a week, some even more, to compensate for all the adversity that took a toll on their personal lives. What they were going through was not a grand experiment of work at home on a global scale. It was *existence* at home. To say that employees are

223

Enterprise Empathy

returning to the office minimizes the pain and suffering that people have endured. Executives and leaders must recognize this and choose their words appropriately. No, people are not returning back to work. They are exploring ways to straddle working remotely and in an office and ascertain what works to be productive.

The Evolution of the Office

According to Gartner, 89 percent of service leaders believe that 20–80 percent of their workforce will work remotely within the next two years. The amount of software utilized within the company heavily influences that percentage; however, I believe that most of the workforce will choose anywhere-work if given an opportunity.[14]

As companies are preparing for people to utilize offices for work, I believe that we will see four primary shifts in working:

1. **Hybrid mode of work will be the norm.** The workforce will adopt some form of working in the office and at home. The optimal ratio for each organization will depend on the appetite and maturity of the organization and the industry vertical.

2. **Employees will focus more on their life experiences and expect a life-work balance.** My take is that the human workforce has crossed the artificial boundaries of work imposed by scientific management (also known as *Taylorism*).[15] People have realized the benefits of working out of their homes. For many, life has become a higher priority, and that notion is soul-stirring.

3. **Organizations will upgrade established processes, workflows, and methodologies to accommodate for a large-scale distributed workforce**. For instance, team agility used to rely heavily on colocation for osmotic learning, bonding,

and collaboration. It is exciting to see how that will evolve to accommodate an anywhere, anytime workforce. Asynchronous communication and collaboration will become essential.

4. **Service leaders will focus on business outcomes and value creation.** The focus will shift from activity performed or hours logged to a project to tangible results. This shift in focus will change the way performance is measured, how leaders will look to promotions, career growth, and MBOs/OKRs. It will elevate the quality of life of the workforce and empower them. This behavioral change is a huge positive from my point of view.

The office will still be a part of our working lives; we will just spend less time physically in it. It will take work for companies to establish a digital culture that fits the culture in the office, so workers who spend more of their time at home don't become isolated and still fit in. The future of work was always heading in this direction. COVID-19 simply accelerated the process. That's a good thing, and it has forced us to grapple with a challenge we were always going to face. As leaders of these organizations undergoing this evolution, we need to empathize with the workforce and help them adapt.

Remote Onboarding

Onboarding has traditionally been a physical activity. Many organizations have processes requiring new employees to be present within an office to complete the onboarding tasks, which have proven challenging in a hybrid or remote working environment. Leaders need to rethink and reimagine these processes to accommodate remote employee onboarding. It is not just a matter of shipping a laptop or work computer accompanied by company swag to the new employee's home address. Joining a new company can be very stressful.

Remote onboarding can be challenging for some people who might not have experienced enterprise culture before. For some of the new hires, this might be their first corporate job, and they will have a lot of trepidation and anxiety. Their understanding of working in an enterprise could come from watching shows and movies or hearing others talk about their experiences.

Leaders must be empathetic and take additional steps to welcome remote employees. Here are a few steps that can achieve this outcome:

1. **Assign a pairing partner.** Pairing is one of the quickest ways to learn the organization, processes, and productivity. It enables the new employee to build trust with the team from day one; a mentor to help navigate the organizational operations, people, and political undercurrents; and a coach to learn from. Pairing reduces anxiety and performance stress and empowers new employees to reduce their learning curve and quickly feel productive.

2. **Have a welcome lunch.** This onboarding activity is standard practice for many organizations and needs to be extended to remote employees. As part of the welcome package, ship a meal kit or provide a food delivery voucher (like DoorDash or Uber Eats) that the remote employee can use to procure lunch. Have a virtual lunch with the team and get to know the new hire. A note of caution: It is tempting to talk about work, the company, and the role that the new hire is entering, but hold that off to a separate meeting or have the assigned pair discuss it. The welcome lunch is for the team to get to know the new hire and vice versa.

3. **Replicate the ambiance of office breakrooms.** Office breakrooms have been a vital part of organizational culture, but it is hard to create a digital twin of the breakroom easily.

Some suggestions are to ship coffee, popcorn, or other break-room items to remote employees regularly. I had hired three remote interns, and the teams went out of their way to make them feel welcome and experience the corporate culture. We shipped them pizzas, cozies, cupcakes, and salted snacks whenever I used to hold my town halls or other team-building events so that they could virtually feel what it would be to snag breakroom pizza or leftover snacks.

4. **Meet them where they are.** This is a simple yet powerful way to welcome new hires and get to know your remote teams. Many organizations fly new hires over to their corporate headquarters as part of orientation and onboarding, but it tends to be a singular event. I recommend meeting the teams where they are. It signals a genuine desire to get to know team members and endears the leader to their teams. It also helps the remote employees get face time with the leader and improves the organization's psychological safety and trust.

From a social perspective, joining a new company is similar to switching to a new tribe. Prior accomplishments, connections, reputation, and relationships might slightly influence the new employee's brand, but everyone starts at the ground level on the organizational status ladder. Empathic leaders recognize this and ensure that the new employees feel safe, valued, and have all the tools at their disposal to be productive.

How to Develop Empathy at Work

You may struggle to show empathy initially—you could be nervous about committing yourself emotionally, or feel unable to do so. But this doesn't mean that you're doomed to fail!

To use empathy effectively, you need to put aside your own viewpoint and see things from the other person's perspective. Then, you can recognize behavior that appears at first sight to be over emotional, stubborn, or unreasonable as simply a reaction based on a person's prior knowledge and experiences.

Practice the following techniques frequently so that they become second nature.

Give Your Full Attention

Listen carefully to what someone is trying to tell you. Use your ears, eyes, and "gut instincts" to understand the entire message that they're communicating.

Start by listening for the keywords and phrases that they use, particularly if they use them repeatedly. Then think about *how* as well as *what* they're saying. What's their tone or body language telling you? Are they angry, ashamed, or scared, for example?

Take this a stage further by listening empathically. Avoid asking direct questions, arguing with what is being said, or disputing facts at this stage. And be flexible—prepare for the conversation to change direction as the other person's thoughts and feelings also change.

Consider Other People's Perspectives

You're likely familiar with the saying, "Before you criticize someone, walk a mile in their shoes." Examine your own attitude and keep an open mind. Placing too much emphasis on your own assumptions and beliefs doesn't leave much space for empathy.

Once you "see" why others believe what they believe, you can acknowledge it. This doesn't mean you have to agree with it, but this is not the time for a debate. Instead, be sure to show respect and keep listening.

When in doubt, invite the person to describe their position some more, and ask how they think they might resolve the issue. Asking the right questions is probably the simplest and most direct way to understand another person.

Take Action

There's no one "right" way to demonstrate your compassionate empathy. It will depend on the situation, the individual, and their dominant emotion at the time. Remember, empathy is not about what you want, but what the other person wants and needs, so any action you take or suggest must benefit them.

For example, you might have a team member who's unable to focus on their work because of a problem at home. It may seem the kind thing to do to tell them they can work from home until the situation is resolved, but work may in fact give them a welcome respite from thinking about something painful. So ask them which approach they would prefer.

And remember that empathy is not just for crises! Seeing the world from a variety of perspectives is a great talent—and it's one that you can use all of the time, in any situation. Random acts of kindness brighten anyone's day.

For example, when you smile and take the trouble to remember people's names, that's empathy in action. Giving people your full attention in meetings, being curious about their lives and interests, and offering constructive feedback are all empathic behaviors, too.

Practice these skills often. When you take an interest in what others think, feel, and experience, you'll develop a reputation for being caring, trustworthy, and approachable—and be a great asset to your team and your organization.

Empathy as a Core Tenet of Organizational Culture

Organizational culture includes the underlying beliefs, values, ways of interacting, and assumptions that create an organization's unique social and psychological environment. This defines the North Star, along with the social and moral compass that the organization follows and drives toward.

To put it in simple words, organizational culture is the way an organization generates value to its customers and its workforce. A great organizational culture is the key to developing the traits necessary for business success. The effects are reflected in the bottom line: companies with healthy cultures have demonstrated they are at least 1.6 times more likely to experience revenue growth of at least 15 percent or more over three years and 2.5 times more likely to experience significant stock growth over the same period.[16] A great culture exemplifies positive traits that lead to improved performance, while a dysfunctional or toxic culture brings out qualities that can hinder even the most successful organizations.

Culture is an essential factor in attracting talent and outperforming the competition. Over 77 percent of applicants consider a company's culture before applying for a role, and almost half of the workforce would leave their current job for a slightly lower-paying opportunity for an organization with a better culture.[17] These numbers will only increase with a remote workforce as the physical limitation of geography is eliminated as a factor in decision making. Also, the way an organization responded to the global pandemic, the adversity that the workforce dealt with, and how the organization supported them throughout are huge deciding factors when assessing whether they want to join the organization.

Culture carries a sense of purpose, self-worth, and value within the organization. It can also be a control system. Culture can also be defined as consistently observable patterns of behavior within organizations. Repeated behaviors and habits are at the core of culture but this does not take into consideration how people think, feel, or what they believe in. Organizational culture is a set of shared assumptions that guide collective behaviors that can then be taught to new organizational members to perceive, think, and feel within an organization.

Westrum's Typology of Organizational Culture

Culture has an immense effect on the performance and success of an organization. It is one of the persistent competitive advantages that a successful organization can have over its competitors. Culture is vital to creating and sustaining a healthy and productive organization. The DevOps movement reinforced the importance of culture as the C in CALMS. (CALMS represents the five pillars of DevOps—culture, automation, lean IT, measurement, and sharing.)

Organizational culture is a patterned way involving the thoughts and actions of the leaders. Ron Westrum, an American sociologist, suggested that culture is directly related to the information flow within the organization. In his research, he considered human factors in the organization concerning system safety coupled with technological domains[18] (see Figure 6.1).

The typology of organizational culture is based on the information processing style and responses to difficulties and opportunities. Westrum described three types of cultures: *pathological, bureaucratic*, and *generative*. Depending on the organizational culture's safety aspect, these types have been categorized by the leaders' and managers' preoccupations.

Enterprise Empathy

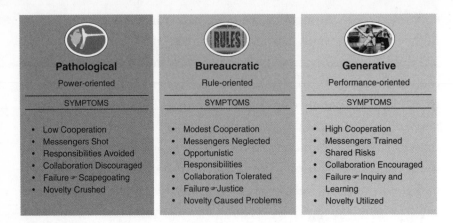

Pathological	Bureaucratic	Generative
Power-oriented	Rule-oriented	Performance-oriented
SYMPTOMS	SYMPTOMS	SYMPTOMS
• Low Cooperation • Messengers Shot • Responsibilities Avoided • Collaboration Discouraged • Failure ☞ Scapegoating • Novelty Crushed	• Modest Cooperation • Messengers Neglected • Opportunistic Responsibilities • Collaboration Tolerated • Failure ☞ Justice • Novelty Caused Problems	• High Cooperation • Messengers Trained • Shared Risks • Collaboration Encouraged • Failure ☞ Inquiry and Learning • Novelty Utilized

Figure 6.1 Ron Westrum's Typology of Organizational culture.

A *pathological* culture is related to personal needs and is highly affected by personal power and glory. It is a power-oriented style with low cooperation among the team culture and overall organizational culture. Responsibilities are either procrastinated or take the shape of a *blame-game*. Power struggles, personal egos, and the concept of departmental fiefdoms impede the flow of value or information through the organization. Information is treated as a commodity and shared sparingly or altered to sabotage political competitors. People in power (it is hard to call them leaders) operate on the dictate, "He who controls information controls the world." This creates a toxic culture and an "us vs. them" mentality within the organization. Further, any attempt of transformation or even the idea of trying new things is crushed.

A *bureaucratic* culture is rule-oriented, where processes and rules profoundly impact the organization's operating model. This culture focuses on passing the correct information to the right person at the right time. The organization enforces standard processes and procedures to ensure information and value flow through the organization. Considerable time is wasted developing processes overloaded with manual oversight, bureaucratic stage gates, and executive sign-off, all

Leading with Empathy

in the name of accountability and consistency. There is modest cooperation between teams. Bridging is tolerated, and any failure in the complex system leads to justice. The messengers are highly neglected, and responsibilities are opportunistic. Failures are analyzed, and countermeasures to prevent these failures are often in the form of supplementing processes with additional manual oversight, rules, or process overhead. At the same, adopting innovation can lead to significant problems within the organizational culture. People in power might champion their department's interest over the organization's mission, hampering systemic thinking and effective decision making.

Psychological safety is a real concern in pathological and bureaucratic organizations, where messengers are either shot or neglected. This threat gets amplified when team members have elevated levels of cortisol and adrenaline in their bodies, causing duress and anxiety. Demonstrating empathy and promoting psychological safety as a leader help reduce stress levels within the workforce, thereby increasing productivity, innovation, and happiness among employees.

The third type of culture is *generative,* and it focuses on the organization's mission, values, and principles. It does not consider needs or positions. Departmental silos are discouraged, and team success is defined by achieving business outcomes, not functional results. This performance-oriented style leads to high cooperation among team cultures and overall healthy organizational culture. The messengers are trained, and teams undertake shared risks to ensure smooth value and information flow in the organization. Failure is not hidden or ignored, instead brought to the surface and celebrated. Failure in the system is also used to learn for future growth. Unlike pathological and bureaucratic cultures, a generative culture highly encourages innovation and lean experimentation. Most organizational cultures that are generative tend to demonstrate high performance and psychological safety.

Having the right organizational culture is imperative for a transformation. More than 70 percent of all change initiatives fail because of the culture or the organization's workforce.[19] We want to have a culture that is positive, is willing to change, and can rally behind the vision and purpose of the transformation. We want to make sure that we do not have majority of the organization as detractors and impeding a transformation. This requires building momentum within the organization and aligning with a common purpose. The workforce needs to have good psychological safety and trust with the leadership for this to work.

Transforming an Organizational Culture

Driving an organization's cultural transformation can be a challenging endeavor as the journey can be unique based on its history, domain, velocity of growth, and assimilation of other cultures through mergers and acquisitions. While the journeys are different, there are similarities in the challenges faced and issues tackled. These challenges are amplified by environmental conditions, stress, anxiety, and an insecure workforce. Transformational leaders need to be sensitive to the following impeding factors and demonstrate their empathetic leadership.

Not knowing why. Conducting a cultural transformation exacerbates employees' insecurity and resistance to change. Therefore, it is imperative that leaders share the company's vision or mission and unequivocally express the organization's *Why* as to an organizational transformation both internally and externally.

No clear definition of done. Cultural transformations are nebulous and continuous in nature and do not have a discrete target to achieve. More often than not, strategic planning performed before embarking on this journey helps identify business outcomes to be achieved and key performance indicators that demonstrate progress. However, these transformational activities also follow the concept of Kaizen[20] or continuous improvement and therefore have no end.

This approach, unfortunately, introduces considerable anxiety and stress to the organization. A never-ending transformation is not sustainable or palatable. Defining the end state will validate the purpose (the *Why*) of the transformation and will signal to the workforce that there is a measurable and achievable end in sight. Measuring accomplishments against the definition of done will also provide opportunities to celebrate successes and achievements along the cultural transformation journey.

Prior communication. A cultural transformation is a complex and challenging endeavor with many moving parts that need coordination and orchestration between multiple teams to ensure that the improved products or processes converge to value streams that drive identified business outcomes. Wiio's laws[21] that focus on human communication state that a message that can be interpreted in several ways usually will be interpreted to maximize the damage. Therefore, having a consistent, succinct, and yet powerful purpose and communicating the *Why*, the definition of done, and the compelling event to the organization via several media and repeatedly will help reduce distortion of messaging.

No incentives to transform. In his book *Drive*, Daniel Pink presents a successful approach to motivating teams through three elements—autonomy, mastery, and purpose:[22]

1. *Autonomy* is the desire to self-direct and be empowered to take decisions within a local scope of influence. It emphasizes the need to provide what needs to be done and allows the how to the individuals or teams.

2. *Mastery* relates to the continuous yearning for some people to improve themselves and get better at skills that they value.

3. *Purpose* feeds the desires for individuals and teams to be part of something bigger than them. It also helps humanize business outcomes and increases customer empathy.

An important assumption made, however, is that extrinsic motivators such as money and recognition have already been addressed, and negative motivators such as reprimands, public shaming, or intolerance to failure have been eliminated from the organization. For instance, this approach would not work with teams that feel severely underpaid and undervalued, and organizations need to address these issues before they embark on a transformational journey.

Crowdsource Empathy

Making empathy part of an organization's culture has to be organic, and leadership cannot mandate empathy as a core tenet for the organization. Having a poster or a desk tchotchke reminding people to be empathic does not work. I hypothesized that the best way to start the empathy engine within a workplace was to crowdsource ideas that improve people's quality of life in the organization and launched an initiative called *Project Athena* to test this hypothesis.[23]

The objective of Project Athena was to improve the quality of life of the people in the organization. I pitched this initiative in my next town hall. I said that this initiative aims to improve work-life balance within the organization, reduce manual toil, and improve team collaboration. The teams were excited about this initiative, and we got to work. We decided that we would call Project Athena successful if we could eliminate two hours of manual toil in a workweek for each team member. The time saved could be used to beat traffic and leave early, use it for working on a favorite project, team bonding, whatever they wanted to do, as long as it was legal and relaxing.

We commandeered the office walls right at the entrance of the elevator banks to create a visual indicator of our work in the form of an initiative board. We not only wanted to radiate our success throughout the organization, but we also wanted people to be curious and join in. Each card on the board had to contain the following information:

- Hypothesis/problem statement
- Amount of time this idea saves per person
- How will this problem be solved
- How will success be measured
- Owner and collaborators' names

Our board was pretty simple. Each idea started in the "Need Collaborators" section, where people would commit to working on the idea. Over the course of this initiative, I observed that for every problem captured on the board, there were enough people sufficiently motivated to eliminate the problem. Once the number of collaborators signed up, the card moved to the "In Progress" section. The collaborators could post a weekly update on the board or our internal communication platform to keep the teams informed of progress. We also had a progress meter on the operations board where we tracked the amount of time saved through Project Athena.

When the collaborators felt that they had accomplished their goal, they had to create a success video. In this video, they had to talk about the problem they solved, how the definition of done was met (proving that the solution saved the amount of time claimed), and what fun activity they would use their saved time on. This success video had to be shared with teams internally. They could also choose to convert it into a case study to tell the story of their experience and share their data.

We reserved Friday afternoons for celebrating completed cards. The card owner had the privilege of progressing the card to the completed column and raising the progress meter by the amount they saved through their idea. We played the success video, and the teams cheered and celebrated with the collaborators.

Project Athena was a huge success. We ran this initiative for three quarters (nine months) and had over 46 idea cards that ran successfully through the board with an average of 2.3 collaborators per idea. We saved around 3.2 hours per person's workweek, eliminated over 18.6 percent of process waste, and reduce manual toil (increase automation footprint) by 23.8 percent overall. Employee Net Promoter Score (eNPS) rose by over 16 points within two quarters, and team collaboration increased considerably. The best value that Project Athena delivered to the organization was compassionate empathy—a genuine desire for the workforce to not only be empathic with their co-workers but take action to reduce the pain.

Hire for Empathy

Another good way to cultivate empathy in an organization is to hire for empathy. But it is just not enough to include empathy as a requirement in the job ads. How do we assess the empathy level of candidates? Do we give them a test and compare empathy scores between candidates? Do we have empathy-based questions in the interviewing process and gauge their empathy in real time? Do we ask them scenario-based questions and evaluate how they think? Would this assessment be objective or subjective? What if the interviewer is empathetic and goes with their emotions in the evaluation?

When hiring for leaders, here are some sample questions to ask:

- Can you share how you dealt with an employee undergoing a crisis?
- How would you work to gain trust with your team?
- How do you ensure collaboration and trust with your peers?

- Can you give an example of conflict where you were able to find common ground?
- What do you do in tense situations?

On the other side of the table, it is a very good sign when the candidate asks many questions around the organization's culture, team norms, how safe the interviewer feels, and queries around innovation, fun, social bonding, and other team-building activities. Evaluating the manner in which these questions are posed, along with their verbal and nonverbal cues, will give additional information about the candidate's empathetic level.

Questions to Gauge Empathy

Over the years, I have changed my interviewing style from technical to situational. Granted, I had the luxury of relying on hiring managers to assess candidates' technical skills, allowing me to focus on the soft skills of interviewees. Here are some of my favorite questions:

- Name one of your role models/inspiration. Why does that person inspire you?
- Have you ever had to let go of someone? Talk me through that scenario and how you handled it.
- What do you try to find in your skip-level meetings?[24]
- Did you ever lose your temper at work?
- Talk about a recent act of kindness. What did you do, and what was the impact?
- How have you used technology for good?
- Are you a member or ally of any employee resource group? What have you done to champion that cause?
- How do you ensure you have a work-life balance?

The Power of a Generative Culture

My previous company, Pivotal, had three explicit organizational principles:

1. Do the right thing.
2. Do what works.
3. Be kind.

As a software company, the organization championed extreme programming (XP) and adapted the XP values of Communication, Respect, Courage, Simplicity, and Feedback in their daily work. These two aspects of organizational culture attracted me to Pivotal and influenced me to accept a position there. These values and principles defined the Pivotal way and enabled us to transform the way the world built software. They also played a vital role as we helped our clients transform their organizations, not only from a technology standpoint but also from a cultural and process perspective.

Pivotal's principles were forces for good and encouraged the workforce to embrace humanity and empathy. *Do the right thing* meant that we had to have integrity in whatever we did, understand the ramifications of our actions, and make sure that we were focusing on the customer's needs and not our own. Doing the right thing was not limited to our customers and software. It was part of every facet of our life. It enabled us to treat people fairly and as equals. We thought of sustainability and the environment. We put ourselves in our customers' shoes and empathize with them, trying to understand their perspective and the rationale behind their request for a software feature or functionality.

Do what works ensured that our focus was on delivering value to the customer and not gold plating our products and services. It also enabled us to be pragmatic in our approach and not expend inordinate amounts of energy trying to make something work just because it worked on paper. It gave us permission to experiment and quickly resolve impediments. We could get something operating swiftly and then look for ways to battle-harden the solution or make it scalable.

Be kind reinforced compassion, kindness, and empathy in the organization. It helped us be human and humble. It guided the way we operated with each other and with customers. Pair programming is an essential component of XP, and the need to be kind with our pairs created stronger bonding, psychological safety, radical candor, and respect within the pairs. We practiced pairing both at a leadership and individual contributor level with respect for one another and kindness as the shared bond. This approach was powerful and enabled us to become trusted advisors to our customers. Our success was defined by our client's success. Our clients appreciated that we were obsessed with their business outcomes rather than treat the relationship as a transaction.

Pivotal's principles and XP values instilled happiness in our teams. Our culture was very welcoming, and our onboarding process was personal and inclusive from day one, even if the new team member was remote. We went out of our way to ensure that new hires were comfortable, authentic, and felt safe. It also checked our entitlement and increased our patience levels in dealing with complex and challenging situations. As XP was our guiding work process, our practices embraced candid feedback, transparent retrospection, and genuine introspection continually, helping us embrace the philosophy of continuous improvement. We had an open, transparent, and generative culture with high levels of candor, respect, and psychological safety.

Pivotal was then acquired by VMware, another great company. Our new leadership went out of their way to make the acquisition easy and psychologically safe for us. As with any complex enterprise acquisition, the transition was challenging, and we hit many snags as the two company cultures melded and our systems integrated. But we pivots (that's what we called ourselves at Pivotal) prided ourselves in embracing change, and this was where our Pivotal culture helped us. We did not have an "us vs. them" mentality during the transition. As leaders, we quickly formed our first team at each level and rallied around our strategic outcomes and our new corporate values.

VMware has a rich, diverse, and vibrant culture. It is committed to empowering its employees to perform their best work and lead from any role or level in the organization. It enables them to constantly learn, grow, and become a better version of themselves. Employees are encouraged to bring their authentic selves to work. It was recognized as one of the best employers for diversity and women in 2020 and 2021 by *Forbes*.[25] It was also identified as one of the best places to work for LGBTQ equality in 2020 by the Human Rights Campaign.[26] The CEO at that time, Pat Gelsinger, was a highly empathic leader and embodied VMware values in his actions, conversations, and dialogue. He was named the best CEO in the United States by employment website Glassdoor in 2019.[27]

VMware's culture is built on its set of shared values expressed through the acronym EPIC$_2$—Execution, Passion, Integrity, Customers, and Community. When we were integrating into VMware, we immediately realized how well the Pivotal principles aligned and resonated with VMware's. We understood that we were not losing our identity but instead were becoming part of something better. VMware's EPIC$_2$ values also embody and champion empathy for the customer, employee, and humankind. Its products and technologies played a crucial role in helping organizations through the global pandemic and its effects. Citizen philanthropy empowers all VMware employees to be active and engaged citizens in their communities and champion their causes. In 2020, more than 26,000 VMware people supported over 14,000 nonprofits in 98 countries. The company has matched donations for many COVID-19 and BLM-related funds.[28] It incentivizes its employees to serve the community by converting 40 service hours per year into a Citizen Philanthropy Investment grant to the nonprofit of their choice. Employees can also join other pro bono activities through VMware's Good Gigs program.

Through its 30 × 30 strategy, VMware has committed to achieve 30 goals spanning trust, equity, and sustainability by 2030. It is investing in co-innovation and collaboration with its expansive ecosystem of partners and customer to redefine together what it means to be a force for good. Equitable pay, diversity and inclusion, net-zero emissions, zero-carbon cloud infrastructure, and an anywhere workforce are some of the goals that it is significantly invested in. VMware believes that technology will play a critical role in building an equitable, accessible, and inclusive digital future and an exemplar of generative culture.

Summary

Organizations must promote empathy and make it part of their organizational culture. Empathic leadership sets an example to the organization and has the important role of leading by example how to handle difficult situations and the best way to achieve results. When a leader can look at a fellow workforce member and put themselves in their shoes, understand the pain and stress they are undergoing, and value their happiness above their own, they are genuinely empathic.

However, we do not see an abundance of empathetic leaders in the workplace and need to create an organizational culture that provides adequate psychological safety for empathic leadership to thrive. Leaders should strive to change an organization's culture from a pathological to generative culture, where the workforce has self-confidence, motivation, and purpose. Generative cultures are open, have positive energy, innovate, and increase productivity. These cultures also champion customer empathy and improve brand recognition. Successful organizations differentiate themselves by promoting a generative culture and being staunch proponents of customer and employee empathy.

Reflections

- What steps has your organization taken to demonstrate empathy to your workforce?
- What are the biggest challenges that your workforce has faced in the last two years?
- Have you surveyed your workforce on whether they want to work remotely or have a hybrid work environment?
- How can you help encourage empathy in your department or division?

Chapter 7

Employee Empathy

People, not technology, are the true value creators within our organization. Technology is only an enabler and can never compensate for an unhappy culture.

E mpathy is necessary now more than ever with ever-increasing diversity in the workforce. From an age-diversity perspective alone, some organizations can have up to four generations of team members, and catering to their needs becomes challenging. Empathy in the workplace can help increase respect and trust among co-workers, and elevate behavior from process or policy-driven to performance or relationship-driven. Empathy demonstrates caring and can increase social bonding in an organization. People feel safer when they have an empathetic boss because they won't be blamed when they fail. They take more risks. When they take more risks, they can innovate better or push themselves harder. They can run more ambitious experiments. They can run smaller experiments with quicker feedback loops and learn from them. They can reach out to others when they are blocked. They do not need to feel worried or have mental blocks when they do not possess a particular skill. They can then improve and grow and learn. This drives a better culture within the organization. Poor performance becomes an opportunity for growth rather than reprimands and negative reviews.

The Benefits of Empathy in the Workplace

We have discussed many benefits of empathy in the workplace. To summarize:

- **Happy people are productive people.** Empathy increases psychological safety, trust, and happiness. When these increase, people are more willing to take risks, and when they take more risks, they innovate better and are more productive.
- **Empathetic businesses have better sales and retention.** Cognitive empathy helps drive sales. It also helps retain loyal customers, since customers can relate and see you as empathetic.
- **Teams bond better, with greater collaboration.** Empathy improves teamwork. Teams better share goals and performance metrics. They understand what impacts other members. They try to reduce the pain that their processes or behavior could inflict on others. They collaborate better to achieve their goals.

Remote Is the New Normal

COVID-19 had a debilitating impact on the operating landscape of organizations in almost every industry vertical. Companies had to switch to a fully remote workforce overnight to accommodate state guidelines regarding shelter-in-place and social distancing. Some verticals such as software development, digital marketing, and other fields—where people were able to work from home more easily— were not impacted as much as others. The retail, hospitality, travel, and healthcare industries have been affected the most, and organizational leaders had to rethink their processes, methodologies, and value streams for a contactless, remote workplace.

Organizations such as hospitals, assisted healthcare facilities, utilities, and first response agencies, unfortunately, do not have that luxury. Healthcare workers, caregivers, first responders, and other essential workers put their lives at risk every day to help humanity, and that's true even without a pandemic. Employees working in manufacturing plants, warehouses, food and service industries, and outreach programs exposed themselves daily to infection, as these roles could not be performed from home.

Empowering Teams

One of my strategic beliefs is that happy people are productive people, and the goal of a transformational leader is to ensure that their teams are happy and enabled. However, interviews with several development and product teams in pathological or bureaucratic enterprises undergoing transformation reveal that, although there might be a well-communicated purpose and a sense of urgency, the teams did not feel empowered.

In my observations, the amount of management/leadership oversight on a strategic task is directly proportional to the business outcome it drives (its value), accountability levels in the enterprise, and the urgency to achieve the outcome.

$$Management\ Oversight\ \alpha\ \frac{Value\ of\ the\ task \times Accountability}{Time\ to\ achieve\ business\ outcome}$$

Remote teams that work on transformational tasks, therefore, suffer from increased management oversight, which usually translates to status reports, deferring decision making to HIPPOs, aggressive deadlines, and loss of work-life balance.[1]

(continues)

(*continued*)

This, in turn, creates a sense of low to no empowerment and lower team morale.

Here are some approaches that I have implemented to counter this effect:

- Emotional intelligence and empathy training to leaders and management
- Increased visual indicators to increase transparency and observability of work
- Retrospectives at the strategic levels and town halls with business leaders where themes are enablement, empowerment, and team appreciation
- Demonstrate connectivity to show how tasks and initiatives are connected to drive business outcomes and goals

As organizations adapt to the inevitability of having some portion of their workforce permanently remote, leaders have to modernize how they empower this workforce in addition to extending organizational culture remotely.

We spent a considerable amount of time exploring the value of empathy as a core tenet for an organization. In addition to empathy, there are four workflow areas that leaders should reinvent to improve business value generation and management in a remote working environment—*execution, collaboration, communication,* and *enablement.* (See Figure 7.1.)

Execution

As teams adapt to more remote workers and days, organization leaders should focus on optimizing the flow of value within the organization and modernizing workforce interaction methods. There are six unspoken laws that we need to consider as governing principles for execution:

1. **Murphy's law: "Anything that can go wrong will go wrong."** This law has its origins with Edward J. Murphy, a major in the US Air Force in the 1940s, whose work involved testing experimental designs in safety-critical systems. The nature of his work exposed Murphy to events, prototypes, and systems that did not conform with the expected response, and this law was coined to describe unpredictable behavior.

2. **Pareto principle: "80 percent of the effects come from 20 percent of the causes."** This is commonly known as the 80/20 rule or the law of the vital few. In essence, the Pareto principle helps us identify the most important assets or inputs for an entity (the vital few or the 20 percent) and utilizing them optimally to create maximum value. We can also interpret it as identifying the most critical inputs, outcomes, or causes and using them to cover 80 percent of target use cases or scenarios. Do not wait until you understand 100 percent of a situation.

3. **Conway's law: "Organizations design systems that mimic the organizational structure."** Conway's law is an aphorism that implies organizations design systems that mirror their communication structure. "Inverse Conway" is a concept introduced by Thoughtworks in 2015 as a mechanism for organization restructuring around better software development. The Inverse Conway maneuver states that the right organizational structure will create the right kind of software feature or function.

    While this is heavily weighted toward software companies—with the reasoning that for a software module or feature to function, multiple teams much communicate with each other—we can extend this law to different industry verticals by substituting software function with value created. Therefore, the broader interpretation of Inverse Conway's law then becomes:

An organizational structure that is designed to optimize the flow of created value within the organization will reduce friction through the organization from idea to consumption of the value that the organization manages.

4. **Brook's law: "Adding more people to a late project only makes it later."** Fred Brooks coined this law in his 1975 book *The Mythical Man-Month*.[2] According to Brooks, the main factors contributing to his law are:

   - People newly assigned to a project have a learning curve and ramp-up time to familiarize themselves with the project, outcomes, features, techniques, and workflows. Even veterans in an industry still need to educate themselves on organization-specific cultures, workflows, and methods. "Hitting the ground running" is an aspirational phrase that project sponsors have when they assign new people to a late project with the hope that they can pull in timelines.

   - The more people on a project, the more complicated communication becomes. Communication overhead rapidly increases with additional people, and logistical challenges of being in sync with ongoing work, being aware of current project status, and being cognizant of project impediments increase drastically with more people on the project.

   - Dividing specialty tasks optimally with many people is sometimes difficult and can result in long wait times, increasing the project's overall duration. Brooks points this out in his book with an example: "While it takes one woman nine months to make one baby, nine women can't make a baby in one month."

5. **Goodhart's law: "When a measure becomes a target, it ceases to become a good measure."** The most cited example

Leading with Empathy

to support this law's effects is the tale of nail factories in the Soviet Union. To measure how performant factories were, central planners decided to use the number of nails manufactured (more widgets created means more productivity, right?) to measure the factory's productivity and issued minimum expected targets. To meet and surpass these targets, factory operators produced millions of tiny nails useless for any practical purposes. When the central planners realized this, they switched the targets to nails' total weight instead (total tonnage of production). The factory operators responded appropriately by producing enormous and heavy nails that exceeded target but were once again useless.

A few digital examples of Goodhart's law incentivizing wrong behavior are using click-through rate (CTR) as a target for advertisements or the number of bugs detected in a test cycle. Imagine the number of spurious defects filed if we incentivize testers by measuring the number of bugs identified in a test cycle. The amount of time it will take for teams to thoroughly address each of these defects would be substantial. Conversely, think of how bloated software would be if developers are measured by how many lines of code they write.

6. **Metcalfe's law: "The more devices connected to a system, the more useful it becomes."** Metcalfe's law was first developed for telecommunications networks and the Internet but has expanded to other areas. For instance, a social platform's value increases as the number of people adopting the platform increases. The same can be said about Uber, Lyft, Doordash, or any digital platform that brings together two different communities. We can also utilize Metcalfe's law for technology adaption within organizations trying to modernize their existing infrastructure and toolset. Unless enough people adapt to new technology, it will not generate enough value

and instead incur technical debt. Therefore, organizations need to look at technologies with low barriers to entry, low integration costs (integration into their existing systems), a low user learning curve, and a good user experience, especially for a highly remote workforce.

Optimize Processes for a Remote Workforce

Each time an organizational process fails, our immediate response is to introduce checks and balances (bureaucratic overhead), manual controls (micromanagement), and stage gates (friction). While these actions originate through good intentions, the net result is bloated, suboptimal processes with considerable manual intervention and hand-offs. With a remote workforce, these processes adversely impact productivity and render teams frustrated. Value stream mapping is a practical approach to identifying waste and points of friction within processes and allows teams to optimize their process flow quickly.

Modernize Your Technology Stack

Process mapping can also help identify areas where technology can eliminate waste or reduce friction for a remote work environment. Introduce technologies that can easily integrate within the value stream to minimize friction. Ensure that these new technologies have a low learning curve and are not intimidating to the workforce. Learning new technologies in a remote setting can be frustrating and could potentially increase stress and anxiety within the workforce.

Signal the End of a Working Day

A challenge of existing from home is losing essential cues that indicate the end of a working day. Introduce the concept of a spindown that serves this purpose.

A *spindown* is a ritual where, every day, the team regroups at the end of the workday and discusses the team's wins for that day. This meeting is scheduled on the team calendar for the same time every day. Next, they call out team members who helped them remove a blocker, taught them something new, or went above and beyond in sharing knowledge or skills. The teams do not talk about existing impediments or blockers (the team discusses these at the beginning of the next day); the ritual aims to have a positive end for a day.

Spindowns help remote teams in many ways:

- They signal the end of a working day, psychologically relax the mind, and reduce stress.
- Talking about what they accomplished provides necessary dopamine and serotonin release to team members.
- The act of callouts releases serotonin and oxytocin in team members and helps them be proud of one another and helps them bond better, which, in turn, increases the team's psychological safety.

Lean, Agile, and DevOps for IT

As IT organizations rethink and reimagine their strategies for a contactless, digital world, leaders are incorporating Lean manufacturing, Agile methodologies, and DevOps practices into their practices. Lean manufacturing helps improve process efficiency by focusing on eliminating waste, reducing inventory and motion, and optimizing work in progress within the organization. Lean software development brings in the concepts of hypothesis-driven development, Lean experimentation, rapid prototyping, and feedback loops to quickly ascertain if the experiment was

(continues)

Employee Empathy

(*continued*)

a failure or a success. Agile methodologies focus on developing working software and shipping features that add value to customers. DevOps practices provide systemic thinking—a holistic view of the software development process, push for automation and reducing manual toil, observing, and measuring events and processes in the organization, and sharing knowledge. (See Figure 7.1.)

Figure 7.1   Lean, Agile, and DevOps are transformational drivers for employee empathy.

Lean, Agile, and DevOps have become transformational drivers for an organization undergoing digital transformation, but introduction of these practices and methodologies has been inconsistent. Humans by nature are averse to change, and transforming an organization requires radically changing the way one thinks, works, interacts, and communicates. This can be overwhelming to many, and invariably a strategy to adapt Lean, Agile, and DevOps ends up trying to figure out how to deliver features quicker through an organization with the least amount of change to the status quo. In cases where organizational leaders are more forceful and drive change within the organization, the level of friction increases drastically, and people then resort to performing the minimal viable change to appease leaders and yet remain within their comfort zone.

This anti-pattern of digital transformation can be countered by developing a strategy that harmoniously utilizes Lean, Agile, and DevOps methodologies rallied around the reason (or purpose) behind *why* the organization needs to undergo a digital transformation. This purpose defines what is valuable within the organization, and the goal of these transformation drivers is to improve the flow of this value through the organization from creation to consumption (by the customer) with the least amount of friction. Dr. Mik Kersten provides a wonderful analysis of flow and value management in his book *Project to Product*.[3]

Collaboration

Collaborating over multiple geolocations and time zones is extremely hard, and this is one of the largest areas of reinvention for organizational leaders. Many Agile frameworks emphasize colocation as essential for high-performing teams. This, however, is a quandary with a highly remote workforce. The concept of a colocated physical location is rarer now; increasingly, teams are remote.

Employee Empathy

The first step that leaders should take is openly acknowledge challenges of distributed collaboration among teams. Teams could span multiple time zones and working hours cannot be mandated to a traditional 9-to-5 routine anymore. Work windows need to be a social contract among team members, and this flexibility improves team bonding, collaboration, and accountability, in addition to productivity.

Next, the organization needs to invest in good tools that strive to provide digital twins of existing experiences. These tools need to be responsive, persistent, and integrate seamlessly with the organization's ecosystem. The tools also need to have good user experience and have a low barrier to adaption. Challenging tools can quickly become sources of anxiety and stress to a remote workforce and will not have the desired impact.

The third step is to introduce pairing at various levels within the organization. There are many studies that demonstrate the benefit of pairing and increased value creation. In addition to those benefits, remote pairing generates better quality of work, better morale, and real-time collaboration. It increases bonding between pairs (oxytocin release), team accountability increases, and immense mentoring capabilities. Teams that practice pairing and pair rotation constantly report higher cohesion and psychological safety within the team—essential in these stressful work conditions.

Finally, leaders have to ensure that there is a single data source that teams operate on. This single source of truth is essential when everyone is working remotely, as they do not have the luxury of osmotic learning or hallway conversations to address any thoughts of data inconsistency. Having this single data source also drives consistent observability, common metrics and data analytics, consistency in inference, and ability to make the right data-driven decisions.

Tips

Demos: Software demos, due to their nature, are usually easier to convert to a digital format. However, leaders should insist on having demos present the business value of the feature, product, or software being shown. Functional demos should be performed when a story is completed and the overarching demo (also called a presentation in many organizations) must showcase the business value of the working software. Recording these demos will also provide video tutorials and training material for others at a later date and should be encouraged.

Retros: Conducting virtual retrospectives can be initially challenging. However there are many free and commercial products in the market that provide digital capabilities to conduct retrospectives online. Leaders need to ensure that the spirit of retrospectives are upheld—blameless retrospectives, freedom to voice one's opinions, teams feeling safe to share feedback, and working on action items that come out of retrospectives. Additional care should be taken to ensure data privacy, and focus has to be on patterns that emerge and not individuals that report problems.

There are some added benefits of conducting virtual retrospectives. First, team members can still express themselves through digital palettes, emoticons, stickers, etc. Second, the team can still read off of nonverbal cues through video interactions and choice of words. Third, many retrospective software also provide the capability of whiteboards, and teams can utilize these to express themselves pictorially. One of the best retrospectives that a team had was when I opened up the whiteboard at the end of

(*continues*)

(continued)

the retro and had the team undertake a silent mapping exercise where I put 15 minutes on the clock and had the team silently express how their iteration felt through pictures and words. The end result was very enlightening, cathartic, and enjoyable to all. I encourage teams to perform this activity once a quarter (or at the end of a program increment).

Communication

Communication was the easiest to adapt to remote working. At the same time, this was also the area that tried to overcompensate for the workforce's needs. People sometimes overcommunicate and use multiple communication methods in fear of not reaching out to their teams appropriately. There has been an explosion of emails and newsletters with large distribution lists. The operating principle has been that it is better to overcommunicate to the workforce multiple times with different methods.

More Noise, Less Relevance

There is, however, a downside to all this: an overabundance of information flowing through various channels and mediums. Indeed, the amount of messages, emails, notifications, newsletters, and communications has grown to the point of becoming work spam. In a closed system such as an organization, the signal-to-noise ratio (SNR) drops significantly, degrading the communication. Taking a cue from radio communication, a method to improve SNR is by introducing an active filter that reinforces positive feedback and amplifies the signal (valuable information) while reducing the noise. Prioritizing quality over quantity will disseminate information more effectively.

Another approach is to use a mixer to modify or shift the signal, which can be accomplished by enriching the information itself as well as the modes of communication used to deliver it. Where possible, use infographics, dashboards, charts, or visual indicators to showcase value to the organization. Doing so also makes communications more impressionable, personable, and relatable. Conveying why the information is relevant to the workforce and how it impacts and improves team members' lives is critical.

Asynchronous Communication

With a remote workforce distributed over geographies and time zones, leaders must discourage synchronous communication such as status meetings to propagate information. Methodologies such as GitOps or ChatOps have taken software development and IT operations into an asynchronous, event-driven world. Leaders need to extend the benefits of these approaches to regular communication. Every organization already has a favorite messaging client (or a few) built for asynchronous communication. Incentivizing the workforce to exchange information on these channels in place of a meeting will be welcomed and appreciated.

A Picture Is Worth a Thousand Words

Images have been used to tell human stories since prehistoric times. Cave paintings, pictograms, hieroglyphs, and other visual imagery are some of the earliest communication methods, and pictures still are some of the most effective forms of human communication. Pictures tend to capture context, emotion, and information in their expression, allowing people to localize their experience while looking at the picture and add their personal commentary. One does not typically experience such emotional responses in tables or spreadsheets. Organizations spend millions of dollars every year on infographics, posters, and other forms of visual communication as they recognize the power of imagery and symbols.

Newsletters, emails, and project statuses are essential modes of communication within the organization. Improve the value of these passive communication methods through visual aids, images, graphs, and infographics to make them more engaging and attention-grabbing. Our minds are trained to zero in on that dash of color contrasted by blocks of text, and we retain the information better. Graphs and charts convey more information than tables or spreadsheets and have been proven to improve messaging credibility.

Real-time dashboards, Kanban boards, operation boards, and progress meters are examples of visual indicators that can be shared across the organization. They can be hosted on the company's intranet home page, providing easy access and visibility to everyone.

Brevity, engagement, and flexibility are the benefits of visual indicators. Pictures transcend the viewers' cultural, ethnic, and language differences and elicit emotional responses from the viewers, making visual indicators impactful on your target audience. Information is retained better and is already packaged to enable storytelling and information propagation within the organization.

Interactive Town Halls

Town halls are a powerful way to communicate with teams, motivate them, excite them, and demonstrate your leadership. They are also a great way to rally people to a common cause, be vulnerable, transparent, and have an open dialogue with the workforce. Achieving similar results can be challenging with a remote work environment, but not impossible. Leaders need to extend their charisma and presence by interacting with their teams differently.

Here are a few tips to make town halls more exciting:

- **Poll the audience.** Send a questionnaire or survey out to teams asking for input on topics they would like to discuss in the town hall and questions they would like to ask. Many organizations time this with a quarterly eNPS survey to optimize data collection. Next, have the teams vote on the top three (to five) items you must cover in the town hall.

- **Have an Ask Me Anything (AMA) session.** Video conference fatigue is real, and your teams will be glad to take off their headphones for a while. Instead of having a traditional town hall, switch it up by having an AMA session on your company's messenger system. People can submit their questions in advance, these can be voted on through the built-in poll feature, and the leadership team can tag-team and address several questions. This method will also illustrate how collaborative, trusting, empathic, and open-minded the leadership team is and demonstrates how the leaders embrace the same organizational communication channels. AMA also indicates that no topic is off the table and has proven effective in many organizations.

- **Align with audience needs.** Structure your town hall around the top items voted by the audience. Share facts, anecdotes, struggles, pains, or other stories around these items.

- **Engage the audience.** During the town hall, have the audience submit questions through the Q&A feature of the video conferencing solution. If this feature is still lacking with your conferencing solution, it probably is time to switch to better software. As an alternative, the audience can use the chat functionality to ask their questions. Assign people to monitor the Q&A and chat during the town hall. Do not forget to record the town hall for team members who cannot attend.

- **Address the audience.** Be empathic, authentic, and vulnerable when addressing your audience. Thank your teams for their hard work through these adverse times. Demonstrate your humility and express your genuine gratitude to represent your teams. Answer questions with conviction.
- **Follow up after the town hall.** Distribute the recording link along with the Q&A (and chat) transcript through email (less desirable) or posting on your organizational channel. If you run out of time during the town hall or AMA, respond to the other pertinent questions in your response. Your teams will genuinely appreciate your going above and beyond to respect their concerns.

Meeting Overload

Proliferation of meetings can overwhelm team members and increase work stress. During the pandemic, many of us have been double, triple, or even quadruple-booked.

The unprecedented increase of meetings during that time can be attributed to the following two factors:

- **Opportunity to socialize.** People lost their physical offices or work environments, and they craved the need for socializing. Meetings therefore became support forms for many people and were a substitute for getting that sense of accomplishment (dopamine release), feeling of belonging and warmth (oxytocin release), or a sense of pride and importance (serotonin release).
- **Low barrier to entry.** People feel that since there is no transit time needed to move from one physical conference room to another, no break room banter, or travel time to go to customer sites, they can always schedule meetings and have a conversations on topics that are top of mind for them.

Things that could have been discussed over email or office messenger tools now become an excuse to have a meeting. This can have severe debilitating consequences to the organization's value stream. In addition, too many meetings can reduce workforce productivity and increase work hours, stress, and employee happiness.

I surveyed teams spanning various industry verticals on meeting proliferation and overload in 2020 compared to the previous year. I asked them how hopeful they were of reducing the number of meetings per day in 2021. Over two-thirds of the people surveyed reported that in 2019, they spend fewer than three to four hours on average in meetings every day. Usage of video conferencing solutions such as Zoom, Microsoft Teams, Google Hangouts, Skype, or Cisco WebEx was low. Such solutions were predominantly used in organizations with distributed teams before the pandemic, and co-location was an essential principle of team agility and collaboration.

As of March 2020, that behavior pendulum swung the other way. Over 65 percent of the respondents reported that they had been spending over five hours on average every day in video conference meetings. A whopping 82.5 percent of the workforce reported being double or triple-booked at least once per week, with almost a quarter of them experience meeting contention at least once a day!

With so many hours of the workday spent on video conferencing, it is inevitable that people spend long hours at work to meet their deadlines, prep for the next day's meetings, or maintain their productivity to meet their key performance indicators (KPIs) or objectives and key results (OKRs) that they are measured on. According to my survey, over 87.5 percent of the workforce report spending at least four additional hours per week to meet their deliverables, with an astounding 62.5 percent of people spending upwards of 1.5 hours per day merely to keep up with their regular workload.

Employee Empathy

To put this into context, almost two-thirds of salaried full-time workers paid to work an average of 40 hours per week now work 47.5 hours per week at a minimum. That's nearly an additional day of work. Two-thirds of the workforce worked almost **300 extra hours** since the pandemic broke out in March 2020.

Not all organizations compensated for this extra work. Several organizations froze promotions, overtime, bonuses, Restricted Stock Units (RSUs), 401(k) matches, and monetary award programs. Others enforced a mandatory pay reduction since they were working from home and not in the office. Some organizations responded with empathy and demonstrated that they valued their employees and their well-being over a short-term revenue impact. In contrast, many organizations chose to take advantage of the economic downturn and increasing unemployment and exploit their employees. The demeanor of these apathetic employers suggested that the workforce should feel fortunate that they still had a paying job and that they were doing a favor to the employees by allowing them to work from home. If COVID-19 response were a social test administered to assess organizational culture, these organizations would fail and be branded toxic.

But the despair did not end there. Over 80 percent of the work-force reported that they did not see any reprieve to meeting overload for 2021. Roughly half of the respondents said they felt the management did not care about the stress that remote work meetings induced and that they were apathetic to how overwhelming each day had become. A quarter of the workforce reported having to start the day as early as 7:00 a.m. and stop working late into the night (around 8:00 p.m.) with hardly any breaks in between.

These statistics are unacceptable, and we as leaders need to make conscious steps to improve our workforce's quality of life and well-being. The next sections discuss some ways to reduce meeting overload in your organization.

Tackling Meeting Sprawl

Lean and Agile methodologies provide helpful guidance around improving value and efficiency of meetings through elimination of waste, clarity in purpose, and focus on value. Here are some points to consider:

- **Is this meeting necessary?** Ask this question before you schedule your meeting. Sometimes, the information that we are seeking can be obtained through other means such as an email, chat, or even a text message. Asking for a status update on your work messaging client provides more visibility and prompter response than a status meeting. Roman voting (thumbs up/down or +1/–1) or online polls and surveys tend to be more efficient and prompt higher participation by being low effort for people.

- **Choose the right participants.** Many meetings are run as support forums and there are way too many participants in them. Unless your meeting is a town hall or an open forum, you will need to choose the right participants for your meeting. Good meeting etiquette dictates that people who will be providing information or taking decisions should be required, and other people optional. If you are including people for visibility or information, a recap email after the meeting should suffice.

- **Smarter meetings.** We humans have bad attention span. This reduces even more when people are stressed or anxious. Normally, the 5 minutes at the start of a meeting are spent with participants acclimatizing themselves to the meeting, and the last 5 minutes of the meeting is spent prepping for the subsequent meeting. If it's a virtual meeting, the context switching occurs during the meeting. Try to implement smarter meetings instead. Reduce a 30-minute meeting to 25 minutes, and a 60-minute meeting to 50 minutes. This not only provides breathing room for participants, it also allows them to refresh themselves before joining so they can be present in your meeting. There are many meeting clients that have smart meetings in their configurations now and have proven to be very beneficial for participant engagement.

- **Clear agenda with expectations.** Vague and ambiguous agendas have unfortunately become common place in the workplace. Meeting participants often find it hard to understand the purpose behind a meeting and end up questioning its value. Having a clear agenda with expectations is important especially with participants being double or triple booked at the same time slot, and this can make the difference between choosing to attend your meeting over other conflicts. Several organizations have empowered their team members to decline meetings if there is no clear agenda or expectations listed. At a minimum, the meeting agenda should contain the reason behind the meeting and what the meeting organizer intends to accomplish. Lacking these two critical pieces of information, the meeting becomes either a status report or a support forum, where known information is rehashed, and conversations drift into hypotheticals and what-if scenarios.

A meeting that does not have a clear purpose ends up being a support forum.

POWER to Make Meetings Valuable

POWER (see Figure 7.2) is a technique taught by my mentor Lyssa Adkins[4] and has proven to be effective in several organizations.

POWER stands for:

Purpose. Start the meeting by stating the purpose of the meeting and why participants are here.

Outcomes. Clearly state the outcomes or deliverables for this meeting. What are your expectations as a meeting organizer?

Figure 7.2 POWER start for a meeting.

What's in it for me (WiiFM). Impress upon the participants what value they will derive from this meeting. People are more involved when they perceive value (their return on investment).

Engage. Engage your participants with excitement and passion. Humans are emotion-driven and reciprocate the feelings of others. Bringing your passion and excitement to the meeting will help participants relate to you and your expectations.

Roles. Be very clear about the roles and responsibilities of participants. Ensure that you are following proper meeting invite etiquette and clearly outline your expectations from your attendees.

Following these approaches will not only increase the signal-to-noise ratio within your organization, it will also drive effective communication and reduce meeting sprawl.

Enablement

There are many mechanisms to provide enablement to a remote workforce. Training, videos, workshops, and conferences are some ways in which teams can upskill themselves remotely. However, this is only one facet of enablement and leaders should consider the following areas for virtual enablement.

Employee Empathy

Connectivity and Relevance

Humans who are impacted by deficiency and growth needs suffer from a need to show relevance and purpose. This feeling is exacerbated in a remote setting, where people feel disconnected or isolated from their professional family (i.e., their team), and by extension, their organization. Leaders need to be able to share the organization's vision in addition to clearly articulating the purpose of strategic initiatives or imperatives that have been implemented.

Leaders also need to emphasize the relevance of each team member by showing connectivity of team projects and initiatives all the way up to strategic imperatives and company goals. Mind maps, KPI dashboards, Management by Business Objectives (MBOs), and OKRs are additional tools that quantify relevance and connectivity and visually represent the value that each team member provides to the organization.

Emotional Intelligence

It is heart-warming to see many organizational leaders demonstrate their increased emotional intelligence along with genuine investment in employee work-life balance and well-being. There are several cases of leaders putting their employees' physiological and psychological safety ahead of traditional business drivers, and that is a win for humanity overall. It enables team members to focus on their loved ones. This not only endears leaders to the workforce but will pay cultural dividends in the long run.

Organizational Culture

Organizational culture represents the collective values, beliefs, and behaviors of an organization's workforce and is driven by a sense of belonging, camaraderie, and common purpose. Co-location has a large impact on the instillation of organizational culture, so building organizational culture with a workforce that is predominantly remote presents a great challenge and an opportunity for many organizations.

Investment in the right organizational tools and technologies not only helps improve the quality of life of the workforce, it also helps drive organizational culture and behaviors that leaders use to instill in a remote workforce.

The global pandemic forced us all to reconsider the foundations of working in an office environment and adapt to a new way of working. It is reasonable to assume that, in many industries, much of the workforce will continue to work remotely, if not full-time, at least a few days of each week. It is therefore imperative for individuals, teams, and companies to adapt to this new norm. Leaders need to embrace the reality that overall productivity of a remote workforce might be low initially as teams learn to adapt to a new way of working.

We are already seeing the effects of remote working in the form of richer asynchronous communication methods, increased acceptance of personal intrusion in professional settings, and improved empathy among teams. This trend of providing digital twins to the remote workforce will continue to be popular, as they provide a platform of familiarity. New ways of working collaboratively, communicating transparently, and demonstrating team empathy are enabling a growth mindset and helping teams discover new norms of productivity and performance. It is definitely a stressful, challenging, yet exciting time to be part of this global experiment.

How to Increase Psychological Safety

Here are some practices to improve psychological safety within the organization:

Increase cooperation. Create stable, balanced, and cross-functional teams that are built around value streams and a common purpose. These teams should have a representative from each functional area in the value stream and be empowered to create value, deliver it to production or to the customer, and manage the value. They need to have a common purpose, shared responsibility, shared OKRs, and shared incentives. This will improve cooperation within the team and introduce shared accountability. It also helps share risks within the team. Quality, security, and resiliency are responsibilities of everyone on the team, and the shared OKRs will drive that behavior. Make sure that the teams have a common toolset as well. Conformity will help camaraderie in this case. It will also enable the team members to help each other when they have challenges with a tool, or there will be consensus in changing toolsets if that doesn't work out for them.

Co-located teams are good solutions if things were not distributed. In remote settings, it's smart to have a common messaging channel, team space, website, common meetings, standups, and so forth. This will also help break down silos within the organization.

Celebrate failure. This means empowering the workforce to be comfortable with failure and not try to hide mistakes. Have blameless post-mortems. When you remove blame, you are removing fear. When fear is removed, people start feeling safer and more comfortable to share information. Encouraging radical candor, conducting blameless post-mortems, and demonstrating that people who speak up will not be punished or face retribution will increase psychological safety of teams. They will start trusting and realize that we are all in it together and that the goal of these activities is to improve quality and increase value, and not have someone pay for mistakes. Embracing failure is one of the best things that can change the organization. Have a failure wall and encourage people to post on there. Have a celebration each town hall where you have a team come and share their failure and validated learning out of that failure.

Encourage experimentation. Promote innovation. Encourage experimentation. Give teams the freedom to explore new ideas and concepts that align with the value that they create. Bake innovation time into product delivery. Promote Lean experimentation and use the right language and words to promote this. Experimentation need not be just product-centric. It can be improving a process, eliminating waste, a new way of working, a new ceremony that the team wants to try out. Reward experiments that increase value.

Promote fun. People spend a lot of time at work and there is no point having them be miserable while working. Encourage fun activities and team events. Don't limit it to obligatory social hour events at the end of the week. While they can start out as fun, pretty quickly it will become a chore, not to mention drop in engagement if it is repetitive. Be quirky. Have a cooking class as a social event. A hack event works well to have fun and encourage experimentation and the comfort of failure.

Lack of Psychological Safety in a Pathological Organization

"If you are a human, you are not welcome here. No human errors allowed," was the headline of a Glassdoor review of a company that my close friend had the misfortune of working for. She experienced firsthand the toxic culture, apathy, and fear-driven management style of totalitarian executives in that organization. She narrated horrifying stories of

(continues)

(*continued*)

harassment and abuse, victimization, and lack of psychological safety. She was under considerable stress and anxiety during her tenure there and admitted that it was the worst place that she had ever worked. She was micromanaged and harassed, and her self-confidence took a nosedive.

I heard about an unfair system where people were severely penalized if they did not meet their numbers, but excuses were made for executives who could not meet their scorecard numbers to claim bonuses. I heard about their phishing failure protocol and how an employee could lose their bonus if they failed a phishing test. Some were even terminated for their first failure, a fact that was conveniently omitted in the hiring process. Favoritism was rampant in the organization, and people who reported offenses were targeted and harassed. Finally, my friend could not take the psychological torture anymore and quit her job.

I read several Glassdoor reviews from prior employees, and it was heartbreaking and disturbing. One review requested an onsite psychologist to support the hundreds of traumatized employees working at the place. Another affirmed the punitive and fear-driven culture within that company's walls. Many reviews spoke of micromanagement, control, punitive measures, and low morale. A feeble attempt to address some of these complaints was made by providing free chips and salsa, and ice cream once a year.

One review that affected me significantly talked about a horrifying tale of abuse and harassment. A long-time employee had tripped in an empty hallway over a piece of carpet that had become bare over time. She went to human resources (HR) and complained about the area where she had tripped and asked HR to address it, as it was a safety hazard. HR conveyed this complaint to the executives, and the employee was called into an executive's office, who questioned her about the incident. A photograph of her shoes was taken as evidence, her account of the incident was captured, and the employee was sent back to work. The next day, an all-employee memo was sent to address safety in the workplace. The employee's story was narrated in the memo and talked about how she had tripped in a hallway because she was wearing improper footwear. The photograph of her shoes was also included, and the executive leadership claimed that this was an example of unsafe footwear that caused the employee to trip and fall. The employee's name was included in the memo, not as an oversight but as a public shaming technique. Rather than thanking the employee for bringing potential safety concerns to their attention, the executives and HR decided to lash back at the employee and publicly humiliate her. She had around a year to go for retirement, but she could not bear the harassment and left the company immediately.

The reviews' overarching themes were lack of psychological safety, apathy, abuse of power, and favoritism. My friend personally underwent considerable trauma as a result of working there. From the stories that I heard, it felt like a terrible place to work, and I have personally seen how toxic cultures can destroy people's will, spirit, and joy. We celebrated when she tendered her resignation, but it took her a long time to recuperate.

A Good Work-Life Balance

Having a good work-life balance is necessary to develop psychological safety and trust and to transform an organization into embracing a generative culture.

Maintaining work-life balance helps in reducing stress and anxiety in people. It also helps in preventing burnout in the workplace. Several studies have researched and documented the effect that long periods of stress have on individuals and their physical, mental, and emotional health. With the challenges of working from home, many individuals lost their familiar cues of daily work, such as commuting to and from work, adhering to public transportation schedules, or even stopping at their favorite coffee shop. Several individuals have reported long workdays—logging in earlier and logging off later than usual—resulting in considerable overtime and increased reports of burnout.[5] Working long hours in front of a screen can also cause mood swings, irritability, fatigue, and even sleep deprivation.

Here are a few questions for you to consider:

- Does work define you and your identity?
- Is working so hard worth sacrificing your time with your family and loved ones?
- Are you expected to work so hard, or is that your assumption?
- Do you have difficulty saying no?

From my personal experience, there is nothing more important than good health and spending time with your family and loved ones. I used to be a workaholic as well and spent needless hours in the office. I hardly took vacations and prided myself on being in the office and spending long hours there. I felt that my work defined me and used to feel anxious if I took some time off. I did not know how to say no to a request and frequently ended up burning the midnight oil working on reports, projects, and presentation decks.

I started getting my tension headaches again after a gap of over 10 years, and that was a wake-up call for me. I recognized the negative behavior patterns that I had embraced and decided I had to do something about it. After all, what is the point of working so hard if you are dead? I decided to take these steps:

- Define what an ideal work-life balance was for me (success criteria).
- Track my work-life balance (human observability).
- Simplify tasks and put life before work as much as possible (prioritization).

Note that work-life balance does not necessarily imply that they have to be of equal weightage, although that would be a good aspiration. Identifying a work-life balance bespoke to you signifies finding a good balance between your life goals and your work goals and endeavoring to maintain that equilibrium. Plan your week and keep track of what you want to accomplish each day. Bring visibility into your nonwork tasks and celebrate their completion as you would with your work. Do not beat yourself up if you do not complete your tasks as intended. Embrace failure. **If things happened the way you wanted them to happen, then it wouldn't be called life.**

Improving your work-life balance does not require radical alteration of your current lifestyle. You can gradually work toward what you have identified as your unique work-life balance. Here are some simple tips to start your journey:

- Start your day with some form of exercise and a healthy breakfast.
- Take some personal time off. It could be mental health days, wellness days, or vacations.

- Spend time with your friends and family (lounging on the couch and watching television together does not count as spending time).
- Make meal prep a family activity.
- Switch to a healthier diet.
- Spend time doing the things that bring you joy and happiness.

Promote a Work-Life Balance

One of the biggest impacts of switching to a full remote working environment is the overnight obliteration of a distinctive line between our professional and personal lives. Many of us have worked from home in the past occasionally (some more than others), but what we experienced during the pandemic was different. Our partners, loved ones, children, and pets were also having their own experiences while cohabiting, and this invariably resulted in our streams intersecting at unpredictable times. This is called *existence at home*, and this experience has been stressful to many.

Promoting a sustainable and harmonious work-life balance has several benefits. It creates a generative organizational culture, improves workforce morale, reduces employee stress, and drives a higher quality of life. The workforce tends to become happier, less stressed, spends more time with their loved ones, and is more collaborative and productive at work. Psychological safety increases, and they take more risks and innovate and become brand ambassadors for their organization, culture, and leadership.

Here are a couple of techniques to improve work-life balance in an organization:

Slow down to accommodate life. Remember why you started working in the first place? It was to make money to support you and your loved ones and have a sense of accomplishment and purpose. We work because we want to live better lives. But what is the point of working so hard if there is no time to live? Whether you are actively engaged in it or not, life occurs all around you. Why not slow down to participate in life events and derive joy and happiness out of them? Because, believe it or not, work will be there when you come back.

As a leader, one must acknowledge this reality and accommodate for joyous interruptions to work. Making life events a priority for your teams is a significant benefit to a remote workforce. It improves morale. It creates a positive environment for your organization and enhances productivity, talent retention, and innovation. Leadership must slow down their expectations of deliverables or extend timelines to allow a sustainable pace. A good rule of thumb is to add a 15–20 percent buffer to timelines to reduce burnout or stress. For Agile software teams, this is analogous to lowering team velocity to achieve a sustainable pace of productivity and delivery.

Reduce your work-in-progress (WIP). Setting a limit on your work-in-progress will not only lessen undue stress on the organization to deliver, it will also increase the probability of success of your current work in flight. Prioritize your initiatives based on value to the customer and organization, identify initiatives or projects that can be put on hold for now, and establish a WIP limit for your teams.

Enable flexible work hours. Life happens. No one plans for unforeseen circumstances. As a leader, empathize with people undergoing anxiety due to unplanned events. It could be as simple as a babysitter not reporting in for work due to illness or needing to perform some task during business hours. Or it could be something more stressful, such as a colicky baby, a sick pet, or even meeting fatigue. Empower your teams to shift their working hours as needed to accommodate for life and other commitments. The concept of a strict 8-to-5 schedule does not exist anymore, and even if it did, there does not seem to be a viable reason for that construct to endure in this new way of working. Teams can adjust their schedules as needed to guarantee that they meet their OKRs, MBOs, or their outcomes and deliverables. As a leader, measure their performance based on these measures.

Encourage downtime. As a leader, this is where your say-to-do ratio should be as close to 1 as possible. Talking about downtime in town halls, company newsletters, or HR memos does not impress employees when the deliverable dates or productivity expectations remain the same. Teams must be enabled to factor in downtime in their roadmaps, project estimates, or deliverable dates. Management should encourage teams to block time on their calendars or take time off as needed. But it is not just encouragement. Managers should respect employees' time off and not disturb them. They should also not expect that work will somehow be magically completed during time off. They should enforce strict device detox for employees and assure them that it is OK not to think about work. It is critical to slow down and reduce WIP if your say-to-do ratio needs to be high.

One of the best rules I implemented with my teams is to require my managers to request my approval for any weekend work. They had to justify the weekend's work and how they would offset this extra time for the employees who had agreed to work over the weekend. This request would also trigger a root cause analysis exercise to identify countermeasures for reducing such occurrences. I am proud that we take employee downtime seriously.

Promote a sustainable pace. We all can endure short bursts of high activity, and almost all of us have pulled an occasional all-nighter to complete our outstanding tasks. Many of us have also experienced bouts of long work hours to accommodate a customer's demand, a critical incident, or an outage. We acknowledge that this is the price of working in an organization and accommodate these occasional stints of stress and activity. It becomes a concern when these events become the norm and impact employee productivity and well-being. Leaders should promote a sustainable pace for their workforce and ensure that management measure and maintain this pace for their teams.

Make working from home comfortable. There is a high probability that your employees working from home for the first time are not equipped with a comfortable setup. Even if your workforce has occasionally worked from home in the past, they may not have the equipment to endure long stints.

During the pandemic, many organizations provided stipends to procure comfortable office furniture and supplies to increase their employees' comfort at home. Others conducted ergonomic surveys for their employee setup and procured office furniture to encourage employee well-being. This simple gesture of empathy endears the workforce to the organization, and they recognize the level that their leaders are committed to their well-being and comfort.

Provide wellness and emotional support resources. Many organizations already provide employee assistance programs for mental health and well-being. If your organization does not currently offer them, it's time to do so.

The good news is that humanity is resilient and highly adaptive, and adversity drives us to discover better and optimal methods of working and in turn elevates our productivity, self-actualization, and overall happiness.

Actualize, Not Just Verbalize

Ajay is a director of customer experience for a large software company. He has to deal with incidents, customer complaints, and other issues daily. He describes how his life spun out of control very quickly during the pandemic. "All of a sudden, we had to switch to a remote way of working. That proved challenging to my teams and to customers. They were so used to meeting us and having a more personal experience. Many complained that video conferencing did not provide the same kind of feeling."

Ajay said that his leadership emphasized that they needed to adapt to this new way of working and supported having a good work-life balance: "We had the CEO, CIO, and the Chief HR Officer (CHRO) talk about remote work, stress, anxiety, and heard how the leadership encourages people to have a work-life balance. The leaders told us that we needed to have downtime and take care of ourselves. We had wellness seminars and virtual happy hours. Our management repeated the words that the leaders said. It felt terrific to hear these things."

But that was where the good intentions and encouragement of leadership and management concluded, according to Ajay. "It is easy to spout these great aspirations and pearls of wisdom when you are by your swimming pool or on your yacht. While we heard the words of encouragement to take time off, nothing tangible happened. Our deadlines didn't shift. Expectations were the same. Our clients were more understanding of our mental health and well-being compared to our leaders. They accommodated us struggling to work from home with our children in virtual school. We even bonded better over common challenges that we were facing."

"But internally, we had no such luck. We were expected to attend all the meetings scheduled and still somehow manage to complete our deliverables or respond to emails immediately. Several peers escalated up their management chain when they did not get a response from me within an hour. Explaining that I was stuck in a meeting that I was not even supposed to be in was not reason enough," he said.

Ajay also lamented about the overload of meetings. "It is so common for me to be double or triple booked at least once a day. People have no regard for others' calendars, and I doubt that they check for meeting conflicts anymore. Knowing that some people might not attend, we now have a situation where three or four of us on each team are invited, with the hope that at least one can attend. Suddenly, we have a situation where we have too many people on a call, and nothing gets accomplished. I remember one situation where we had 35 different people on a project call, but that meeting ended with no action items or decisions. Except for the decision to have a follow-up meeting. It was a colossal waste of time, not only for each attendee but for the company overall. Imagine how costly that meeting was if you factor in the cost of an hour of each attendee and add them all up!"

Even though the organization's leaders had good intentions, it can all be to naught when their say-to-do ratio is low. Unfortunately for Ajay and his teams, his leaders stopped at verbalizing and did not actualize.

(continues)

Employee Empathy

(continued)

Reflection

- On a scale of 1 to 5 (1 being you don't relate and 5 being you relate entirely to Ajay's story), where does your experience with your teams fall?
- What actions have your organization's leaders taken to reduce your workload and promote a sustainable pace?
- What arguments have you heard opposing a slowdown of delivery velocity for your teams? How have you tackled these arguments?

Virtual Team Building

When teams are co-located or in close physical proximity, they have many team-building exercises to improve collaboration and social bonding. Almost everyone who has worked in an enterprise has competed in building tall structures with spaghetti and marshmallows. Others have engaged in Nerf gun or paintball wars.

Virtual team building extends these concepts and has many advantages over physical activities. For one, the team does not have to be geographically co-located to participate. As long as they are willing to overcome time zone limitations, anyone around the world with a good Internet connection can participate. For another, there is no need for extensive planning and logistical coordination such as booking venues, travel time, and so forth for these events. They can be agile and spur of the moment, making them much more natural and enjoyable. The downside is that they increase screen time for the participants who are already struggling with long hours online. It can become monotonous and devolve into another meeting.

The goal, therefore, is to incentivize people to participate in these team-building exercises, during regular work hours if possible. Virtual gaming is a good way to encourage team building. Encourage the team to have a fun-o-meter, a progress bar that tracks how much of time was saved through smarter meetings, decision making that did not require scheduling meetings, and other ways of saving time. Once a certain amount of time is saved, have the team decide what online game or team-building exercise they would like to participate in. Traditional examples are online console gaming, trivia, quizzes, drawing games, or even scavenger hunts. Virtual talent shows have been a hit during the lockdown. Show your furry friend or talk about your hobby and how you have been maintaining your sanity during lockdown. Virtual meetings give an opportunity for teams to enter each other's personal lives in ways that were not possible before.

It does not always have to be online. The team can start a book club and read a book offline, with the only time that they get on a virtual meeting is when they are discussing it. Or the teams can submit their favorite recipe, vote on the most popular one, and cook that recipe, sharing the results either asynchronously through team messaging applications in the form of pictures, a small video describing the dish and how it tasted, what it reminded them of, and the teams can share common emotions and strengthen their social bonds. The remote working environment has enabled teams to become creative and interact in various ways.

Virtual Happy Hours

Virtual happy hours can be a simple method of team bonding and sounds attractive and compelling. After all, what is the downside of having a drink with your team and swapping stories? Results from a survey that I conducted, however, tell a different story. The respondents' overall consensus was that the novelty of a virtual happy hour faded away quickly, and it became an event that they avoided. Here are two popular reasons why:

1. **Yet another meeting.** A virtual happy hour is another video conferencing meeting on the calendar. It immediately sucks the fun and spontaneity of a traditional happy hour. The fact that it is a repetitive event makes it a chore. "I just want to finish my meetings and end my week on a high note," said one employee. "I would rather spend my time relaxing with my family and my dog rather than be stuck on another Zoom meeting with the same people that I have spent so much time with already."

2. **It may not be optional.** Another person responded, "I can understand why management schedules these virtual happy hours, but once it is scheduled on my calendar, I don't really have much choice, even though it is marked as optional. It is supposed to be a team-bonding exercise, and I am worried that management might misconstrue my absence from these events as not being a team player. I then feel compelled to attend these meetings. And I don't even enjoy drinking so much."

Reflections

- What are your experiences of virtual happy hours or virtual team-building exercises?
- What worked for you and your team?
- How did you introduce fun into your teams during the lockdown?

  I would love to hear from you on these topics. Please email me at gpallapa@pm.me with your responses or share them on your favorite social medium using the hashtag #leadwithempathy.

A Good Work-Life Balance Is Achievable

If you cannot invest in yourself, how can you expect a company to invest in you?

We cannot help our employees achieve a good work-life balance without investing in ourselves first. It is not enough for organizations and leaders to promote a work-life balance and provide the means to improve the quality of life of their workforce. It is incumbent upon you as a leader to take necessary action to improve your work-life balance and set a good example. Awareness of your current work-life balance and taking concrete steps to reduce your stress and improve the time you spend on your life is imperative. Some simple steps all workers should consider are:

1. **Make your work area comfortable.** Have an extra monitor if possible and a comfortable, ergonomic chair with good back and neck support. Good lighting is also essential. If your organization allows you to purchase a sit-stand desk, procure one.

2. **Take regular breaks.** Force yourself to get up and walk around every 55 minutes. If possible, block 5–10 minutes after each meeting to unwind and step away from all devices. Check on your loved ones (physically, not through a device), walk through your home, water your plants, pet your cat—perform an activity that does not require interacting with a screen or electronics. For those of you anxious to check your social feeds or Reddit, dedicate the last 1–2 minutes of your break to those activities. The goal is to allow your brain to relax a little.

3. **Ensure you have downtime.** Force yourself to refrain from your work devices for a specific window. Ideally, you want to

end your workday and not think about it until the next morning, but that is a luxury to many employees. Instead, dedicate a block of time for your family, loved ones, or for your non-work activities and adhere to it. Discipline is essential for this activity, as this downtime is meant for you to relax and rejuvenate.

4. **Embrace a healthier lifestyle.** Social distancing enabled some people to embrace a healthier lifestyle. Make small tweaks to your intake to eat healthier. Also, remember to hydrate and exercise. It could be as simple as stretching, moving, or bending and touching your toes in between meetings. If possible, move around the home and take a call or two while standing to perform these stretches. Small changes can add up, making you feel healthier and happier.

Summary

A hybrid model for working is inevitable. People have embraced a contactless, digital-first experience with a redefined level of instant gratification. We have elevated our expectation of work from an 8-to-5 grind in a physical location to an anywhere-anytime mode, making planning and workplace logistics both exciting and challenging. We need to evolve our mindset and thought leadership to rethink and reimagine how we upgrade our existing processes and procedures. But we are still human, and therefore, physical interaction will still play a vital role in the way we work. As leaders, we need to use empathy as our core tenet as we embark on this transformation. It is definitely an exciting time to be a leader.

Reflections

- What efforts did your organization undertake to improve employee empathy during the pandemic?
- How bad is meeting overload at your organization? What steps have you taken to reduce it?
- What is your WIP limit, and what steps have you taken to promote a sustainable pace?
- How have you encouraged your workforce to log off and have downtime?

Chapter 8

Optimism, Evolution, and Empowerment

To build high-performing teams, leaders need to prioritize trust, empowerment, and empathy over deadlines and performance.

2020 was the year that we lost our comfort and safety. COVID-19 forced organizations to change their ways of working. It made them stop and evaluate their current processes and business models, and pressure-test their ability to pivot quickly in a dynamic setting. It was also a year where words like *unprecedented* and *new normal* became trending topics and were used by almost everyone.

It was also the year of the introvert and a chance for everyone to become a video celebrity with the number of conferences attended. As a society, we finally learned the importance of washing hands, sanitizers, and social distancing. 2020 was the year of the teachers who heroically had to abandon their teaching methods and quickly adapt to an entirely new platform and way of engaging students. Kudos and immense respect to them, and even more so for teachers who had their own children in school.

2020 was indeed the year of digital. Everything had to switch to a contactless, digital platform. Zoom meetings, virtual classrooms, virtual enrichment, subscription-based online physical fitness, virtual social hours, happy hours, eDates, and eCommerce.

Adversity in 2020

2020 also taught us that we are a fragile and delicate species despite all our technological and medical advancements. Our hubris of development was decimated by nature and put us back in our place. We learned how we have not really evolved and how people still hoard, loot, exploit others, and how we are greedy and highly self-centered, and try to justify our actions through financial excuses. We suffer from social anxiety and an unhealthy obsession with ourselves, not from inner beauty but a superficial, cosmetic appearance.

The outburst of the COVID-19 global pandemic brought the world to its knees. Many individuals became stressed by this unprecedented surge, and in one way or the other, they had to engage in the remote workforce. Businesses and organizations were not spared, either. With this pandemic's impact, there has been a dire need for transformational change, a call to action for people to step up and lead with empathy.

2020 was a challenging year for all of us. The world has seen immense adversity in a short time frame. Apocalypse bingo was a reality, and it has impacted humanity on many levels—a global pandemic, racial inequality and injustice, natural disasters, economic instability, and unemployment. People lost their livelihood, source of income, sense of security, and their social constructs overnight. The personal cost of this pandemic was inordinate, and we are not in the clear yet. The many variants of COVID-19 loom large, and some countries are battling a second wave of infections.

This feeling of fear and desperation is not limited to a deadly pathogen alone. It sometimes feels like we have five pandemics raging at the same time with no resolution in sight:

- The COVID-19 global pandemic
- Racial injustice (Black, Asian, Hispanic)
- Economic inequality

- Privilege and elitism (white, politically connected, male)
- Anti-intellectualism (anti-vaxxers, flat earthers, conspiracy theorists, deniers)

The COVID-19 Global Pandemic

COVID-19 brought the entire world to its knees. It severely impacted every facet of our life, fundamentally disrupting, and in many areas, debilitating, various industry sectors, including travel, hospitality, retail, healthcare, and education. Unemployment skyrocketed, world economies were weakened and destabilized, and companies had to close down or declare bankruptcy. Schools and universities shut down overnight, disrupting education for generations. Hospitals and healthcare facilities were overwhelmed and strained beyond capacity.

The global pandemic forced society to reimagine and reinvent business processes, engagement models, and interactions. These drastic changes have introduced a substantial contrast to how we live, work, interact with our fellow humans, and generate significant stress, anxiety, and insecurity. These emotions are amplified by the challenging environmental conditions and the socioeconomic impact that the global pandemic has inflicted on humanity.

As we heal and repair from the worst of the pandemic, we must realize that aftermath will be here to stay for years. Psychologically, financially, professionally, socially—we have healing to do. The future may look a lot different than prepandemic times.

Racial Injustice

Racial injustice has been on the rise over the last decade. Since 2013, the Black Lives Matter (BLM) movement has transformed the debate around police brutality in the United States. However, the tangible impact of the demonstrations became visible only after the death of

George Floyd in May 2020. These demonstrations are reminiscent of those during the Civil Rights era due to their anti-racist agenda. However, the crucial roles played by social media and the decentralized form of leadership are two factors that set apart these movements.

Some of the cases are heart-wrenching. For instance, Secoriea Turner, an 8-year-old girl, was shot and killed on July 4, 2020, near a Wendy's during the BLM riots in Atlanta, Georgia. Twelve-year-old Tamir Rice of Cleveland, Ohio, was brutally killed in 2014. Tamir was playing with a toy gun in a park, and within two seconds of arriving at the part, Officer Timothy Loehmann had shot and killed Tamir. Police then tackled Tamir's 14-year-old sister Tajai to the ground, handcuffed her, and put her in the back of their car. Officer Loehmann and Officer Frank Garmbark, who was with him at that time, were not indicted.

There are so many victims of racial injustice against the Black community, but I wanted to highlight a few names of people senselessly killed:

George Floyd, Breonna Taylor, Ahmaud Arbery, Tony McDade, Dion Johnson, Rayshard Brooks, Daniel Prude, Laquan McDonald, Atatiana Jefferson, Walter Scott, Aura Rosser, Stephon Clark, Samuel DuBose, Botham Jean, Philando Castille, Alton Sterling, Michelle Cusseaux, Freddie Gray, Tanisha Fonville, Eric Garner, Akai, Gurley, Gabriella Nevarez, Tamir Rice, Michael Brown, Tanisha Anderson.

While the BLM movement has its roots in the United States, it has garnered widespread international support with local demonstrations in at least 60 countries and across every continent. This is due to the issues of racism and discrimination being familiar in almost every society. As in the United States, governments around the world have for too long ignored the issues of systemic racial injustice. Ethnic minorities have been repeatedly denied equitable access to opportunities, services, and fundamental human rights. While many of these localized protests began in solidarity with their American counterparts, many have taken on new forms and led to different debates as they adapt to different national contexts.

For instance, the recent surge of hate crimes targeted at Asians and Asian Americans in the United States is a reminder that this feeling of racism is deep-rooted. The senseless killing of Asian women at the spa incident in Atlanta and increasing hate crimes against Asians in the San Francisco Bay Area are recent examples. There was even a rumor of a "Slap an Asian" challenge on social media, demonstrating how low humanity can stoop down. The Center for the Study of Hate and Extremism released a report that documented a 146 percent increase in Asian hate crimes since 2020 in the United States.[1]

We have observed a similar uptick in hate crimes toward the Hispanic and Latino community when the United States' previous president called Mexicans drug dealers, criminals, and rapists. These observations demonstrate how easily inflammatory and explicitly racial remarks embolden certain people and give them license to express their deeply held prejudices.

Researchers have aptly dubbed this the "Trump effect" or "emboldening effect."[2] This is a particularly recent and compelling example of how important it is for our leaders to model empathy and compassion rather than hate and fear. A sad reality is that racism is deeply rooted in the human psyche and is amplified by privilege and elitism.

The pandemic of racial injustice has brought several critical issues to the forefront. Politicians and lawmakers worldwide have started much-needed dialogue for reform and equality of all people with a renewed sense of urgency. Generations of empathic people have become activists, championing the discriminated groups along with underrepresented minorities. Social media has helped bring episodes of racial injustice to light sooner than before, and awareness is at an all-time high. But we are far from becoming a utopia. We need to continue working on diversity, equity, and inclusion.

Privilege and Elitism

Privilege is a principal reason for social inequality and a key driver of social injustice. It is a benefit enjoyed by an individual or group that is not accessible to others. Privilege has been a part of our history. Social classes, caste/feudal systems, colonialization/subjugation by other countries and races, slavery, and immigration status are prominent examples of lack of privilege that exist even to this day.

White privilege has been one of the most visible and sordid aspects of societal rights. The mere fact that some people enjoy tremendous benefits due to the color of their skin has been a contentious point for centuries.

Gender privilege is another challenge in our society. Numerous studies have been conducted to prove gender inequality in every walk of life, and the United Nations has identified gender equality and women empowerment as one of its top six goals.[3] Many corporations have also pledged to reform policies on gender equality and increase hiring of genders other than cis male and underrepresented minorities in their organizations. Despite these advancements, discrimination and outdated social norms continue to prevail and impede progress toward gender equality. The COVID-19 pandemic has also exacerbated these inequalities and, in some cases, reversed any tangible progress made.[4]

Socioeconomic privilege and legal status privilege are additional privileges that impact the progress in our communities. There have been several accounts of the wealthy and influential people getting off scot-free for severe crimes—a stark contrast to experiences of the poor and the plebians. Each country also has its unique challenges with legal status privilege, and there are numerous accounts of immigrants or people seeking asylum that are heart-wrenching.

Being cognizant of one's privilege is an essential step in demonstrating empathy. It reduces the probability of exhibiting signs of patronization, misunderstanding, and elitism. Remember, having privilege means that one has an advantage over others that was not earned or requested. The lack of privilege is how power is distributed within our communities. This characteristic makes privilege the face of oppression.

Economic Inequality

The global pandemic and its after-effects have accentuated economic inequality in our societies. We saw the impact of this inequality in 2007 with Occupy Wall Street protests and the sub-prime mortgage crises. COVID-19 increased the divide between the rich and the poor, with many developed countries reporting an almost nonexistent middle class. There have been events such as hedge funds vs. WallStreetBets and an extremely volatile stock market in recent times. The pandemic led to skyrocketing unemployment rates, with many industries laying off their workforce. States and countries implementing forbearance measures to prevent landlords from evicting tenants during the pandemic, which unfortunately created a housing inventory shortage and, therefore, a housing bubble waiting to burst. Millions have suffered from homelessness, poverty, or fear of losing a roof over their head. Adversity is on the rise for humanity at a global level. We are slowly course-correcting, but we have a ways to go.

Anti-Intellectualism

Despite our advances in science, culture, and technology, there has also been a steady increase in anti-intellectualism. This phenomenon of disregarding facts and scientific methods just because they do not align with one's convictions is appalling and concerning. Even in this modern time, some question whether the earth is actually round. There are conspiracy theorists and deniers of scientific fact. Anti-vaxxers question the efficacy of vaccines and spread falsehoods and misinformation, resulting in risking children's health, and have caused morbidity rates of infections and diseases that could be easily contained. In a recent study, Facebook,[5] Instagram, and Twitter identified that only a small group of accounts are responsible for over half of the anti-vaxxer propaganda and misinformation.[6] Social media has considerably changed the definition of truth and news over the last few years and has drastically amplified the voice of anti-intellectualism.

Let's Be Optimistic about Our Future

To be fair, it was not all desperation, gloom, and disaster. These recent issues were challenging for many industry verticals to take a step back and evaluate their business models critically, question their purpose, and adapt to a changing landscape. Technology became an accelerator for progress, and quality of life became a priority for many people worldwide.

We are constantly bombarded by articles, news reports, and media coverage of hard and trying times. But as humans, we tend to look for inspirational or motivational themes even in the face of adversity. I consider myself an eternal optimist and therefore want to identify five positive trends that have emerged as proverbial "silver linings" to the dark clouds of these stressful and challenging times.

People Are More Empathic Than Before

For many, seeing another person in pain and responding with indifference or even outright hostility seems utterly incomprehensible. People are stepping up to help their fellow humans and are demonstrating empathy more than ever. Many have gone out of their way to truly be present and create a safe space for others. Doctors, nurses, healthcare workers, and first responders are risking their lives every day to ease the pain and suffering of others, reduce their stress and anxiety, and administer vaccines to a pandemic-fatigued population. There are several reports of healthy youth and adults helping the elderly and disabled with groceries, food, medication, supplies, transportation, and other necessities.[7]

These past few years have underscored the consequences of racial injustice, homelessness, poverty, societal biases, and ineffective policies. The COVID-19 pandemic hit communities of color the hardest, and as a society, we have realized that there have been long systemic biases against communities of color. Many charities, crowdsourced donation websites, petitions, and forums have been created to champion, fund, and support social change, diversity, inclusion, and equity causes. Socioeconomic injustice has been highlighted and sets the stage for open dialogue, reform, and better policy.

There's an Increase in Employee Empathy

Organizational leaders, for the most part, have increased their emotional intelligence (EQ) and employee empathy. According to Maslow's hierarchy of needs, physiological needs (breathing, food, water, warmth, rest) and safety (security in clans, morals, employment, health) are the most important needs for humans, followed by the need for love or belonging. The pandemic attacked our fundamental needs and made us very insecure.

When the pandemic started, some people were scared even to get food and water. Focus shifted to foraging—finding cleaners and toilet paper, chicken and pasta—giving some the feeling that they were in a throwback to the Stone Age. Everything was a threat, and that induced considerable stress. Then, as the pandemic went on, social distancing measures, virtual schooling, and shelter-in-place affected our sense of belonging. People in several sectors became unemployed through no fault of their own, health became a concern, there was a separation between families and friends, and even the sense of belonging that employees had by visiting a physical office was impacted by remote work measures. It is therefore heartwarming to see the majority of organizational leaders demonstrate their understanding of the sheer stress that their employees were undergoing.

Remote Work Has Become More Acceptable

Working from home has become more acceptable. Companies understand that many need the freedom and flexibility that comes from working at home. Organizations with concerns about allowing their workforce to operate remotely[8] have not observed a noticeable decrease in productivity.[9] Many firms are exploring the possibility of a four-day workweek,[10] allowing families to spend more time together and enjoy life.[11]

While we all are collectively working on finding the right work-life balance, we are also embracing good behavior, such as turning off work email notifications at nights and on weekends and not logging into our work computers over weekends, to have some device downtime.

Companies saved considerable travel and entertainment expenses, conference and event costs, and other essentials such as breakroom and cafeteria costs. Many are exploring the possibility of closing their physical offices and allowing their employees to work virtually. There are many examples of large organizations moving from expensive cities into other locations to save on cost.[12]

Working from home also gives more options to disabled workers, parents, and military spouses who can work remotely, keep the same position when or if they move house, and work the most convenient hours.

There Are Newer Ways of Collaboration

A challenge for distributed and remote Agile teams is to ensure effective collaboration during pair programming, iteration planning, research, or architecture discussions. New additions to the standard developer productivity toolset are conferencing and screen-sharing tools. Several innovative applications that try to mimic physical interactions—such as watercooler conversations, hallway chats, drivebys, and so on—are popular with remote teams, This trend of providing digital twins to the remote workforce will continue to become popular, as they provide a platform of familiarity. Better ways of collaboration will emerge with tenets in design thinking, Lean, and Agile methodologies, with empathy at the core.

The Digital Landscape Is More Egalitarian

I believe that the pandemic and its economic aftermath equalized the technology playing field from a digital landscape. Before COVID-19, startups had a considerable headstart on the incumbents with advantages of no brownfield applications in their portfolio or infrastructure management pains. Enterprises in the same space were in various stages of their business transformation journey, and some organizations were contemplating their strategy to transform their heritage applications into a cloud-native portfolio.

The pandemic provided the compelling event that organizations were looking for to transform. With economic downturns following a global shutdown, several startups experienced funding challenges, requiring them to slow their pace. This creates a unique opportunity for incumbent companies to prudently invest in innovation and strategic business transformation and reduce the technological gap between their disruptors and contenders. This is also an economic climate for interesting coopetition (cooperation and competition) and newer business models that target and positively exploit the new consumer and market dynamics that have emerged.

Leapfrogging Innovation and Evolution

COVID-19 impacted the physiological and safety needs of people at a global level. Habits were disrupted and social lives were curtailed, and this drastically reduced joy from extrinsic factors. The workforce had to switch to a remote working setting virtually overnight. If we were lucky enough to still be employed, all these physical locations collapsed into our homes.

There were challenges with new technologies, and a drop in productivity impacted people's esteem needs. Work converted into switching from one video conference to another, with hardly any time for us to context-switch, take a rest, or even a break sometimes. People had to adapt to being on camera all the time. Accessories such as 4K web cameras, selfie ring lights, microphones, and headphones were in demand. People became conscious of their appearance and on guard lest their loved ones, children, or pets entered the room and disrupted a team meeting. The phrase "You're on mute" was one of the most common phrases used during the pandemic.

These events of the pandemic adversely affected our needs, severely stressing us and increasing our anxiety levels. This experience was not a grand experiment of working from home. Instead, it was a global condition of existence from home.

Throughout history, existential crises have driven evolution and adaption by leaps and bounds.

Where do we go from here? How can we leverage the positive repercussions of a global pandemic and advance the human race? After all, we have evolved and progressed by adapting to adverse conditions over the centuries. Contactless, digital-first, and remote have become necessities for many of us.

One positive effect of the pandemic on the workforce was that many leaders and team members became empathetic to people's personal needs. We invited our teams into our homes through video conferencing, and it was not uncommon to see unexpected guests in our video conferencing, such as children, pets, and loved ones. People became comfortable abandoning the unrealistic expectation of having a stoic and professional facade at work and became more authentic, empathetic, and human. We learned to embrace life and all of its varied facets.

Four predominant areas have evolved into a digital-first approach due to the pandemic and its aftereffects, improving the quality of life for humanity globally:

1. **Execution.** People adapted to different methods of remote work in all aspects of their lives. The definition of productivity and impact has shifted from deadlines to outcomes, from artifacts generated to value created, and from manual intervention to governed automation. Lean, Agile, and DevOps practices are not limited to software development anymore. Many techniques, such as backlog management, prioritization, and flow management, have intersected with personal life and have optimized value creation.

   Social distancing and lockdown protocols inspired people to increase planning, prep work, and scheduling in their daily lives. Task-based checklists evolved into value-driven activities. Digital became the go-to mode to accomplish actions, and many businesses were focused on improving customer interaction experience online and adapting to contactless methods at their physical locations. In the workplace, processes were optimized for a remote workforce, with newer technologies. Lean, Agile, and DevOps practices were introduced to reduce manual toil and increase workforce productivity to enable quicker delivery of customer-delighting features. Organizations and teams were acutely aware that no idea has value unless their customers derive benefit and happiness from it; they are striving to reduce the time from ideation to implementation, thereby improving their flow of value within the organization.

2. **Collaboration.** With the world switching to a remote work environment en masse almost overnight, people adapted quickly to newer and more innovative collaboration methods to ensure consistent delivery of value. Organizational leaders started to openly acknowledge the challenges of distributed collaboration among teams spanning multiple geolocations and time zones.

   There has been considerable investment in responsive, persistent, user-friendly tools that strive to provide digital twins of existing experiences. Teams adopted high-value collaboration techniques such as pairing remotely, enabling the workforce, increasing empathy, reducing stress in team members, and driving innovation, team camaraderie, and knowledge management in their organizations. These collaboration techniques also increase team cohesion, psychological safety, and innovation among team members, reduce attrition, and transform organizational culture from pathological to generative.

3. **Communication.** In-person interaction was not an option in many places, so virtual meetings, emails, and other digital offerings became the primary mode of communication. However, people were sometimes overcommunicating and using multiple communication methods in fear of not reaching out to their teams appropriately, with the underlying principle that it is better to overcommunicate to the workforce numerous times through different modes. As with all complex systems, it takes time to achieve equilibrium, and organizations are finding bespoke ways of communication, tailor-made to their unique culture.

Asynchronous communication and messaging applications have been helping reduce noise, and image-based communication such as infographics, graphs, and charts are becoming increasingly influential in communicating large volumes of data to a remote workforce. Digital town halls have become more interactive, and there is increased demonstration of empathic leadership within a workplace. Good leaders have become more open, authentic, accessible, and approachable, improving the organization's culture. Meeting overload will be actively addressed in several organizations, as it has become evident of their adverse impact on value generation.

4. **Enablement.** There are many mechanisms to provide enablement and upskilling opportunities to a remote workforce, such as online training, videos, workshops, and conferences. Leaders can share the organization's vision and clearly articulate the purpose of strategic initiatives and the relevance of each team member by showing the connectivity of team projects and initiatives all the way up to strategic imperatives and company goals. Mind maps, key performance indicator (KPI) dashboards, management by business objectives (MBOs), and objectives and key results (OKRs) are additional tools that quantify relevance and connectivity and visually represent the value that each team member provides to the organization.

It is heartwarming to see many organizational leaders demonstrate their increased emotional intelligence and genuine investment in employee work-life balance and well-being. Leaders have put their employees' physiological and psychological safety ahead of traditional business drivers by relaxing deadlines, slowing down throughput, and allowing the workforce to stay healthy and happy, at the cost of potential revenue or profits. This enables team members to focus on their loved ones when necessary. Small gestures rooted in empathy endear leaders to the workforce and pay cultural dividends over the long run.

Leading with Empathy

We are in an interesting time right now. The global pandemic revealed how delicate, fragile, and interdependent our lives are, and how inequitable conditions are across the world. While the pandemic created a huge amount of angst globally, there still are signs of positivity and growth that we can look to. The encouraging fact is that humans are tenacious, persistent, and adapt well in the face of adversity. I am optimistic that with some work, we will be more connected, collaborative, and innovative as a human race, post-COVID-19.

Thanks to the hard work of scientists, doctors, and healthcare professionals worldwide, pandemic infection and mortality rates dropped, despite a resurgence of variants. Society is feeling hopeful again. People look forward to planning their vacations. The excitement of having a meal with loved ones at a restaurant. Visiting a favorite club or bar. Meeting friends and having a good time. A date night. Attending a concert or sporting event. Sales executives, vendors, and partners are looking forward to meeting their clients onsite and helping them achieve their business outcomes. Schoolchildren and college students are excited to go back to school and interact with their classmates, peers, and teachers. I am looking forward to traveling and meeting people in person again at conferences and workshops. People are going through their celebration lists—things that they wanted to do once safe to do so. Last year, my son said that he would consider himself lucky if we could celebrate his birthday at the Ghirardelli chocolate factory in San Francisco, California. He was ecstatic when I took him there this year and savored every minute of the visit. We have all started to appreciate the small things in life.

The pandemic gave us a chance to spend more time with our families and build genuine and stronger relationships. In some cases, family bonds were strengthened, and children communicated better with their parents. Technology enabled increased communication and collaboration, and people found more ways to reconnect with their loved ones as sources of mutual support, advice, and care. As life slowed down due to social distancing and lockdown protocols, people acknowledged, conversed, and in some cases, cared for their neighbors and the community's health and well-being. People cooked meals for the needy, offering emotional and even financial support to those in need, and performed supermarket runs for those unable to leave their homes. We became a well-functioning community again.

We also digitally transformed the world by creating digital twins of physical world interactions with comparable user experiences. We evaluated our processes with a newfound perspective of remote working and exploring ways to reduce manual toil. The focus shifted to value, and many companies focused on high-value activity while enabling systems to handle mundane tasks. We also started extending Lean, Agile, and DevOps practices into our personal lives. Productivity, efficiency, and optimization became common themes between personal and professional lives, uplifting humanity overall.

Organizations that promoted empathy and made it part of their organizational culture are the ones poised for success and positive change going forward. Empathic leadership is at the core of these cultural transformations, and change agents are striving hard to change the organizational culture from pathological to a generative. These empathic leaders are also championing customer and employee empathy. There is a dire need for collaboration, compassion, kindness, and empowerment, and empathy provides the ability to emotionally understand what other people

Optimism, Evolution, and Empowerment

feel, see things from their perspective, and imagine yourself in their place.

Your actions to improve people's quality of life make you an empathetic leader.

As you read this, I am sure that you are thinking fondly of all the activities that you have completed so far. Maybe you are thinking of items on your celebration list that you are yet to accomplish. Perhaps you are on vacation right now and making new memories. People are enjoying life to the fullest. We are constantly learning and evolving, and continuous improvement has become part of our lives. There is more positivity and empathy within the world as it bounced back quickly. We have proven that collectively we are strong and resilient and can work together as a society for a better future.

Living and surviving through a pandemic has not been easy, but we have persevered, and once again, we have demonstrated an abundance of grit and determination as a human race. Empathy, once a scarce resource in our society, has become a defining trait of humanity. Recognize that you do not need permission to lead with empathy. There is a profound difference between reducing pain and building happiness. Reducing pain is momentary; building happiness is persistent. When you perform actions to encourage happiness in others and reduce the pain they are going through, you are acting as an empathic leader and are empowering humanity, which is especially critical during times of adversity.

Chapter 9

Actions for Empathy

If you cannot invest in yourself, how can you expect an organization to invest in you?

The world has been transforming at a rapid pace over the last few years. It is hard to keep up with the sheer velocity of change introduced in our lives. But it is not just the last couple of years. I would venture to say that this entire millennium has been a crazy rollercoaster, starting with Y2K. It has indeed been a trial by fire for many of us. But we are resilient as a human race, and we continue to adapt to adversity, emerging stronger each time.

In this chapter, I include some ways to develop empathy as an adult. It also covers how to encourage empathy in children. I provide some tips and techniques that you can follow to lead with empathy in your personal and professional life. If there are exercises and techniques that have helped you develop empathy, I would love to learn about them! At the end of this chapter, I included ways to share your information to help others.

Empathy for Adults
Tips for Practicing Empathy

Fortunately, empathy is a skill that you can learn and strengthen. If you want to build your empathy skills, there are a few things that you can do:

- Work on listening to people without interrupting.

- Pay attention to body language and other types of nonverbal communication.
- Try to understand people, even when you don't agree with them.
- Ask people questions to learn more about them and their lives.
- Imagine yourself in another person's shoes.

Preparing for Hybrid Work

Organizations are surveying their workforce, discussing with their leadership, and evaluating their technology strategies to define their unique hybrid work model. It will take some time for these new processes and technologies to become familiar and achieve equilibrium. For the foreseeable future, organizations will be running several experiments to achieve their productivity aspirations.

While each company is in a state of flux, there are essentials that the workforce and leaders must embrace as table stakes. Here are some salient requirements of working remotely:

- **A safe and comfortable work environment.** An ergonomic chair and table, proper lighting and airflow, a good headphone and mic setup, comfortable working equipment, a good webcam (external preferred), and a stress ball/toy. An external monitor is preferred but optional. A printer is optional as well.
- **A stable Internet connection with decent bandwidth.** Video conferencing is a bandwidth hog, and so the Internet has become an essential utility on par with electricity and water.
- **A whiteboard or scratch pads to doodle, draw, or express yourself.** Also, stickie pads and markers. One of the things that I have been missing is walking to a whiteboard and drawing architecture or flow diagrams. Being visual and kinesthetic,[1] this activity helped me deconstruct complex problems,

and I dearly missed holding a marker in my hand until I installed a whiteboard in my home office. Somehow, using an electronic pencil and a tablet did not satisfy my need. Your mileage may vary.

- **Some exercise equipment in the house.** It could be a treadmill, elliptical machine, a cycle (stationary or street-ready), or weights. Working remotely for long durations tends to atrophy muscles, so make sure that you can exercise when you have some time.
- **An alternate comfortable chair or couch where you can spend time out of your home office.** It is vital to break the tedium and prevent yourself from feeling sequestered in a single location.

Exercises for Empathy

Here are some exercises that can help develop and strengthen empathy:

- *Six Thinking Hats*. Edward De Bono's *Six Thinking Hats*[2] is a beautiful tool to increase empathy within your peer network or leadership team. It enables people to examine a problem from multiple perspectives and reveal various cause-and-effect relationships before attempting to solve the problem as a group.
- Famous author and life coach Martha Beck has created an *empathy workout*[3] that people can follow to develop and strengthen their empathy levels, akin to a cardio workout.
- Empathizing with users is the first stage of design thinking.[4] Many product companies and design schools[5] have developed customer empathy[6] and user experience exercises[7] that people can follow.

Random Acts of Kindness

In Chapter 5, I shared some examples of acts of kindness that do not require you to go out of your way to perform. Here are a few more examples of acts of kindness:

- Smile.
- Gift a friend chocolates or flowers for no apparent reason to show that you cherish the relationship.
- Greet people cheerfully.
- Write a blog post about someone who inspires you and share it on your social media feed.
- Write motivational quotes or draw pictures with chalk on your sidewalk or driveway.

Challenge your loved ones, children, or your friends to a kindness challenge, where each of you perform a random act of kindness for a month, and track what each one did, either through social media or your personal messaging group. Keep it spontaneous and do not bring competition into this challenge, because that will defeat the purpose of random acts of kindness.

Volunteering

Perform an act of kindness by volunteering at a soup kitchen or event to feed the homeless or needy. Several organizations supporting the homeless need help sponsoring meals as well. For example, we sponsored meals for the homeless for an entire month in my mother's memory. We had the honor of visiting the center and handed out sandwiches and packed lunches for the homeless as a family. My son was excited to be handing out lunches to the attendees.

There are several ways in which you can volunteer and genuinely make a difference. Community projects such as Habitat for

Humanity, coaching and mentoring underprivileged and underrepresented minorities, or offering your skills to people in need are some ways to volunteer. You could also volunteer at hospitals and read to patients or children. If you can handle the stress and anxiety, you could also volunteer at hospices and ease patients' pain there. Several websites welcome volunteers, so look for local organizations that you can visit.

Encouraging Empathy in Children

Here are a few ways to teach children empathy:

- Help your child express their emotions. In chapter 5, I describe how you can enable your child to understand what they are feeling and name their emotion through the help of emojis.
- Do not be afraid to explore why your child is acting out, misbehaving, or throwing a tantrum. Your calming voice will soothe your child, and together, you can get to the root of your child's behavior.
- Do not teach your child to say sorry and move on. My opinion is that the expectation is for the child to apologize for any misdoing is necessary but not sufficient. Once your child has apologized, use the incident as a teaching moment to explore different perspectives. Use this opportunity to explore what the other person would have experienced.
- Take your child to a volunteering event if it is safe for them to be in that venue. Demonstrating compassion is one of the best ways to instill empathy in children. They observe you being empathetic and associate it as a behavior that they should emulate.
- Read to your children. Similar to the effect books have on adults, children are influenced by characters in books and

stories with morals. Choose books with diverse characters—female protagonists, underprivileged kids, children of color—so that children can appreciate different perspectives. Do not be afraid to choose books that talk about race, gender identity, prejudice, inequality, diversity, and inclusion.

- Children are innocent and curious by nature. This combination could result in them asking questions about some sensitive topics such as racism, bias, gender discrimination, income level, or other societal differences.[8] Have open, transparent, and candid conversations with your child. Do not try to avoid the question, misrepresent critical topics, brush the questions off, or silence children.[9] Isn't it worth overcoming your discomfort and embarrassment?

- Teach your child to fight stereotypes. We want our children to realize that they live in a world of freedom and opportunity, where they can accomplish anything they put their minds to, and that there are no barriers to hold them back. Discourage stereotypical and aged statements such as "girls aren't good at math" or "boys don't play with dolls or cry." If you hear children speak such sentences, address them immediately by asking questions such as, "Would you say that your teacher is not good at math?" or, "Does it seem fair that dolls are only for girls?"

- Empower your child to fight discrimination or bullying by standing up for their rights or the rights of children experiencing discrimination. Enable them to say "Stop" or stand in solidarity with the child being targeted. Also, teach them to find a trusted adult if needed.

- Actively listen to your child when they are expressing themselves. Put your device down, pause what you are doing, and genuinely show interest in what they are saying. Connecting with your child at an emotional level makes your bond stronger and instills empathy within your child. It also helps develop

312

Leading with Empathy

emotional intelligence, which makes your child strong, resilient, and compassionate.

Playdough Emotions

If you have a younger child or do not want to introduce the rigorous approaches mentioned elsewhere, playdough emotions is a good technique to help with your child's emotional development in a fun and expressive way.

- Decide on a few different emotions, and use a different color of playdough to represent each one.
- Draw a simple face to show each emotion, and place a blob of each color dough by each face. This will be your reference chart.
- Discuss a scenario with your child, factual or hypothetical, and then identify together which emotions they might feel.
- Take colors and quantities of playdough that accurately represent how they feel—for example, being home from school might be half sad (missing friends), a quarter happy (spending more time with family), and a little bit worried and excited.
- Squish them together and mix them up to demonstrate that we can feel lots of different emotions all at the same time.

Adopting a Pet

Take your child to your local animal shelter and allow them to spend time with the animals there. If possible, adopt a pet. Taking care of a pet is immensely valuable from a psychological, emotional, and even physiological perspective. You will not only be providing love, affection, and security to an animal, you will be elevating your life as well through the unconditional love that many animals provide. This act of empathy can enrich all of your lives.

Donate Toys, Games, and Books

We encourage our son to donate his toys, games, and books twice a year—once around his birthday and once during the holiday season. A few of our friends have also adopted this tradition. They report that it is an invaluable opportunity for their children to assess their current possessions and choose what they want to give away. Some children even use their pocket money to buy new toys to donate, empathizing with the less fortunate children.

Help in a Voluntary Capacity

Take your child with you when you volunteer, or have them sign up to perform a voluntary act once a month if possible. Cleaning up the neighborhood, recycling drives, or spending time with seniors are all good ways to improve emotional intelligence and empathy for your child.

Read to Children in Hospitals

If you have teenagers, you could encourage them to volunteer at hospitals and read to children or other patients. This act of kindness is an excellent opportunity for them to interact with people in need, overcome any social inhibitions or public speaking fears that they might have, and even reduce their device time.

Guessing Emotions

Most children are exposed to emoticons and emojis early, even more so now due to virtual schooling. Here is a fun activity that has proven helpful to develop empathy in young children. Hand each child a sheet of paper and a pencil or crayon. If you have emoji stickers, that will make this activity even more involving. Narrate a scenario in which a few characters interact and express emotions. It could be a favorite fairy tale or a personalized hypothetical scenario with the children. Instruct the children to draw (or stick) the emoji that comes to mind as they listen to each sentence. At the end of the scenario, have the children display the emojis and explain why they drew them in that sequence.

I have always been amazed at how children interpret interactions and express themselves succinctly whenever we played this game. Emojis are unquestionably the hieroglyphics and, in some cases, primary forms of communication with the younger generations.[10]

Emotions Collage

This is a good activity for a classroom setting or supervising many children (think babysitting, playdates, and sleepovers). Buy a large sheet of posterboard, art supplies, glue sticks, markers, or (if you are brave enough) glitter/tinsel/pipe cleaners. Bring a stack of magazines and hand them out to the children. Invite them to identify pictures of people expressing emotions and ask them to cut those pictures from the magazines and stick them on the posterboard to create an emotions collage. Encourage them to group similar sentiments and have them decorate or color the groupings to express how those emotions make them feel. Then have them choose one person to talk about each group of emotions and prompt them with thoughtful questions to explore their empathic sides.

Share Your Stories

I would love to hear your stories of how you overcame adversity and led with empathy in your personal or professional life. If you have tips or exercises that have helped you and your family cope with painful events, introduced empathy, and enabled you to lead with empathy, please share them with the world. Your validated learning is precious, and sharing it with the world increases its value tremendously.

Here are some hashtags to use when you are sharing your thoughts and ideas on social media: #leadwithempathy and #empathicleadership.

You could also send me an email at gpallapa@pm.me. I would love to hear from you and learn how you led with empathy. Together, we can improve the quality of human lives through compassion, kindness, and love.

Notes

Chapter 1

1. Kim, H. H., & Jung, J. H. (2021). Social isolation and psychological distress during the COVID-19 pandemic: a cross-national analysis. *The Gerontologist* 61 (1): 103–113. https://doi.org/10.1093/geront/gnaa168

2. The implications of COVID-19 for mental health and substance use, Nirmita Panchal, Rabah Kamal, Cynthia Cox, and Rachel Garfield; Published Feb 10, 2021, www.kff.org.

3. Daly, M., & Robinson, E. (2020). Psychological distress and adaptation to the COVID-19 crisis in the United States. *Journal of Psychiatric Research* 136: 603–609. https://doi.org/10.1016/j.jpsychires.2020.10.035

4. Hartnett, K. P., Kite-Powell, A., DeVies, J., et al. Impact of the COVID-19 Pandemic on Emergency Department Visits—United States, January1, 2019–May 30, 2020. MMWR Morb Mortal Wkly Rep 2020;69:699–704. DOI: http://dx.doi.org/10.15585/mmwr.mm6923e1

5. Woolf, S. H., Chapman, D. A., Sabo, R. T., & Zimmerman, E. B. (2021). Excess deaths from COVID-19 and other causes in the US, March 1, 2020, to January 2, 2021. *JAMA* 325 (17): 1786–1789. https://doi.org/10.1001/jama.2021.5199

6. Heist, T., Oct 19, S. B. P., & 2020. (2020, October 19). *Trends in Overall and Non-COVID-19 Hospital Admissions*. KFF. https://www.kff.org/health-costs/issue-brief/trends-in-overall-and-non-covid-19-hospital-admissions/

7. Lawrence, E. (2020, May 27). Nearly half of Americans delayed medical care due to pandemic. Kaiser Health News. https://khn.org/news/nearly-half-of-americans-delayed-medical-care-due-to-pandemic/

8. Hauck, G. (2021, February 3). Cutting, bribing, stealing: Some people get COVID-19 vaccines before it's their turn. *USA Today*. https://www.usatoday.com/story/news/health/2021/02/03/covid-vaccine-some-people-cutting-bribing-before-their-turn/4308915001/

9. Lorenz, E. N. (March 1963). Deterministic nonperiodic flow. *Journal of the Atmospheric Sciences* 20 (2): 130–141.

10. As of August 18, 2021. Data from Johns Hopkins University Coronavirus Resource Center, https://coronavirus.jhu.edu/map.html.

11. Action Against Hunger. (2018, July 12). *World hunger: Key facts and statistics 2021*. Action against Hunger. https://www.actionagainsthunger.org/world-hunger-facts-statistics

12. Nebehay, S. (2020, April 29). Nearly half the global workforce risks losing livelihoods during the pandemic—ILO. World Economic Forum. https://www.weforum.org/agenda/2020/04/nearly-half-of-global-workforce-risk-losing-livelihoods-in-pandemic-ilo/

13. Raynor, L. (2021, April 5). The pandemic has hit women's wallets: How financial brands can help, *Forbes Business Council,* https://www.forbes.com/sites/forbesbusinesscouncil/2021/04/05/the-pandemic-has-hit-womens-wallets-how-financial-brands-can-help/?sh=925740b79c31

14. United Nations (2020). *The Sustainable Development Goals: Our Framework for COVID-19 Recovery*. United Nations Sustainable Development, https://www.un.org/sustainabledevelopment/sdgs-framework-for-covid-19-recovery/

15. Globally, as of July 22, 2021. On a positive note, as of July 22, 2021, 3.75 billion vaccine doses have been administered.

16. World Health Organization. (2021). *WHO COVID-19 dashboard*. Covid19.Who.int; World Health Organization. https://covid19.who.int/

17. The Visual and Data Journalism Team. (2020, September 18). See the devastation of the US wildfires in maps. *BBC News*. https://www.bbc.com/news/world-us-canada-54180049

18. Know your meme. *2020 Bingo*. Know Your Meme. Retrieved July 22, 2021, from https://knowyourmeme.com/memes/2020-bingo

19. Fowers, A., & Wan, W. (2020, May 26). A third of Americans now show signs of clinical anxiety or depression, Census Bureau finds amid coronavirus pandemic. *Washington Post*. https://www.washingtonpost.com/health/2020/05/26/americans-with-depression-anxiety-pandemic/

20. Centers for Disease Control and Prevention. (2020, May 28). *Mental Health – Household Pulse Survey – COVID-19*. www.cdc.gov; https://www.cdc.gov/nchs/covid19/pulse/mental-health.htm

21. Barroso, A. (2021, January 25). *For American couples, gender gaps in sharing household responsibilities persist amid pandemic*. Pew Research Center. https://www.pewresearch.org/fact-tank/2021/01/25/for-american-couples-gender-gaps-in-sharing-household-responsibilities-persist-amid-pandemic/

22. Francis, S. (2020, October 20). Council Post: Women hit hardest by economic damage resulting from pandemic. *Forbes*. https://www.forbes.com/sites/forbesfinancecouncil/2020/10/20/women-hit-hardest-by-economic-damage-resulting-from-pandemic/?sh=764dcaf455c1

23. Our World in Data. *Number of births and deaths per year*. Our World in Data. Retrieved July 21, 2021, from https://ourworldindata.org/grapher/births-and-deaths-projected-to-2100?country=~OWID_WRL

24. United Nations. (2020, April 28). *COVID-19 could lead to millions of unintended pregnancies, new UN-backed data reveals*. UN News. https://news.un.org/en/story/2020/04/1062742

25. Mostafavi, B. (2021, June 3). *Researchers Predict COVID Baby Boom*. University of Michigan Health Lab. https://labblog.uofmhealth.org/rounds/researchers-predict-covid-baby-boom

26. United Nations Committee for Development Policy. (2021). *Comprehensive Study on the Impact of COVID-19 on the Least Developed Country Category*.

27. Hinnant, L., & Mednick, S. (2020, July 27). *Virus-linked hunger tied to 10,000 child deaths each month*. AP NEWS. https://apnews.com/article/virus-outbreak-africa-ap-top-news-understanding-the-outbreak-hunger-5cbee9693c5 2728a3808f4e7b4965cbd.

28. Osendarp, S., Akuoku, J. K., Black, R. E., Headey, D., Ruel, M., Scott, N., Shekar, M., Walker, N., Flory, A., Haddad, L., Laborde, D., Stegmuller, A., Thomas, M., & Heidkamp, R. (2021). The COVID-19 crisis will exacerbate maternal and child undernutrition and child mortality in low- and middle-income countries. *Nature Food* 2 (7): 476–484. https://doi.org/10.1038/s43016-021-00319-4

29. Usher, K., Bhullar, N., Durkin, J., Gyamfi, N., & Jackson, D. (2020). Family violence and COVID-19: Increased vulnerability and reduced options for support. *International Journal of Mental Health Nursing* 29 (4). https://doi.org/10.1111/inm.12735

30. Boserup, B., McKenney, M., & Elkbuli, A. (2020). Alarming trends in US domestic violence during the COVID-19 pandemic. *The American Journal of Emergency Medicine* 38 (12). https://doi.org/10.1016/j.ajem.2020.04.077

31. Fielding, S. (2020, April 3). In quarantine with an abuser: Surge in domestic violence reports linked to coronavirus. *The Guardian*. https://www.theguardian.com/us-news/2020/apr/03/coronavirus-quarantine-abuse-domestic-violence

32. Refuge. (2020, April 9). Refuge sees online traffic to its National Domestic Abuse Helpline website rise by 700%. Refuge Charity – Domestic Violence Help. https://www.refuge.org.uk/refuge-sees-700-increase-in-website-visits/.

33. Boserup, B., McKenney, M., & Elkbuli, A. (2020). Alarming trends in US domestic violence during the COVID-19 pandemic. *The American Journal of Emergency Medicine* 38 (12). https://doi.org/10.1016/j.ajem.2020.04.077

34. UN Women. (2020). The Shadow Pandemic: Violence against women during COVID-19. UN Women. https://www.unwomen.org/en/news/in-focus/in-focus-gender-equality-in-covid-19-response/violence-against-women-during-covid-19

35. Tribune News. (2020, November 1). Covid-19 & the flickering lights of Diwali. Tribuneindia News Service. https://www.tribuneindia.com/news/features/covid-19-the-flickering-lights-of-diwali-164217

36. TOI Staff. (2021, January 1). Gutted by pandemic, tourism to Israel saw 81% drop in 2020. *Times of Israel*. www.timesofisrael.com. https://www.timesofisrael.com/gutted-by-pandemic-tourism-to-israel-saw-81-drop-in-2020/

37. Karadsheh, J., & Qiblawi, T. (2020, July 29). "Unprecedented" Hajj begins – with 1,000 pilgrims, rather than the usual 2 million. CNN. https://www.cnn.com/travel/article/hajj-2020-coronavirus-intl/index.html

38. A formal ruling or interpretation on a point of Islamic law given by a qualified legal scholar.

39. Bailey, S. P. (2020, March 30). More than half of Americans have prayed for the end of coronavirus, poll finds. *Washington Post*. https://www.washingtonpost.com/religion/2020/03/30/prayer-coronavirus-church-faith-americans/

40. Pew Research Center. (2020, March). Most Americans say coronavirus outbreak has impacted their lives. Pew Research Center's Social & Demographic Trends Project. https://www.pewresearch.org/social-trends/2020/03/30/most-americans-say-coronavirus-outbreak-has-impacted-their-lives/

41. CDC. (2020, February 11). Coronavirus disease 2019 (COVID-19). Centers for Disease Control and Prevention. https://www.cdc.gov/coronavirus/2019-ncov/daily-life-coping/animals.html

42. May, R. (2021, February 2). Pets are helping us cope during the pandemic—but that may be stressing them out. Animals. *National Geographic*. https://www.nationalgeographic.com/animals/article/pets-are-helping-us-cope-during-the-pandemic

43. Moric, M. (2020, July 29). US divorce statistics during COVID-19. Legal Templates. https://legaltemplates.net/resources/personal-family/divorce-rates-covid-19/#divorces-increase-in-couples-with-children

44. Felix, M. (2020, November 25). A growing number of Americans are going hungry. *Washington Post*. https://www.washingtonpost.com/graphics/2020/business/hunger-coronavirus-economy/.

45. Strochlic, N. (2020, November 24). One in six Americans could go hungry in 2020 as pandemic persists. History. *National Geographic*. https://www.nationalgeographic.com/history/article/one-in-six-could-go-hungry-2020-as-covid-19-persists

46. Kolomatsky, M. (2021, January 28). People of color face the most pandemic housing insecurity. *The New York Times*. https://www.nytimes.com/2021/01/28/realestate/people-of-color-rent-mortgage-pandemic.html

47. International Labour Organization. (2020, April 29). ILO: As job losses escalate, nearly half of global workforce at risk of losing livelihoods. www.ilo.org. https://www.ilo.org/global/about-the-ilo/newsroom/news/WCMS_743036/lang--en/index.htm

48. Williams, W. (2021, May 28). Unemployment rates: The highest and lowest in the World. Investopedia. https://www.investopedia.com/articles/personal-finance/062315/unemployment-rates-country.asp

49. Falk, G., Romero, P. D., Carter, J. A., Nicchitta, I. A., & Nyhof, E. C. (2021). *R46554, Unemployment Rates During the COVID-19 Pandemic*. Congressional Research Service. https://crsreports.congress.gov/product/pdf/R/R46554

50. Bourzac, K. (2020, September 25). Covid-19 lockdowns had strange effects on air pollution across the globe. *Chemical & Engineering News*. https://cen.acs.org/environment/atmospheric-chemistry/COVID-19-lockdowns-had-strange-effects-on-air-pollution-across-the-globe/98/i37

51. Blumberg, S. (2020, April 9). Data shows 30 percent drop in air pollution over Northeast U.S. NASA. https://www.nasa.gov/feature/goddard/2020/drop-in-air-pollution-over-northeast

52. Zaki, Jamil (2019). *The War for Kindness: Building Empathy in a Fractured World*. Crown.

53. Quintana, D. S., Rokicki, J., van der Meer, D., Alnæs, D., Kaufmann, T., Córdova-Palomera, A., Dieset, I., Andreassen, O. A., & Westlye, L. T. (2019). Oxytocin pathway gene networks in the human brain. *Nature Communications* 10(1). https://doi.org/10.1038/s41467-019-08503-8

54. A *nuclear family* is a family group that consists of parents and their children (one or more).

Chapter 2

1. https://skift.com/2016/03/27/the-travel-industry-now-supports-nearly-10-percent-of-worlds-jobs/

2. Grossman, E. R., Benjamin-Neelon, S. E., & Sonnenschein, S. (2020). Alcohol consumption during the COVID-19 pandemic: A cross-sectional survey of US adults. *International Journal of Environmental Research and Public Health* 17 (24): 9189. https://doi.org/10.3390/ijerph17249189

3. Nussey, S. (2021, July 18). First competitors in athletes' village infected with COVID-19. Reuters. https://www.reuters.com/lifestyle/sports/athlete-covid-19-infections-rise-tokyo-2021-07-18/

4. Takenaka, K., & Lies, E. (2021, August 6). *Factbox: Coronavirus cases at the Tokyo Olympics*. Reuters. https://www.reuters.com/world/asia-pacific/coronavirus-incidents-tokyo-olympics-2021-07-15/

5. International Labor Organization. (2021). World Employment and Social Outlook: Trends 2021.

6. World Bank. *GDP (current US$), Data*. Worldbank.org. Retrieved July 20, 2021, from https://data.worldbank.org/indicator/NY.GDP.MKTP.CD?most_recent_value_desc=true

7. Falk, G., Romero, P. D., Carter, J. A., Nicchitta, I. A., & Nyhof, E. C. (2021). *R46554|Unemployment Rates During the COVID-19 Pandemic*.

Congressional Research Service. https://crsreports.congress.gov/product/pdf/R/R46554

8. International Labour Organization. (2020, April 29). *ILO:* As job losses escalate, nearly half of global workforce at risk of losing livelihoods. www.ilo.org. https://www.ilo.org/global/about-the-ilo/newsroom/news/WCMS_743036/lang--en/index.htm\

9. Ranney, M. L., Griffeth, V., & Jha, A. K. (2020). Critical Supply Shortages—The Need for Ventilators and Personal Protective Equipment during the Covid-19 Pandemic. *New England Journal of Medicine, 382*(18). https://doi.org/10.1056/nejmp2006141

10. Dunklin, R., & Pritchard, J. (2020, March 19). $10 toilet paper? Coronavirus gouging complaints surge in US. AP NEWS. https://apnews.com/article/virus-outbreak-health-us-news-ap-top-news-weekend-reads-53bf1ac57c50df34336c284bfe939212

11. Martineau, P. (2020, March 16). The "Surreal" Frenzy Inside the US' Biggest Mask Maker. *Wired*. https://www.wired.com/story/surreal-frenzy-inside-us-biggest-mask-maker/

12. Newcomb, A. (2020, March 20). Brothers who hoarded 17,700 bottles of hand sanitizer forced to donate to charity. TODAY.com. https://www.today.com/news/brothers-who-hoarded-17-700-bottles-hand-sanitizer-forced-donate-t176028

13. Gressin, S. (2020, April 24). *FTC sends COVID-related warnings to MLM companies*. Consumer Information. https://www.consumer.ftc.gov/blog/2020/04/ftc-sends-covid-related-warnings-mlm-companies

14. Wakefield, A., Murch, S., Anthony, A., Linnell, J., Casson, D., Malik, M., Berelowitz, M., Dhillon, A., Thomson, M., Harvey, P., Valentine, A., Davies, S., & Walker-Smith, J. (1998). RETRACTED: Ileal-lymphoid-nodular hyperplasia, non-specific colitis, and pervasive developmental disorder in children. *The Lancet* 351 (9103): 637–641. https://doi.org/10.1016/s0140-6736(97)11096-0

15. CDC. (2020, March 2). *Tuskegee Study - Timeline - CDC - NCHHSTP*. Centers for Disease Control and Prevention. https://www.cdc.gov/tuskegee/timeline.htm

16. Press, J. H. T. A. (1972, July 26). Syphilis victims in U.S. study went untreated for 40 years. *The New York Times*. https://www.nytimes.com/1972/07/26/archives/syphilis-victims-in-us-study-went-untreated-for-40-years-syphilis.html

17. Lynch, S. (2020, June 19). Fact check: Father of modern gynecology performed experiments on enslaved Black women. *USA TODAY*. https://www.usatoday.com/story/news/factcheck/2020/06/19/fact-check-j-marion-sims-did-medical-experiments-black-female-slaves/3202541001/

18. Holland, B. (2018, December 4). The "Father of Modern Gynecology" Performed Shocking Experiments on Slaves. HISTORY. https://www.history.com/news/the-father-of-modern-gynecology-performed-shocking-experiments-on-slaves

322

Notes

19. Farzan, A. N. (2021, January 26). Wealthy couple chartered a plane to the Yukon, took vaccines doses meant for Indigenous elders, authorities said. *Washington Post*. https://www.washingtonpost.com/nation/2021/01/26/yukon-vaccine-couple-ekaterina-baker/

20. Wick, J., Nelson, L. J., & Lau, M. (2021, February 24). False claims in texts, emails led to misuse of vaccine codes intended for those in need. *Los Angeles Times*. https://www.latimes.com/california/story/2021-02-24/false-claims-in-texts-emails-misuse-of-vaccine-codes-intended-for-those-in-need

21. The Associated Press Staff. (2021, February 19). Florida women dressed as elderly caught trying to get COVID-19 shot. Coronavirus. https://www.ctvnews.ca/health/coronavirus/florida-women-dressed-as-elderly-caught-trying-to-get-covid-19-shot-1.5316253

22. Soucheray, S. (2020, August 14). US blacks 3 times more likely than whites to get COVID-19. CIDRAP News. https://www.cidrap.umn.edu/news-perspective/2020/08/us-blacks-3-times-more-likely-whites-get-covid-19

23. Lindaman, D., & Viala-Gaudefroy, J. (2020, April 22). Donald Trump's "Chinese virus": The politics of naming. *The Conversation*. https://theconversation.com/donald-trumps-chinese-virus-the-politics-of-naming-136796

24. Rogers, K., Jakes, L., & Swanson, A. (2020, March 18). Trump defends using "Chinese Virus" label, ignoring growing criticism. *The New York Times*. https://www.nytimes.com/2020/03/18/us/politics/china-virus.html

25. Stop AAPI Hate. https://stopaapihate.org/

26. Yam, K. (2021, March 9). Anti-Asian hate crimes increased by nearly 150% in 2020, mostly in N.Y. and L.A., new report says. NBC News. https://www.nbcnews.com/news/asian-america/anti-asian-hate-crimes-increased-nearly-150-2020-mostly-n-n1260264

27. Donlevy, K. (2020, September 24). Anti-Asian hate crime jumps 1,900 percent. *Queens Chronicle*. https://www.qchron.com/editions/queenswide/anti-asian-hate-crime-jumps-1-900-percent/article_f007a05b-f43e-54ca-a3c6-1b5493333dea.html

28. Meng introduces legislation to promote the teaching of Asian Pacific American history in schools; Measure seeks to help combat bigotry and discrimination against Asian Americans. (2021, May 4). Congresswoman Grace Meng. https://meng.house.gov/media-center/press-releases/meng-introduces-legislation-to-promote-the-teaching-of-asian-pacific-0

29. Katersky, A., Shapiro, E., & Deliso, M. (2021, February 27). Asian man stabbed in back in Chinatown, suspect charged with attempted murder. ABC News. https://abcnews.go.com/US/asian-man-stabbed-back-york-citys-chinatown-suspect/story?id=76133248

30. Rozner, L. (2021, March 3). *Manhattan DA Says Evidence Does Not Support Hate Crime Charges in Stabbing of Asian-American Man*. CBS New York. https://newyork.cbslocal.com/2021/03/03/manhattan-da-asian-attack-no-hate-crime-charges/

31. Beer, T. (2021, February 27). Jeremy Lin won't publically name player he says called him "Coronavirus." *Forbes*. https://www.forbes.com/sites/tommybeer/2021/02/27/jeremy-lin-wont-publically-name-player-he-says-called-him-coronavirus/?sh=798574ec6f02

32. Sheets, M. (2021, March 2). California teacher uses "slant eyes" to explain racism to students. Mail Online. https://www.dailymail.co.uk/news/article-9316717/California-high-school-teacher-used-slant-eyes-explain-Asian-stereotypes-students.html

33. Bogel-Burroughs, N. (2021, May 11). Atlanta spa shootings were hate crimes, prosecutor says. *The New York Times*. https://www.nytimes.com/2021/05/11/us/atlanta-spa-shootings-hate-crimes.html

34. Farivar, M. (2021, April 30). Attacks on Asian Americans spiked by 164% in first quarter of 2021, *Voice of America – English*. www.voanews.com. https://www.voanews.com/usa/attacks-asian-americans-spiked-164-first-quarter-2021

35. CNN, J. C. (2021, May 5). Anti-Asian hate crimes surged in early 2021, study says. CNN. https://www.cnn.com/2021/05/05/us/anti-asian-hate-crimes-study/index.html

36. Haynes, S. (2021, March 22). The Atlanta shooting highlights the painful reality of rising Anti-Asian Violence around the world. *Time*. https://time.com/5947862/anti-asian-attacks-rising-worldwide/

37. Shaw, D. O., & Kidwai, S. A. (2020, August 21). The global impact of the Black Lives Matter movement, Part-2. *The Geopolitics*. https://thegeopolitics.com/the-global-impact-of-the-black-lives-matter-movement/

38. European Union Agency for Fundamental Rights. (2021). Fundamental Rights Report 2021. https://fra.europa.eu/sites/default/files/fra_uploads/fra-2021-fundamental-rights-report-2021_en.pdf

39. Diallo, R. (2021). Racism: The comparison with the United States is not absurd. *Ufahamu: A Journal of African Studies* 42 (2). https://doi.org/10.5070/f742253953

40. Chwałek, T., Greszta, A., Belisario, K., Rycroft, C. E., Underwood, T., & King-Okoye, M. M. (2021). COVID-19 Among ethnic minorities: How missing data and colour-blind policies perpetuate inequalities in the United Kingdom and the European Union. *Interdisciplinary Perspectives on Equality and Diversity* 0(X). http://journals.hw.ac.uk/index.php/IPED/article/view/107

41. Madgavkar, A., White, O., Krishnan, M., Mahajan, D., & Azcue, X. (2020, July 15). COVID-19 and gender equality: Countering the regressive effects. *McKinsey & Company*. https://www.mckinsey.com/featured-insights/future-of-work/covid-19-and-gender-equality-countering-the-regressive-effects

42. Coury, S., Huang, J., Kumar, A., Prince, S., Krivkovich, A., & Yee, L. (2020, September 30). Women in the Workplace, *McKinsey*. Www.mckinsey.com. https://www.mckinsey.com/featured-insights/diversity-and-inclusion/women-in-the-workplace

43. UN WOMEN. (2020, September 16). COVID-19 and its economic toll on women: The story behind the numbers. UN Women. https://www.unwomen.org/en/news/stories/2020/9/feature-covid-19-economic-impacts-on-women

44. Kashen, J., Glynn, S. J., & Novello, A. (2020, October 30). *How COVID-19 Sent Women's Workforce Progress Backward*. Center for American Progress. https://www.americanprogress.org/issues/women/reports/2020/10/30/492582/covid-19-sent-womens-workforce-progress-backward/

45. #metoo movement - https://metoomvmt.org/

46. Lopez, L., & Snyder, C. (2017, December 13). Tarana Burke on why she created the #MeToo movement—and where it's headed, *Business Insider*. https://www.businessinsider.com/how-the-metoo-movement-started-where-its-headed-tarana-burke-time-person-of-year-women-2017-12

47. *Diversity, Equity & Inclusion*. (2021, May 31). VMware. https://www.vmware.com/company/diversity.html

48. *Mansplaining* is a pejorative term implying a man explaining something to a woman in a condescending and overconfident manner—often in an inaccurate or overly simplistic way.

49. Sherman, N. (2020, June 2). Zoom sees sales boom amid pandemic. *BBC News*. https://www.bbc.com/news/business-52884782#:~:text=Use%20of%20the%20firm

50. Ali, F. (2021, February 15). Ecommerce trends amid coronavirus pandemic in charts. Digital Commerce 360. https://www.digitalcommerce360.com/2021/02/15/ecommerce-during-coronavirus-pandemic-in-charts/

51. Moore, K. (2020, April 17). Retailers Selling Non-Essentials See Double & Triple-Digit Increases in Online Sales During COVID-19 Crisis. *Forbes*. https://www.forbes.com/sites/kaleighmoore/2020/04/17/retailers-selling-non-essentials-see-double--triple-digit-increases-in-online-sales-during-covid-19-crisis/?sh=52cddbf96431

52. Carlyle, E. (2020, August 10). Demand for home design and remodeling soars amid pandemic. *Houzz*. https://www.houzz.com/magazine/demand-for-home-design-and-remodeling-soars-amid-pandemic-stsetivw-vs~139312337

53. Hazelton, S. (2020, November 10). The best is still to come for the US home improvement market. *IHS Markit*. https://ihsmarkit.com/research-analysis/best-still-come-us-home-improvement-market.html

54. Popken, B. (2021, June 28). How the lumber industry misread Covid and ended up with a global shortage and sky-high prices. NBC News. https://www.nbcnews.com/business/economy/how-lumber-industry-misread-covid-ended-global-shortage-sky-high-n1272542

55. Nepogodiev, D., & Bhangu, A. (2020). Elective surgery cancellations due to the COVID-19 pandemic: Global predictive modelling to inform surgical recovery plans. *British Journal of Surgery* 107 (11). https://doi.org/10.1002/bjs.11746

56. Aref, M. (2020, September 28). How COVID-19 Impacted Travel & Tourism Industry Globally. *Infomineo*. https://infomineo.com/covid-19-impacted-travel-tourism-industry/

57. World Travel & Tourism Council. (2020). *Economic Impact, World Travel & Tourism Council (WTTC)*. wttc.org. https://wttc.org/Research/Economic-Impact

58. Bouver, J., Saxon, S., & Wittkamp, N. (2021, April 2). Five profound shifts in the post-pandemic aviation sector | McKinsey. www.mckinsey.com. https://www.mckinsey.com/industries/travel-logistics-and-infrastructure/our-insights/back-to-the-future-airline-sector-poised-for-change-post-covid-19

59. Dogra, S. (2020). *COVID-19:* Impact on the hospitality workforce. Hospitalityinsights.ehl.edu. https://hospitalityinsights.ehl.edu/covid-19-impact-hospitality-workforce

60. Roy, A. (2021, July 11). India reports 41,506 new COVID-19 cases in last 24 hours. Reuters. https://www.reuters.com/world/india/india-reports-41506-new-covid-19-cases-last-24-hours-2021-07-11/

61. India: WHO Coronavirus Disease (COVID-19) Dashboard. (2021, July 16). Covid19.Who.int. https://covid19.who.int/region/searo/country/in

62. Brunner, J. (2020, June 1). Complete List of Distilleries (Including Anheuser-Busch) Making Hand Sanitizers Instead of Spirits. *Parade*: Entertainment, Recipes, Health, Life, Holidays. https://parade.com/1011922/jerylbrunner/distilleries-making-hand-sanitizer/

Chapter 3

1. Sun Tzu's Art of War, ss. 3.18: Attack by Stratagem.

2. World Health Organization. (2020, January 30). *Statement on the second meeting of the International Health Regulations (2005) Emergency Committee regarding the outbreak of novel coronavirus (2019-nCoV)*. www.who.int. https://www.who.int/news/item/30-01-2020-statement-on-the-second-meeting-of-the-international-health-regulations-(2005)-emergency-committee-regarding-the-outbreak-of-novel-coronavirus-(2019-ncov)

3. Mind Tools content team. (2009). The Holmes and Rahe stress scale understanding the impact of long-term stress. Mindtools.com. https://www.mindtools.com/pages/article/newTCS_82.htm

4. Maslow, A. H. (1943). A theory of human motivation. *Psychological Review* 50 (4): 370–396. https://doi.org/10.1037/h0054346

5. Koltko-Rivera, M. E. (2006). Rediscovering the later version of Maslow's Hierarchy of Needs: Self-transcendence and opportunities for theory, research, and unification. *Review of General Psychology* 10 (4): 302–317. https://doi.org/10.1037/1089-2680.10.4.302

6. Mayo Clinic. (2017). Agoraphobia—Symptoms and causes. Mayo Clinic. https://www.mayoclinic.org/diseases-conditions/agoraphobia/symptoms-causes/syc-20355987

7. Feuer, W. (2021, March 5). WHO says pandemic has caused more "mass trauma" than WWII. CNBC. https://www.cnbc.com/2021/03/05/who-says-pandemic-has-caused-more-mass-trauma-than-wwii-and-will-last-for-years.html

8. Scagliusi, A. L. (2021, July 1). What is post-pandemic stress disorder? How to spot the signs, and what to do next. *Vogue.* https://www.vogue.com/article/what-is-post-pandemic-stress-disorder

9. Gopinath, G. (2020, April 14). The Great Lockdown: Worst economic downturn since the Great Depression. IMF Blog. https://blogs.imf.org/2020/04/14/the-great-lockdown-worst-economic-downturn-since-the-great-depression/

10. Tucker, MD., P., & Czapla, MD, C. S. (2021, January 8). Post-COVID stress disorder: Another emerging consequence of the global pandemic. *Psychiatric Times.* https://www.psychiatrictimes.com/view/post-covid-stress-disorder-emerging-consequence-global-pandemic

11. Cerbara, L., Ciancimino, G., Crescimbene, M., La Longa, F., Parsi, M. R., Tintori, A., & Palomba, R. (2020). A nation-wide survey on emotional and psychological impacts of COVID-19 social distancing. *European Review for Medical and Pharmacological Sciences.*

12. Czeisler, M. É. (2020). Mental Health, Substance Use, and Suicidal Ideation during the COVID-19 Pandemic—United States, June 24–30, 2020. *MMWR. Morbidity and Mortality Weekly Report, 69*(32). https://doi.org/10.15585/mmwr.mm6932a1

13. Coman, C., Țîru, L. G., Meseșan-Schmitz, L., Stanciu, C., & Bularca, M. C. (2020). Online teaching and learning in higher education during the coronavirus pandemic: Students' perspective. *Sustainability* 12 (24): 10367. https://doi.org/10.3390/su122410367

14. UNICEF. (2021, March 2). COVID-19: Schools for more than 168 million children globally have been completely closed for almost a full year, says UNICEF. www.unicef.org. https://www.unicef.org/press-releases/schools-more-168-million-children-globally-have-been-completely-closed

15. GBD 2017 Disease and Injury Incidence and Prevalence Collaborators (2018). Global, regional, and national incidence, prevalence, and years lived with disability for 354 diseases and injuries for 195 countries and territories, 1990–2017: A systematic analysis for the Global Burden of Disease Study 2017. *Lancet (London, England)* 392 (10159): 1789–1858. https://doi.org/10.1016/S0140-6736(18)32279-7

16. Ritchie, H., & Roser, M. (2018). Mental health. Our World in Data. https://ourworldindata.org/mental-health

17. National Alliance on Mental Illness. (2021, March). Mental health by the numbers. Nami.org. https://www.nami.org/mhstats

18. SingleCare. (2020, August 4). Mental health statistics 2020. The Checkup. https://www.singlecare.com/blog/news/mental-health-statistics/

19. Raypole, C. (2020, May 28). Visualization meditation: 5 exercises to try. Healthline. https://www.healthline.com/health/visualization-meditation

20. Thoma, M. V., La Marca, R., Brönnimann, R., Finkel, L., Ehlert, U., & Nater, U. M. (2013). The Effect of music on the human stress response. *PLoS ONE* 8 (8): e70156. https://doi.org/10.1371/journal.pone.0070156

21. McDermott, A. (2016, September 26). *Try this: 18 essential oils for anxiety*. Healthline; Healthline Media. https://www.healthline.com/health/anxiety/essential-oils-for-anxiety

22. Crichton-Stuart, C. (2018, August 1). *9 foods that help reduce anxiety*. www.medicalnewstoday.com. https://www.medicalnewstoday.com/articles/322652

23. Raypole, C. (2019, September 27). How to increase endorphins: 13 tips. Healthline. https://www.healthline.com/health/how-to-increase-endorphins

24. Mayo Clinic Staff. (2020, March 6). Caffeine: How much is too much? Mayo Clinic. https://www.mayoclinic.org/healthy-lifestyle/nutrition-and-healthy-eating/in-depth/caffeine/art-20045678#:~:text=Up%20to%20400%20milli-grams%20(mg

25. Menges, S. (2019, November 5). The 3 biggest advantages of human touch may surprise you, *PlushCare*. https://plushcare.com/blog/advantages-of-human-touch-hugs/

26. CDC. (2021, March 30). *Benefits of physical activity*. Centers for Disease Control and Prevention. https://www.cdc.gov/physicalactivity/basics/adults/health-benefits-of-physical-activity-for-adults.html

27. Peterson, L. A. (2017, March 23). Decrease stress by using your breath. Mayo Clinic. https://www.mayoclinic.org/healthy-lifestyle/stress-management/in-depth/decrease-stress-by-using-your-breath/art-20267197

28. Azami, M., Shohani, M., Badfar, G., Nasirkandy, M., Kaikhavani, S., Rahmati, S., Modmeli, Y., & Soleymani, A. (2018). The effect of yoga on stress, anxiety, and depression in women. *International Journal of Preventive Medicine* 9 (1): 21. https://doi.org/10.4103/ijpvm.ijpvm_242_16

29. Mayo Clinic. (2020, December 29). Yoga: Fight stress and find serenity. https://www.mayoclinic.org/healthy-lifestyle/stress-management/in-depth/yoga/art-20044733

30. Mayo Clinic Staff. (2018, August 29). Your crew matters: How to build social support. Mayo Clinic; https://www.mayoclinic.org/healthy-lifestyle/stress-management/in-depth/social-support/art-20044445

31. Wein, H. (2018, March 6). The Power of Pets. NIH News in Health. https://newsinhealth.nih.gov/2018/02/power-pets

32. Smyth, J. M., Johnson, J. A., Auer, B. J., Lehman, E., Talamo, G., & Sciamanna, C. N. (2018). Online positive affect journaling in the improvement of mental distress and well-being in general medical patients with elevated anxiety symptoms: A preliminary randomized controlled trial. *JMIR Mental Health* 5 (4): e11290. https://doi.org/10.2196/11290

33. Mayo Clinic Staff. (2021, March 18). 12 tips to tame stress. Mayo Clinic; https://www.mayoclinic.org/healthy-lifestyle/stress-management/in-depth/stress-relievers/art-20047257

34. Healthwise Staff. (2019, December 16). Stress management: Managing your time. HealthLink BC. https://www.healthlinkbc.ca/health-topics/av2103

35. Mischoulon, D. (2018, August 3). Omega-3 fatty acids for mood disorders. Harvard Health Blog. https://www.health.harvard.edu/blog/omega-3-fatty-acids-for-mood-disorders-2018080314414

36. Gunnars, K. (2018, June 29). 12 proven health benefits of avocado. Healthline. https://www.healthline.com/nutrition/12-proven-benefits-of-avocado

37. Julson, E. (2018, May 10). 10 best ways to increase dopamine levels naturally. Healthline; Healthline Media. https://www.healthline.com/nutrition/how-to-increase-dopamine

38. Stevenson, S. (2012, June 25). There's magic in your smile. *Psychology Today Canada*. www.psychologytoday.com. https://www.psychologytoday.com/ca/blog/cutting-edge-leadership/201206/there-s-magic-in-your-smile

39. Intermountain Healthcare. (2020, February 12). Cuddle and hug your way to better health. Intermountainhealthcare.org. https://intermountainhealthcare.org/blogs/topics/live-well/2015/02/cuddle-and-hug-your-way-to-better-health/

40. Mayo Clinic. (2017). Seasonal affective disorder (SAD)—Symptoms and causes. Mayo Clinic, https://www.mayoclinic.org/diseases-conditions/seasonal-affective-disorder/symptoms-causes/syc-20364651

41. Vinalli, M. (2021, February 23). Lavender for anxiety: The best way to use this calming herb. Healthline. https://www.healthline.com/health/anxiety/lavender-for-anxiety

Chapter 4

1. Brown, B. (2018). *Dare to Lead: Brave Work. Tough Conversations. Whole Hearts*. Ebury Publishing.

2. Twenty One Toys. (2017, December 6). Dr Brené Brown: Empathy vs Sympathy. Twentyonetoys.com. https://twentyonetoys.com/blogs/teaching-empathy/brene-brown-empathy-vs-sympathy

3. Beetz, A., Uvnäs-Moberg, K., Julius, H., & Kotrschal, K. (2012). Psychosocial and psychophysiological effects of human-animal interactions: The possible

role of oxytocin. *Frontiers in Psychology* 3 (234). https://doi.org/10.3389/fpsyg.2012.00234

4. Zachos, E. (2017, November 10). Bonobo apes express empathy, willingly help strangers. *National Geographic*. https://www.nationalgeographic.com/animals/article/bonobo-help-stranger-behavior-animals-speed

5. Titchener EB (2014). Introspection and empath (PDF). *Dialogues in Philosophy, Mental and Neuro Sciences*. 7: 25–30. Archived from the original (PDF) on July 26, 2014.

6. Stueber, K. (2008). Empathy. *Plato.stanford.edu*. https://plato.stanford.edu/archives/fall2019/entries/empathy/

7. Twenty One Toys, 2017.

8. Google Trends - https://trends.google.com/

9. Christov-Moore, L., Simpson, E. A., Coudé, G., Grigaityte, K., Iacoboni, M., & Ferrari, P. F. (2014). Empathy: Gender effects in brain and behavior. *Neuroscience & Biobehavioral Reviews* 46 (4): 604–627. https://doi.org/10.1016/j.neubiorev.2014.09.001

10. Heilweil, R. (2021, April 15). Seems like everyone hates Instagram for kids. Vox. https://www.vox.com/recode/22385570/instagram-for-kids-youtube-facebook-messenger

11. Taylor, J. (2021, March 19). Facebook building a version of Instagram for children under 13. *The Guardian*. https://www.theguardian.com/technology/2021/mar/19/facebook-building-a-version-of-instagram-for-children-under-13

12. Don't judge a man until you have walked a mile in his shoes. (n.d.) *Farlex Dictionary of Idioms*. (2015). Retrieved July 19 2021 from https://idioms.thefreedictionary.com/don%27t+judge+a+man+until+you+have+walked+a+mile+in+his+shoes

13. Sinek, S. (2013). *Start with Why: How Great Leaders Inspire Everyone to Take Action*. Portfolio/Penguin.

14. National PTA. (2018). *Reflections Arts Program | National PTA*. pta.org. https://www.pta.org/home/programs/reflections

Chapter 5

1. Vago, D., & David, S. (2012). Selfawareness, selfregulation, and selftranscendence (SART): A framework for understanding the neurobiological mechanisms of mindfulness. *Frontiers in Human Neuroscience* 6: 296. https://www.frontiersin.org/article/10.3389/fnhum.2012.00296

2. Robbins Research Inc. (n.d.). *Top 20 Inspirational Quotes About Life & Success, Tony Robbins*. Tonyrobbins.com. https://www.tonyrobbins.com/tony-robbins-quotes/inspirational-quotes/

3. Salmansohn, K. (n.d.). *Be The Reason Someone Believes in the Goodness of People*. NotSalmon. Retrieved July 21, 2021, from https://www.notsalmon.com/quotes/be-the-reason-believes-goodness/

4. Cedars-Sinai Staff. (2019, February 19). *The Science Behind Random Acts of Kindness, Cedars-Sinai*. Cedars-Sinai.org. https://www.cedars-sinai.org/blog/science-of-kindness.html

5. D Goleman. (1996). *Emotional intelligence: Why it can matter more than IQ*. Bloomsbury.

6. Fegert, J. M., Vitiello, B., Plener, P. L., & Clemens, V. (2020). Challenges and burden of the Coronavirus 2019 (COVID-19) pandemic for child and adolescent mental health: a narrative review to highlight clinical and research needs in the acute phase and the long return to normality. *Child and Adolescent Psychiatry and Mental Health* 14 (1). https://doi.org/10.1186/s13034-020-00329-3

7. Relaxio s.r.o. *Daylio – Journal, Diary and Mood Tracker*. Daylio. https://daylio.net/

Chapter 6

1. Edmondson, A. C., & Lei, Z. (2014). Psychological Safety: The History, Renaissance, and Future of an Interpersonal Construct. *Annual Review of Organizational Psychology and Organizational Behavior* 1 (1): 23–43. https://doi.org/10.1146/annurev-orgpsych-031413-091305

2. De Smet, A., Rubenstein, K., Schrah, G., Vierow, M., & Edmondson, A. (2021, February 11). *Psychological safety and leadership development, McKinsey*. Www.mckinsey.com. https://www.mckinsey.com/business-functions/organization/our-insights/psychological-safety-and-the-critical-role-of-leadership-development

3. Dwoskin, E. (2020, October 1). Americans might never go back to the office, and Twitter is leading the charge. *Washington Post*. https://www.washington-post.com/technology/2020/10/01/twitter-work-from-home/

4. Redazione. (2018, June 18). Satya Nadella: When empathy is good for business. *Morning Future*. https://www.morningfuture.com/en/2018/06/18/microsoft-satya-nadella-empathy-business-management/

5. 11/30 Update: Verizon is prepared to serve customers during COVID-19 crisis. (2020, November 30). www.verizon.com. https://www.verizon.com/about/news/update-verizon-serve-customers-covid-19.

6. Sottrup, T. (2019). Why empathy is the secret to great customer service. Dixa. https://www.dixa.com/blog/why-empathy-is-the-secret-to-great-customer-service/

7. Nightingale, E. (2007). *Earl Nightingale's the Strangest Secret*. Gardners Books.

8. Topolosky, J. (2010, June 25). Apple responds to iPhone 4 reception issues: You're holding the phone the wrong way. Engadget. https://www.engadget.com/2010-06-24-apple-responds-over-iphone-4-reception-issues-youre-holding-th.html

9. Baker, M. (2020, March 19). Gartner HR survey reveals 88% of organizations have encouraged or required employees to work from home due to coronavirus. Gartner.

10. OWLLabs. (2020). *State of Remote Work 2020*. https://resources.owllabs.com/state-of-remote-work/2020

11. Gallup Inc. (2020, October 13). COVID-19 and Remote Work: An Update. Gallup.com. https://news.gallup.com/poll/321800/covid-remote-work-update.aspx

12. Boland, B., De Smet, A., Palter, R., & Sanghvi, A. (2020, June 8). Reimagining the office and work life after COVID-19, *McKinsey*. www.mckinsey.com. https://www.mckinsey.com/business-functions/organization/our-insights/reimagining-the-office-and-work-life-after-covid-19

13. Miller, S. (2020, April 1). Pandemic forces employers to cut pay. SHRM. https://www.shrm.org/ResourcesAndTools/hr-topics/compensation/Pages/pandemic-forces-employers-to-cut-pay.aspx

14. Omale, G. (2021, February 18). Future of work from home for service and support employees. www.gartner.com. https://www.gartner.com/smarterwithgartner/future-of-work-from-home-for-service-and-support-employees/

15. Drury, H. B. (1915). *Scientific Management; a History and Criticism*. New York. [Web.] Retrieved from the Library of Congress, https://lccn.loc.gov/15015984.

16. Wong, K. (2020, May 7). Organizational culture: Definition, importance, and development. *Achievers*. https://www.achievers.com/blog/organizational-culture-definition/

17. Calvello, M. (2020, November 19). 62 recruitment statistics every HR professional needs to know. G2. https://www.g2.com/articles/recruitment-statistics

18. Westrum, R. (2004). A typology of organisational cultures. *Quality and Safety in Health Care* 13 (suppl_2): ii22–ii27. https://doi.org/10.1136/qshc.2003.009522

19. Nohria, N., & Beer, M. (2000). Cracking the code of change. *Harvard Business Review*. https://hbr.org/2000/05/cracking-the-code-of-change

20. Kaizen is the Japanese word meaning "change for better." It is a Lean Six Sigma concept where organizations embrace the need to continuously improve all functions and processes within the organizations.

21. Wiio, O. A. (1978). *Wiion lait- ja vähän muidenkin*. Weilin + Göös. ISBN 9789513516574

22. Pink, D. H. (2018). *DRIVE: The Surprising Truth About What Motivates Us*. Canongate Books Ltd. (Original work published 2009).

23. Named after the ancient Greek goddess of wisdom, handicraft, and war.
24. A skip-level meeting is when a higher-up manager (employee's supervisor's supervisor or higher) meets with the employee to discuss employee well-being, improvement opportunities, pain points, ideas for new products and initiatives, sentiment around company, departmental, and individual goals, and pain points in a safe environment.
25. Stoller, K. (2021, April 20). America's Best Employers for Diversity 2021. *Forbes.* https://www.forbes.com/best-employers-diversity/#5928b6fd9b9e
26. Leona O' Sullivan. (2021, February 5). *VMware Earns Perfect Score for LGBTQ Equality on the 2021 HRC Corporate Equality Index – VMware Careers.* VMware Careers. https://blogs.vmware.com/careers/2021/02/vmware-earns-perfect-score-for-lgbtq-equality-on-the-2021-hrc-corporate-equality-index.html
27. Haranas, M. (2019, June 19). VMware's Pat Gelsinger Voted Best CEO in America: Glassdoor. CRN. https://www.crn.com/news/virtualization/vmware-s-pat-gelsinger-voted-best-ceo-in-america-by-glassdoor
28. VMware Foundation, We are all Citizen Philanthropists. VMware. https://www.vmware.com/company/foundation.html

Chapter 7

1. Highest Paid Person's Opinion.
2. Brooks, F. (1995). *The Mythical Man-Month.* Addison-Wesley.
3. Kersten, M. (2018). *Project to product: How to survive and thrive in the age of digital disruption with the flow framework.* IT Revolution Press.
4. Lyssa Adkins, https://lyssaadkins.com/
5. Davis, M. F., & Green, J. (2020, April 23). *Three Hours Longer, the Pandemic Workday Has Obliterated Work-Life Balance.* Bloomberg. https://www.bloomberg.com/news/articles/2020-04-23/working-from-home-in-covid-era-means-three-more-hours-on-the-job.

Chapter 8

1. Report to the Nation: Anti-Asian Prejudice & Hate Crime. (2021). In *Report to the Nation: Anti-Asian Prejudice & Hate Crime (April 30, 2021) - Corrected.* https://bit.ly/3BqrLZw
2. Newman, B., Merolla, J. L., Shah, S., Lemi, D. C., Collingwood, L., & Ramakrishnan, S. K. (2020). The Trump Effect: An Experimental Investigation of the Emboldening Effect of Racially Inflammatory Elite Communication. *British Journal of Political Science,* 1–22. https://doi.org/10.1017/s0007123419000590

3. United Nations. (2018, September). *Sustainable Development Goals*. United Nations Sustainable Development; United Nations. https://www.un.org/sustainabledevelopment/sustainable-development-goals/

4. United Nations. (2020). *The Impact of COVID-19 on Women (9 April 2020)*. https://www.un.org/sites/un2.un.org/files/policy_brief_on_covid_impact_on_women_9_apr_2020_updated.pdf

5. Dwoskin, E. (2021, March 14). Massive Facebook study on users' doubt in vaccines finds a small group appears to play a big role in pushing the skepticism. *The Washington Post*. https://www.washingtonpost.com/technology/2021/03/14/facebook-vaccine-hesistancy-qanon/

6. Bond, S. (2021, May 14). Just 12 people are behind most vaccine hoaxes on social media, research shows. *NPR*.org. https://www.npr.org/2021/05/13/996570855/disinformation-dozen-test-facebooks-twitters-ability-to-curb-vaccine-hoaxes

7. Shirvell, B. (2020, April 1). These teens are helping self-isolating seniors stay connected. *Teen Vogue*. https://www.teenvogue.com/story/teens-helping-seniors-coronavirus

8. McKinsey Global Institute. (2021, February 18). The future of work after COVID-19. *McKinsey*. Www.mckinsey.com. https://www.mckinsey.com/featured-insights/future-of-work/the-future-of-work-after-covid-19

9. Marinova, I. (2021, July 4). 2021's Remote work statistics (productivity, income, trends). *Review42*. https://review42.com/resources/remote-work-statistics/

10. Choudhury, P. (Raj). (2020, November 1). Our work-from-anywhere future. *Harvard Business Review*. https://hbr.org/2020/11/our-work-from-anywhere-future

11. Villegas, P., & Knowles, H. (2021, July 7). Iceland tested a 4-day workweek. Employees were productive—and happier, researchers say. *Washington Post*. https://www.washingtonpost.com/business/2021/07/06/iceland-four-day-work-week/

12. Kelly, J. (2020, December 14). Wall Street banks and tech companies are fleeing New York and California. *Forbes*. https://www.forbes.com/sites/jackkelly/2020/12/14/wall-street-banks-and-tech-companies-are-fleeing-new-york-and-california/?sh=1b11e31f661a

Chapter 9

1. Leite, W. L., Svinicki, M., & Shi, Y. (2009). Attempted Validation of the Scores of the VARK: Learning Styles Inventory with Multitrait–Multimethod Confirmatory Factor Analysis Models. *Educational and Psychological Measurement* 70 (2): 323–339. https://doi.org/10.1177/0013164409344507

2. Edward De Bono. (2017). *Six Thinking Hats*. Penguin Life, An Imprint Of Penguin Books. (Original work published 1985).
3. Beck, M. (2013, March 24). *The Empathy Workout*. Martha Beck. https://marthabeck.com/2013/03/the-empathy-workout/
4. Yu Siang, T. (2009). *What Is Design Thinking?* The Interaction Design Foundation; UX courses. https://www.interaction-design.org/literature/topics/design-thinking
5. Such as Stanford D.school - https://dschool.stanford.edu.
6. Liedtka, J. (2018, August 28). *Why Design Thinking Works*. Harvard Business Review. https://hbr.org/2018/09/why-design-thinking-works
7. Winter, J. (2017, July 11). *Three Exercises to Teach Your Team Empathy | UX Booth*. UX Booth. https://www.uxbooth.com/articles/three-exercises-to-teach-your-team-empathy/
8. Anderson, A., & Dougé, J. (2019). *Talking to Children about Racial Bias*. HealthyChildren.org. https://www.healthychildren.org/English/healthy-living/emotional-wellness/Building-Resilience/Pages/Talking-to-Children-About-Racial-Bias.aspx
9. Stern, C. (2000, February). *Talking to Young Children about Bias and Prejudice*. Anti-Defamation League. https://www.adl.org/education/resources/tools-and-strategies/talking-to-young-children-about-prejudice
10. Have you heard of Emojicode? https://www.emojicode.org/

About the Author

Dr. Gautham Pallapa is the founder of Transformity, an organization that transforms humanity through empathy and technology, and an executive advisor at VMware. He works with C-suite and executives at Global 2000 enterprises in transforming their strategy, processes, technologies, culture, and people to achieve their business outcomes. Having almost succumbed to stress early in his career, he employed that wake-up call to help improve the quality of life for people working in enterprises. His mantra is *"Transform with Empathy,"* and he works passionately to promote empathy for employees, enterprises, and communities.

Dr. Pallapa is an Agile coach, a Lean Six Sigma Black Belt, a SAFe Agilist, and an Ambassador for the DevOps Institute. He writes/talks/works on transformation, elevating humans, helping underprivileged people, and giving back to the community. He was awarded the 2018 Tech Leader of the Year award by AIM for his contributions. Gautham lives in the San Francisco Bay Area with his wife and son. He can be reached via email at gpallapa@pm.me.

You can learn more about Transformity at https://transformity.info or follow Dr. Pallapa on LinkedIn: https://www.linkedin.com/in/gpallapa/ or Twitter: @gpallapa.

Index

341

Index

344

Index